# Modern French Jewish Thought

THE TAUBER INSTITUTE SERIES FOR
THE STUDY OF EUROPEAN JEWRY
Jehuda Reinharz, General Editor
ChaeRan Y. Freeze, Associate Editor
Sylvia Fuks Fried, Associate Editor
Eugene R. Sheppard, Associate Editor

THE BRANDEIS LIBRARY OF MODERN JEWISH THOUGHT
Eugene R. Sheppard and Samuel Moyn, Editors
This library aims to redefine the canon of modern Jewish thought by publishing
primary source readings from individual Jewish thinkers or groups of thinkers in
reliable English translations. Designed for courses in modern Jewish philosophy,
thought, and intellectual history, each volume features a general introduction
and annotations to each source with the instructor and student in mind.

*Modern French Jewish Thought: Writings on Religion and Politics*
    Sarah Hammerschlag, editor
*Jewish Legal Theories: Writings on State, Religion, and Morality*
    Leora Batnitzky and Yonatan Brafman, editors
*Sabbatian Heresy: Writings on Mysticism, Messianism, and the Origins of Jewish Modernity*
    Paweł Maciejko, editor
*Modern Middle Eastern Jewish Thought: Writings on Identity, Politics, and Culture, 1893–1958*
    Moshe Behar and Zvi Ben-Dor Benite, editors
*Jews and Diaspora Nationalism: Writings on Jewish Peoplehood in Europe and the United States*
    Simon Rabinovitch, editor
*Moses Mendelssohn: Writings on Judaism, Christianity, and the Bible*
    Michah Gottlieb, editor
*Jews and Race: Writings on Identity and Difference, 1880–1940*
    Mitchell B. Hart, editor

FOR THE COMPLETE LIST OF BOOKS THAT ARE FORTHCOMING IN
THE SERIES, PLEASE SEE HTTP://WWW.BRANDEIS.EDU/TAUBER

# Modern French Jewish Thought

Edited by
Sarah Hammerschlag

WRITINGS ON

RELIGION AND

POLITICS

Brandeis University Press

Waltham, Massachusetts

BRANDEIS UNIVERSITY PRESS

An imprint of University Press of New England

www.upne.com

© 2018 Brandeis University

Designed by Eric M. Brooks

Typeset in Albertina and Verlag by Passumpsic Publishing

For permission to reproduce any of the material in this book,
contact Permissions, University Press of New England, One Court
Street, Suite 250, Lebanon NH 03766; or visit www.upne.com

*Credits appear on page 269.*

Library of Congress Cataloging-in-Publication Data

NAMES: Hammerschlag, Sarah, editor.

TITLE: Modern French Jewish thought: writings on religion and
politics / edited by Sarah Hammerschlag.

DESCRIPTION: Waltham, Massachusetts: Brandeis University Press,
[2018] | Series: The Tauber Institute series for the study of
European Jewry | Series: The Brandeis library of modern Jewish
thought | Includes bibliographical references and index.

IDENTIFIERS: LCCN 2017048761 (print) | LCCN 2017050151 (ebook) |
ISBN 9781512601879 (epub, mobi, & pdf) | ISBN 9781611685268
(cloth: alk. paper) | ISBN 9781512601862 (pbk.: alk. paper)

SUBJECTS: LCSH: Jews—France—Intellectual life—20th century—
Sources. | Jews—France—Intellectual life—21st century—
Sources. | Judaism—France—History—Sources. | Jews—
France—Identity—Sources. | Jewish philosophy—France—
20th century—Sources. | Jewish philosophy—France—
21st century—Sources. | France—Ethnic relations.

CLASSIFICATION: LCC DS135.F83 (ebook) |
LCC DS135. F83 M646 2018 (print) | DDC 305.892/4044—dc23

LC record available at https://lccn.loc.gov/2017048761

5  4  3  2  1

# Contents

## IV | Identification, Disidentification  179

# Foreword

The French scene has often been marginal to the interpretation of the modern experience of the Jewish people, even though it has a famous centrality in the early history of political emancipation and despite the fact that, since the Holocaust, it has hosted the third-largest Jewish community in the world. Not least, while German-speaking lands have long boasted the thinkers canonized in the tradition of modern Jewish thought, from Moses Mendelssohn to Franz Rosenzweig, today such narratives often end in France. There, the French-Lithuanian philosopher Emmanuel Levinas elaborated a compelling vision of ethics as Judaism's contribution to world affairs and several thinkers inspired by him, most notably Jacques Derrida (an Algerian Jew by birth), were moved to write on Jewish themes. As Sarah Hammerschlag demonstrates in this magnificent volume, it is important to regard French Jewish intellectual life, so often neglected in the Anglophone world, as a rich source for scholars and students. Far from coming from nowhere, the most recent surge in prominence of French Jewish thought presupposed the longer sequence of authors that Hammerschlag's curatorial work and valuable introduction reconstitute for the first time in the English language. As such, this volume provides an indispensable starting point for thinking about how contemporary Jewish thought was forged. Indeed, many of the contributions remain current for readers to treat as sources for their own thinking about secularism, difference, and persecution.

*Eugene R. Sheppard and Samuel Moyn, Editors*
The Brandeis Library of Modern Jewish Thought

# Introduction

In his eponymously titled anthology, Nahum Glatzer in 1977 defined Modern Jewish Thought as a form of reflection on "life and human existence," based on Jewish sources. From this definition alone, we can glimpse the historical, disciplinary, and philosophical negotiations that underlie the field, and the questions that inevitably follow from the very attempt to think about Judaism's capacity to speak to universal questions. Is the task of reflecting on "life and human existence" in its broadest form not philosophical? But if this inquiry is dictated by Jewish canonical sources should it be classified as theology? Are both these categories—philosophy and theology—themselves not already colored by their cultural origins and thus Greek and Christian? Are Jewish concerns religious? Is the term "religion" even appropriate for categorizing Judaism or should the tradition be understood otherwise?

Clearly modern Jewish thought has been not merely reflection on "life and human existence" based on Jewish sources, but rather engagement with all the ensuing questions that follow from such a claim. Modern *French* Jewish thought, from its initial attempts to conceptualize Judaism in terms of the legacy of modern France and the revolutionary ideals of 1789, has been particularly preoccupied with the terms of this negotiation. Thus the texts selected for this anthology do not merely invite the questions delineated above; many of them ask these questions and sometimes they pose answers. In so doing they are never divorced from political-historical questions, even if they may sometimes appear to be.

The anthology is organized in roughly chronological order, to highlight the connections between the religious, political, and historical. There is much about the intersections of these concerns as they develop around Judaism that is unique to France not only because of the particular contingencies of French history but also in terms of the questions and concepts relating to Jewish identity, politics, and religion that the events of modern French history bring to the fore, particularly in so far as the Jewish Question has continually resurfaced in many of France's major moments of crisis. From the Dreyfus Affair to the Vichy regime, in the Algerian War and surrounding colonial conflicts, then during the events of May 1968, and even in the most recent debates about the nature and value of French secularism, discourse on the position of Jews within the nation has been central.

It is important to note that attention to these historical concerns does not make this a source volume of French Jewish history. The texts collected here are not provided primarily as historical documents, nor are they edifying in any sense that would allow them to be read without reference to their history. Rather it is in the task of thinking about how the ideas and arguments collected here arose in relation to the national history of France that they become paradigmatic of Jewish modernity and thus relevant far beyond their context.

### Historical Background: "To Live like God in France"

While this collection focuses on the late nineteenth century onward, to conceptualize the significance of French Judaism for modern Jewish thought we must first revisit France's role in the late European emancipation of the Jews.

The Yiddish proverb "Leben vi Got in Frankraykh" (To live like God in France) sums up the general perception of life for French Jews among the Eastern European diaspora until the Second World War.[1] The first among nations to emancipate the Jews, France was widely seen in the nineteenth century as a kind of utopia for *les Israélites*.[2] Unlike in Germany, where Jewish rights were alternately proffered and rescinded throughout the century, stabilizing finally only with Germany's unification under the leadership of Bismarck, in France citizenship arrived *almost* concurrently with the French Revolution. The "almost" is important here, however, because in fact neither Jews nor Protestants were originally understood to be included under the Declaration of the Rights of Man. Final equality under the law came about only through protracted debate on the perceived conflict between Jewish law and French civil law. It was not until 1791 that all Jews in France were granted citizenship, and then only with the explicit contention that French citizenship replaced the corporate membership of Jews in their *kehilot*, their religious communities. As the Count of Clermont-Tonnerre famously said, "The Jews should be denied everything as a nation, but granted everything as individuals."[3] The count's assertion was a response to the debate over the Jews' capacity for *régéneration*.

It was a debate that itself preceded the Revolution and took its more insidious form in Voltaire's *Dictionnaire philosophique*, which used Judaism as a foil to attack fanaticism but in the process described Jews in uncompromising terms as "ever vagrants or robbers or slaves . . . They are still vagabonds upon the earth and abhorred by men, yet affirming that heaven and earth and all mankind were created for them alone."[4] The reform-minded saw Jews as capable of citizenship but in need of *"régéneration."* The particular situation of Alsatian Jews aroused concern and debate beyond the French context when their community leader Cerf Berr sought the help of the Jewish luminary Moses Mendelssohn in Berlin in response to anti-Jewish actions and propaganda regarding Jewish moneylenders in the community. The result was Wilhelm von Dohm's tract, solicited by Mendelssohn, *On the Civic Improvement of the Jews*, written in German in 1781 but soon translated into French. A number of events followed, including Holy Roman Emperor Joseph II's Edict of Toleration for Austrian Jews, which banned certain forms of discriminatory taxation but also included measures aimed at promoting Jewish acculturation. Then, in 1785, the Royal Society of Arts and Science in Metz held an essay contest, following up on von Dohm's essay with the prompt, "Are there means of making the Jews happier and more useful in France?"

Among the three prize winners was the French liberal priest Henri Grégoire, whose descriptions of contemporary Jewish life were not much more flattering than Voltaire's but who spoke in less ontologically damning terms. Abbé Grégoire saw Jews as a victim of their circumstances. He imagined a unified France no longer mired in dialects or regional identities and saw Jewish difference as something to be eradicated through political and social reform. That these debates about regional identity never fully disappeared in France is evident in Richard Marienstras's 1975 essay included here, "The Jews of the Diaspora, or the Vocation of a Minority," in which Marienstras returns to the earlier debate to argue for the political value of minority populations, and to position Judaism as exemplary on this issue. In the late eighteenth century, Jews were already something of a testing ground for progressive ideals and their emancipation was seen as one means to prove the efficacy of these principles.[5] The success of Jewish assimilation was premised on the idea that, when granted the means and the rights to participate in the life of the nation, Jews would gladly sacrifice the forms of life that had kept them apart and different from their fellow countrymen.

The religious situation of French Jews was not formally resolved until the end of the first decade of the nineteenth century. Complaints and suspicions about Jewish fitness for citizenship accompanied their new status and flared up around charges of usury. The practice of Jewish moneylending was itself viewed as symbolic of the Jews' foreign nature.[6] In response to calls to revoke Jewish citizenship, Napoleon sought a means to enforce his influence by assimilating Jews into the nation. In 1806, he convoked the Assembly of Notables with representatives from Jewish communities around the nation. Their task was formally to dispel suspicions about their tradition by answering a series of queries posed to evaluate the fitness of Judaism to serve as a national religion. The assembly thus answered the questions with an eye toward convincing Napoleon's representatives of the fitness of Judaism for modern political life, even when that meant bending certain facets of Jewish law to fit the bill. Not unaware that such would be the case, Napoleon then resurrected the Sanhedrin, the ancient legislative body of Second Temple Judaism, to ratify the responses of the assembly and to give a sense of world-historical importance to the task. The role of the Sanhedrin, a legislative body made up mostly of members of the original Assembly of Notables, was to transform the assembly's responses into concrete reforms. Consequences of this process included a very clear definition of Judaism in religious terms, the subordination of its legal prescriptions to French civil law, and the circumscription of the role of rabbis to one equivalent to the leaders of the nation's other faiths: "preaching morality in the temples, blessing marriages, and pronouncing divorce."[7] Following the precedent set in 1802 for Protestants, in an 1808 decree Napoleon established the consistory system, a state-sponsored hierarchy for French Judaism, with a central consistory and departmental representatives. These representatives were responsible for regulating Judaism on the local and national level but also for securing the tradition as itself an agent of state values.[8] Some of Napoleon's actions were less popular and more punitive, such as the "Infamous Decree," which annulled debts to Jewish moneylenders by married women, minors, and soldiers, canceled any debt with an interest rate over 10 percent, restricted Jewish commerce and moneylending for ten years, banned Jewish settlement in certain areas of Alsace, constrained freedom of movement for Jews, and required the adoption of official last names. Nonetheless, Napoleon's actions ultimately secured his legacy as a great hero to the Jews and established France's reputation as a Jewish utopia.

The effects of the process on French Jewish thought were far-reaching. While Judaism did not disappear in France, as both Abbé Grégoire and Napoleon had in fact hoped, the identification with their fatherland that it produced among French Jews was profound. By the 1830s the very concept of *régéneration* had been transformed into a movement of internal Jewish reform, including a focus on Jewish scholarship. Scholars such as Adolphe Franck and Salomon Munk turned to the sources of the Jewish canon, studying Talmud, Kabbalah, and Jewish philosophy; through this study, and through the production of critical editions and translations, such as Munk's edition of *The Guide for the Perplexed*, they sought to return Judaism to what they conceived of as its pristine past.[9]

Among the stipulations that emerged from the Sanhedrin was the reformation of the synagogue service so that it did not conflict with patriotic values. Additionally, there were calls for the reeducation of Jews in the more conservative communities of Alsace. Even as some of these efforts met with resistance among the more traditional communities, French Judaism ultimately exceeded early hopes, crafting a version of modern Judaism that sought to promote the values of France not only to Jews within France but also to Jewish communities around the world. By the centenary of the Revolution, French Jews had come to see France itself as the inheritor of the Mosaic legacy.[10] It was in France that the first international Jewish aid organization was established, the Alliance israélite universelle, with the express mission of spreading French values to Jewish people across the Mediterranean basin and indeed around the globe. As the Alliance urged in its mission statement, "if . . . you believe that the influence of the principles of '89 is all powerful in the world . . . that the example of peoples who enjoy absolute religious equality is a force . . . [then] *Israélites* of the entire world, come give us your membership, your cooperation."[11] As some scholars have argued, this mission itself almost replaced the traditional modes of practice as a means of asserting Jewish identity for a particularly successful sector of the Parisian Jewish world. Jewish statesmen and scholars chose the religion of civilization and the task of spreading the ideals of morality and freedom over observance of Torah.[12]

Paradoxically, it was this identification between Judaism and France that made Jews an easy target of anti-Republican sentiment by the end of the century. Jews were a convenient scapegoat for populations opposing the Third Republic from the Right and the Left. Insofar as Jews were seen to have gained from the Revolution, they could also be blamed for its ills. *La Croix*, the leading Catholic newspaper, referred in 1889 to the Centenary Celebration as "the Semitic Centenary." Édouard Drumont's vituperative and wildly popular *La France juive*, published in 1896, argued that the Jews were the true beneficiary of the Revolution and were simultaneously responsible for the corrosion of the values of the nation.[13]

With the Dreyfus Affair, which commenced with the arrest of Captain Alfred Dreyfus on the charge of espionage in 1894 and did not ultimately conclude until his final exoneration in 1906, the Jewish Question took center stage in France as a means by which the nation itself debated its relation to its past and its trajectory forward. The question of whether France was a culture built from blood and soil with a Catholic, monarchist sensibility or a nation identified with its Revolution and the abstract ideals of *liberté, egalité,* and *fraternité* was fought over the back of one Jew. The outcome was the 1905 edict separating church and state. It promised religious freedom and defined the state and its institutions in secular terms, thus establishing the current parameters of the notion of *laïcité*. It is a concept that has had long-lasting influence on the French conception of religion and the public sphere, unexpectedly coming to inhibit Jews' and Muslims' capacity to express their religious identity and practice their traditions in France. Its influence continues to reverberate today in recent debates over the nature of French secularism, an issue now co-opted by right-wing parties, which had originally fought to maintain Catholicism's influence on the state.

While the Dreyfus Affair has been often credited with motivating Theodor Herzl to write *Der Judenstaat*, thus officially launching the Zionist movement, French Jews were, as a group, probably the least receptive of any European Jewish population to the idea that Zionism was the answer to antisemitism.[14] At the height of the Dreyfus Affair, in 1898 after the publication of Zola's famous "J'accuse," Herzl, disgruntled by the complacency of the French Jewish community, complained that "they are no longer [even] Jews."[15] While some pro-Zionist voices did emerge from the scandal, including Bernard Lazare's and those of the poets and writers André Spire and Edmond Fleg, the major organs of French Judaism persisted in their resistance to, or at least ambivalence toward, the Zionist movement into the 1940s. It seemed a given among the community's dominant strands that the very terms of the Zionist project were at odds with the character of French Judaism. Where French Judaism had defined itself in confessional terms, as a parallel faith to Catholic and Protestant Christianity, Zionism redefined the Jews as a nation. French Jewish scholars and activists tended to see the Dreyfus Affair as a battle to protect the ideals of French humanism. The Zionists, at least implicitly, in shaping their own ethnocentric politics acknowledged and legitimized the arguments of the very ethnic separatists against whom the Dreyfusards had fought so avidly. "But the spirit of Judaism as it is reflected in its history is the condemnation of Zionism," stated a 1907 article in the traditionalist Jewish review *Univers israélite*.[16] From the 1890s to 1940, the political views held by France's Jewish population would grow more diverse as the community was fed by new sources.[17]

During these years France saw an influx of Jewish immigrants, streaming in first in response to the pogroms in the Pale of Settlement and then later to escape the Nazi regime. The Jewish population of France increased by about a third by 1914 and doubled by 1939. These new immigrants brought with them a myriad of Jewish sensibilities, from Hasidism to Bundist and Zionist perspectives.[18] In the long run this community did much to change the standing of Zionism in France. In the short run the *Ostjuden* in their poverty and with their distinctive dress were often viewed as a dangerous spectacle, a provocation to antisemitism. Even while Jewish organizations strove to improve the social welfare of this population, the majority of which congregated in the 4th and 11th arrondissements of Paris, the language they used to describe their predicament, referring to them even in print as "les sales Juifs," often smacked of condescension.[19] And yet it was by means of these immigrants that French Judaism not only became more pluralistic but also advanced the depth of its learning.[20]

The greatest Jewish teachers of the 1930s, 1940s, and 1950s arose from the ranks of refugees. Jacob Gordin, for example, in the sweep of his migration from revolutionary Russia to Weimar Berlin and finally into France, brought with him the teachings of Kabbalah that he had acquired while traveling in Russia and then the neo-Kantian philosophy he had studied in Germany, as well as a great knowledge of medieval Jewish philosophy, finally disseminating these riches to a generation of thirsty young Jews during and in the years immediately following the Second World War. And Emmanuel Levinas credited the mysterious and nomadic Chouchani, supposedly himself from Lithuania, for teaching him everything he knew about the Talmud.[21] The German Leo Cohn introduced what he called neo-Hasidism to young Jews in the South of France during the war. And Rav Zalman Schneerson, the brother of the Chabad Rebbe, founded children's homes during the war and later taught Kabbalah out of his apartment in the 10th arrondissement of Paris into the 1960s. Thanks to these masters and others, French Jews became the students of German and Russian Jews whose culture and practices they often had not acknowledged before the war.[22]

There can be no doubt that the Second World War altered the terms of French Judaism, the self-understanding of French Jews, and the project and mission of the nation's Jewish organizations. When all was said and done, French Jews fared better in the war than the Jews of almost any other nation occupied by the Nazis, but its impact was far-reaching nonetheless. It is generally estimated that a quarter of the Jews in France during the war perished as a consequence of the occupation. Of the three hundred thousand present in France, some seventy-five thousand were deported, very few of whom returned. The survival of so many was a consequence of a number of factors, among which was a network of successful underground operations sheltering Jews on farms and in convents across the South of France.[23] Nonetheless, during and after the war Jews in France had to come to terms with the fact that it was not the Nazis who first instituted race laws against them, but their own government. The first race laws went into effect in October 1940 and were instituted by General Pétain's military government, which ruled the unoccupied section of France after the armistice agreement of June 22. As scholars have successfully demonstrated, these statutes did not follow from Nazi orders but rather grew out of the convictions of France's own right wing. The first statute of October 3 was aimed at eliminating Jewish influence by dismissing Jews from all elected bodies, civil, military, and judiciary service, including teaching posts and positions in journalism and the media. The second, issued on October 4, authorized the internment of foreign-born Jews, and the third, following on October 7, repealed the Crémieux Decree of 1870, which had granted French citizenship to the Jews of Algeria.[24]

One consequence of these ordinances was that many in the highly educated sector of the Jewish population were not only dislocated—driven south by the invasion—but barred from their professions and stripped of a patriotic orientation that had informed their sense of identity. These young Jews, for whom service to their nation had been a guiding principle, now lacked not only an occupation but also a worldview. Already during the war a reorientation of Jewish life and identity began to take place at farm schools, in study circles, and in children's homes. In the spring of 1941, the Jewish poet Edmond Fleg and the leader of the Jewish scouting movement Robert Gamzon held a camp for former officers, functionaries, and professors at Fleg's summer home in Beauvallon. The object was to redirect these figures to a new calling: the revival of Judaism. While certainly this movement reached only a small minority of young Jews, inspiring many of those to emigrate to Palestine, one can clearly trace the beginnings of a new approach to Judaism and to Jewish thought in France to this movement and those it affected.

In Algeria, the revocation of the Crémieux Decree, which had granted Jews French citizenship in 1870, setting them apart from their Muslim neighbors, also initiated something of a soul-searching process among North African Jews, a calling into question of identity and allegiance, which would then be further complicated by the Algerian War and the effects of decolonialization. For some, like the writer Albert Memmi, the statutes motivated a reassertion of Jewish identity, if not in religious terms, then at least in political ones. For others, like the philosopher Jacques Derrida, the statutes prompted an examination of the very terms of belonging and even the nature of what it meant to possess a language and an identity, an experience he would thematize in *Monolingualism of the Other* as having only one language, which was not his own.

In the initial years following the war, the Jewish community had much to do merely to rebuild infrastructure in France, to relocate displaced persons, and to house and clothe orphans. But already by 1946, French Jews were reflecting on the way forward, as well as looking back: forward to a future in Palestine and to a Judaism defined now by the relationship between the Diaspora and the new homeland; back into the tradition, into its sources as a site of wisdom and teaching, and also back into the history of the relationship between Judaism and the French state.

For a number of French Jewish thinkers, this meant questioning the assimilationist and apologetic postures that had characterized Judaism's self-definition in France before the war. Instead of attempting to show the myriad of ways in which Judaism was consonant with French values, Jewish thinkers began looking to Judaism for an alternative to the wisdom of the Christian West. André Neher, one of the most important figures in the postwar movement, called in 1963 for a reformulation of what it meant to be a French Jewish intellectual. Instead of referring to "the lost child of Judaism," the intellectual would now use his intellect in the service of Judaism.[25] Judaism emerged as a source uncontaminated by the violent irruptions of the twentieth century, a tradition that had, as Hegel suggested and Rosenzweig reaffirmed, been excluded from the playing field of world history, but which for that very reason could now speak to contemporary social and political dilemmas. Postwar French thinkers sought, as Levinas himself put it in a 1968 essay titled "The Jewish Cultural Renaissance in Continental Europe," "to receive the light of the world through Hebrew, through the arabesques that make up the square letters of the prophetic, Talmudic, rabbinic, and poetic texts, a bit as one receives the light through the cathedral windows, through the verses of Corneille, Racine, or Victor Hugo."[26]

For some, however, the endgame to this process was ultimately the abandonment of Jewish life in France. A huge turning point for many was the 1967 Six-Day War, not only because the drama highlighted their attachment to the fate of the Israeli nation but also because they were catalyzed by the French response to the war: the arms embargo imposed after Israel's preemptive strike and de Gaulle's infamous comment after the war that the Jews were "an elite people, sure of themselves and domineering." From 1965 to 1971, nearly seven thousand French Jews emigrated to Israel, among them André and Renée Neher, Léon Ashkénazi, and Stéphane Mosès, all figures prominent in the postwar renaissance of French Judaism and included in this volume. While this number does not compare to the waves of French immigration to Israel of the past few years—2014 alone exceeded this figure with 7,200 French Jews making aliyah —the nascent community created the foundation for what has become one of the largest and most prominent immigrant groups in Israel, one that is largely acknowledged to be among the most religiously committed to Zionism. While this represents a strong reversal from the early trends in French Judaism, it might in fact be explicable in terms of French Judaism's earlier orientation. The nineteenth-century Jewish establishment in France, represented most clearly by the authorities of the consistory system, went to great lengths to define Judaism in religious terms. Thus in the early years of the Israeli state, even after the majority of French Jews had come to embrace Zionism, French Jewish intellectuals persistently criticized what they perceived to be the Zionist project's lack of religious investment. Hence, as the community came to embrace the state after the Second World War, and many emigrated there, they embraced its project in religious terms.

These postwar years involved as well a shift in Jewish demographics; as the process of North African decolonization accelerated, Jews from North Africa came to make a home in France. At the end of the Second World War, North Africa was home to some five hundred thousand Jews. Beginning with Tunisia's shift to internal autonomy in 1954, then Morocco's proclamation of independence in 1955, the Suez Crisis of 1956, and finally with the Algerian War, which lasted from the late 1950s to Algeria's declaration of independence in 1962, some 250,000 North African Jews emigrated to France. By the mid-1980s they constituted the majority of the French Jewish population. This population is often credited with adding new life and vigor to French Jewish cultural practice. Like the Eastern European Jews who had arrived in the early part of the century, they brought with them a tradition less profoundly affected by the demands of assimilation and an emphasis on traditional observance.[27]

At the same time, the experience of cultural alienation was often doubled or even tripled by the sequence of events that affected North African Jews. After the revoking of their French citizenship, they faced Islamic nationalism, which developed in the first few decades after the war, and their exclusion from the nascent African nations further highlighted their isolation. For those without a strong Jewish upbringing and allegiances, there was furthermore no shelter within Judaism. The experience of being Jewish thus became synonymous with alienation. Certainly not a new sentiment among Jews, and attested here as well in Jacqueline Mesnil-Amar's essay among others, it was experienced differently in light of new historical realities.

No doubt the phenomenon of a new French antisemitism in the last decade or so, driven from one direction by anti-Israel sentiment on the Left, from the other by the traditional nationalist Right, and additionally by growing tensions between France's Muslim and Jewish populations, has only intensified the experience of alienation for some. Reflecting on the attacks on the *Charlie Hebdo* offices and the Hyper Cacher supermarket in January 2015, Daniel Cohn-Bendit—the German Jewish leader of the May 1968 student revolt, in which "Nous sommes tous des Juifs allemands" was a rallying cry of identification among students storming the streets in mass protest—noted that the slogan "Je suis juif" that surfaced after the 2015 attacks was not a means by which non-Jews identified with Jewish victims, but by which Jews took stock of the fact, once again, that the victims had been killed merely because they were Jewish.

The fate of Judaism in France is thus once again at an important juncture. On the one hand, critical attention to the history of Jews in France and to French Jewish thought is on the rise, driven by a younger generation of scholars inside and outside France. On the other hand, with each new antisemitic outbreak or terrorist attack directed at Jews, a new spate of articles appears; they replace the old Yiddish saying "To live like God in France" with the question, "Is it time for the Jews to leave France?"[28]

*Thinking along with History*

Against this background, let us return, then, to the argument with which we began: that it is by correlating its texts with the historical events that motivated them and to which they respond that modern Jewish French thought gains its capacity to signify beyond its context. The historical background provided above is a story that can be graphed along two axes, one between Jewish universalism and particularism, the other between identification and disidentification of France's Jews with the nation of France. Although I have used these themes to organize the last two parts of the volume, they pervade the first two as well, which are more strictly historical in their organization.

We begin with those scholars from the second half of the nineteenth century whose work runs roughly parallel to the contributions of the *Wissenschaft des Judentums* tradition in Germany. I have, however, included passages from Joseph Salvador and James Darmesteter that focus not on their contributions to the field of Orientalism or on the investigation of the early relationship between Jesus' followers and the Jews, but rather on their own efforts to identify in the writings of the ancient Jewish prophets a spirit consonant with the Republican spirit.[29] For Salvador this went as far as predicting a new era for *Mosaïsme*, a new religion informed most prominently by the Jewish tradition, which would have its basis in Jerusalem, imagined as a new world center. This new faith would be thoroughly ecumenical and would acknowledge the contributions of the world's great philosophical and religious leaders.[30]

What distinctly set French thinkers apart from their German counterparts was the way in which they conceived the relationship between the particular and the universal, history and the present. Rather than tracing an organic development or evolution in Judaism, they sought to locate directly in ancient Judaism the sources of modern moral and political ideals.[31] These nineteenth-century thinkers also reflected, already, on the issue that would continue to obsess French Jewish thinkers for the next hundred years: that of the relationship of the particular to the universal. Very few French Jewish thinkers up to the present context have been willing to completely forgo a claim to Jewish universalism. Even as this notion is variously conceived, showing that Judaism embodies the universal remains a consistent concern, from Chief Rabbi Zadoc Kahn to the postwar Algerian Léon Ashkénazi.

The volume's first part goes on to examine the confrontation between Judaism and the Dreyfus Affair and its consequences. On the one hand, this was a time in which the identification between Jews and the state was perhaps at its strongest, when Jewish scholars and intellectuals had risen to great prominence in the academy as well as in the government. The three most important branches of philosophy in the early decades of the twentieth century had assimilated Jews as their figureheads. Léon Brunschvicg, whose references to "religion" eschew Judaism for Hellenic and Christian sources, was the leading figure in French Idealism.[32] Émile Durkheim, son of a rabbi, was the leader after Comte of French positivist thought, and Henri Bergson, whose Jewish background can perhaps be detected only in the vehemence of his rebellion against the legalist nature of Judaism, was the guiding light of spiritualism.[33] I have not included here Durkheim's essay "Individualism and Intellectualism," which defends the individualism of the Dreyfusard intellectuals as a new religion of humanism rather than egoism. It could, however, be considered the outgrowth of the assimilated Jews' identification with the revolutionary ideals of the Declaration of the Rights of Man. As Durkheim himself puts it in the essay, this form of universalistic humanism arising from Kantianism sees moral weakness in those actions "that can be logically justified only by . . . my social condition, by my class or caste interests." A counterpoint to this extreme is another of Dreyfus's defenders, Bernard Lazare, for whom the affair was an experience of disillusion-ment with the promise of assimilation. Instead, he came to claim the identity of the Jew over and against the *Israélite*, the Jew as a minority figure, a member of the downtrodden who pretends that there is no distinction between himself and his fellow Jew but lives behind invisible ghetto walls. The poets and essayists André Spire and Edmond Fleg follow in Lazare's footsteps and exemplify how reassertions of Jewish pride and indeed of Jewish communal identity began to emerge in the decades before the Second World War, but nonetheless as expres-sions of a kind of universal humanism, for which Judaism was the best instan-tiation. As Fleg wrote in his 1928 essay "Why I Am a Jew," "I am Jewish because in every place where there are tears of suffering, the Jew cries. . . . I am Jewish because the promise of Israel is the universal promise."[34]

The second part of the volume focuses on the French Jewish experience during the Second World War. Included here are responses to the fissure that opened up during the war between the Jew and his state as well as meditations on the resources within Judaism to cope with such an event. Simone Weil's let-ter to the Vichy minister of education uses the criteria by which Judaism was established as a religion in France—on the basis of belief and practice—to argue that by such criteria, she should not be considered Jewish. For others, such as Emmanuel Levinas, Jewish suffering became the source of a reaffirma-tion of Judaism, not only as a reaction to persecution by the dominant culture but also because the experience of persecution could itself be understood as a sign of Jewish election. It is clear that the postwar renewal of Judaism was in part inspired by such reactions. Thus I have included a lesson that Jacob Gordin taught at the end of the war on the Jewish vocation as exile, on the idea of the Jews as the heart of the world, but also its *ménagère*, its housewife or cleanup squad, a teaching that drew both from Hermann Cohen and Lurianic Kabbalah. The philosopher Vladimir Jankélévitch, in a paper he presented at the first meet-ing of the Colloque des intellectuels juifs de langue française, discusses how the war brought him to appreciate his Jewish identity out of the profound sense of loneliness that he felt during the conflict. For Robert Gamzon, the leader of the Jewish scouting movement, the war paradoxically provided an opportunity to finally develop a modern Jewish way of being in the world. Though writing during the chaos of war, he conceived of a philosophy of Judaism founded on the principle of harmony. The aim of this part is thus to show how this period was both a time of unprecedented loss but, also, the crucible in which postwar French Jewish thought began to take shape.

The third part offers texts responding to the rebuilding of the French Jewish community and the expansion of its institutions, but also to the birth of the State of Israel and thus the reconceptualization of Jewish dispersion in this context, and to the Six-Day War, which marked a radical shift in this relationship. This period included the establishment of the Colloque des intellectuels juifs de langue française in 1957, the first concerted effort among Jewish thinkers to conceive of how the Jewish sources could speak to contemporary conflicts and issues. Out of this endeavor emerged a whole new spate of modern Jewish thought, but one for which the meta-questions surrounding such an endeavor were never merely implicit. Its participants certainly borrowed the tools of philosophy and theology to interrogate Jewish sources and reveal their contemporary relevance, but they also marked off the borders between Jewish modes of thinking and those traditionally categorized in the West under the rubrics of philosophy and theology.[35]

Without attempting to document the Jewish response to each major political event of the second half of the twentieth century in France, this part reveals how different positions on the political spectrum between universalism and particularism were tested. It also shows how new models of synthesis emerged, new means for arguing that, in their particularity, Jews were universal. Richard Marienstras's argument for a Diaspora nationalism, which would resist the center of gravity that Israel had become for Jews, represents one means of asserting Jewish particularity in France, and Henri Atlan's exploration of concrete universalism represents another.

The final part explores the question of what it means to identify as a Jew. While this part overlaps significantly with the previous one, it is concerned primarily with the generation that came of age during and after the war and participated in the student movement of 1968, as well as those Jews who came to France from North Africa, for whom both Jewish identity and French identity remained an uneasy fit. For this generation, Jewish identification is a fraught oscillation between embracing communitarianism and contending with the French heritage of laïcité. The relation between the universal and the particular is central here too, but so are questions concerning the nature of political identity, forms of hybridity, and the relation between the Jew and the project of decolonialization. The part, and the volume as a whole, concludes with an essay by Stéphane Mosès, which considers not only how modern Jewish thought elegantly accommodates the desire to return to Jewish sources and see how they can speak to contemporary issues, but also the historical and theological discontinuity between the post-Holocaust era and the world represented in these texts. Mosès reflects on some of the figures who have been hardest to categorize under Nahum Glatzer's terms, including literary figures such as Franz Kafka and Paul Celan but also the philosopher Jacques Derrida. What all these figures share is that their use of Jewish forms itself reflects a dialectic of identification and disidentification that marks the modern Jewish experience.

### French Jewish Thought: Continuity and Discontinuity

Julius Guttman's classic 1933 text *Philosophies of Judaism* ends with Franz Rosenzweig. In 1977, when Nahum Glatzer published his collection *Modern Jewish Thought*, he did not include a single French Jewish thinker. Reading these texts now, one might almost think that European Jewish thought came to an end with the destruction of German Jewry.[36] But as we have seen here and as this collection demonstrates, the history of French Jewish thought both runs parallel to the canonical history of modern Jewish thought and yet also provides a new chapter. In fact, one of its important contributions is precisely that French Jewish thought in the second half of the century enables us to consider how Rosenzweig's ideas were received in a community that had survived the war, for which the notion of the remnant was more than a prophetic reference. For not only was Levinas reading and interpreting Rosenzweig throughout the 1940s and 1950s, but little-known figures such as Léo Cohn and Jacob Gordin introduced his philosophy to young Jews in France during the war. And afterward it was Stéphane Mosès who wrote one of the first commentaries on Rosenzweig's *Star of Redemption*. For these new thinkers to conceive of the Jewish people as standing outside history was, however, an altogether different task than it had been for Rosenzweig. The State of Israel was now no longer a mere aspiration, more even than a viable alternative. Instead, for a generation of French Jews rebuilding and reinterpreting Jewish life in Europe, Israel was the continental exit ramp toward which all signs were pointing, the logical solution against which remaining in the European diaspora needed to be conceptualized and justified. At the same time, for those French Jews who embraced the state, whether during the 1940s or after the Six-Day War, the state itself had to be justified in terms consonant with Jewish universalism, thus often in messianic terms. As Arnold Mandel wrote in the journal *L'Arche*, reflecting on Israel's victory in 1967, "already one thing is sure: the Jewish Messiah just entered the optic field of our apprehension."[37] It was only as an instantiation of these universal ideals that nationalism and universalism could remain consonant. One contribution of this volume is to show

how the idea of Jewish universalism changed and evolved from the 1860s to the 1980s in order to accommodate the idea of the Jewish state, originally an anathema to its principles.

In recent years the choice between French Jews' staying in Europe or moving to Israel has once again been in the spotlight. While the media has primarily emphasized the external forces pushing French Jews to emigrate to Israel, there is also a particular story to be told about the shifting landscape of French Jewish thought and its internal dynamics, one that ends perhaps with a renewed identification between French Jews and the State of Israel, but that offers possibilities for thinking about the Diaspora in ways that contest that outcome. As I have argued in this introduction, one thing that makes French Jewish thought unique is its attempt to formulate and reformulate itself in the face of shifting understandings of the very terms of religious identity in the French state. This story is a compelling one leading up to the Second World War, but after the war it is unique. For not only did the circumstances of Jewish thought in France give rise to creative attempts to think through the terms of Jewish identification, its relation to universalism and particularism, but they also reveal the creative synthesis that results from the confrontation between the tradition and European philosophy and literature. It is what happens when, as Levinas wrote, one attempts to receive the light of the world through the lens of Judaism, but also, and perhaps more accurately, to receive and pass on Jewish thought and identity under the extraordinary pressure of world events.

NOTES

1. The other common alternative is "Men ist azoy wie Gott in Frankreich."

2. This was the preferred term by which French Jews identified themselves until the postwar period, when the very terms of Jewish belonging in France became a hotly debated issue within the Jewish community.

3. For a longer excerpt from Count Clermont-Tonnerre's speech, see Mendes-Flohr and Reinharz, *The Jew in the Modern World*.

4. Voltaire, *Dictionnaire philosophique* (Paris: Cluny, 1930), 278–79. The first edition was published in 1764.

5. Already in the 1780s, the issue of Jewish emancipation was a major topic of public debate. Christian Wilhelm von Dohm's *Über die bürgerliche Verbesserung der Juden* (On the Civic Improvement of the Jews), published in Berlin in 1781, is generally credited as the first major treatment of the subject. This text itself was written at the urging of Moses Mendelssohn who was responding, in turn, to Herz Cerfberr, a community leader in Alsace who sought help for his community from the world's most prominent Jewish figure. For more on the depiction of

Jews in von Dohm's treatise and those that followed, see Graetz, *The Jews in Nineteenth-Century France*, 29–34.

6. This specific claim was made by Louis Poujol, a Parisian lawyer from Alsace. See Berkovitz, *The Shaping of Jewish Identity*, 41.

7. Tama, *Transactions of the Paris Sanhedrin* (London: C. Taylor, 1807), 207. For a look at the proceedings themselves, see Mendes-Flohr and Reinharz, *The Jew in the Modern World*, 125–36.

8. See Phyllis Albert, *The Modernization of French Jewry* (Hanover, NH: Brandeis University Press, 1977).

9. See Graetz, *The Jews in Nineteenth-Century France*, 128–49.

10. As Chief Rabbi Aron of Strasbourg put it at a celebration of the centenary of the Revolution: "*Israélites*, the flag that today flies above the national courtyard of the French Republic is the sacred banner . . . that the Eternal one entrusted to Moses . . . It is the symbol of the rights of humanity, which our prophets righteously proclaimed." *La Révolution française et le rabbinat français*, 98.

11. Hyman, *The Jews of Modern France*, 78.

12. See Leff, *Sacred Bonds of Solidarity*; Berkovitz, *The Shaping of Jewish Identity*.

13. Drumont's volume sold over a hundred thousand copies in its first year alone and was reprinted two hundred times.

14. The view that the Dreyfus Affair did in fact influence Herzl has largely been discredited by Jacques Kornberg in *Theodor Herzl: From Assimilation to Zionism* (Bloomington: Indiana University Press, 1993), which contends that Herzl's preoccupation with European antisemitism went back at least to 1892 as a response to Austrian antisemitism (89).

15. Raphaël Patai, ed., *The Complete Diaries of Theodor Herzl* (New York: Herzl Press and Thomas Yoseloff, 1960), entry from September 30, 1898. Cited in Catherine Nicault, "Zadoc Kahn et le sionisme," in *Zadoc Kahn: Un grand rabbin entre culture juive, affaire Dreyfus et laïcité* (Paris: Editions de l'Éclat, 2007), 187.

16. August 23, 1907, 714; quoted in Hyman, *The Jews of Modern France*, 132.

17. Catherine Nicault, *La France et le sionisme, 1897–1948* (Paris: Calmann-Lévy, 1992); Abitbol, *Les deux terres promises*.

18. The Jewish population of France was close to 100,000 by the 1860s, and Hyman (*The Jews of Modern France*) estimates that some 44,000 Jews arrived in France from Eastern Europe from 1881 to 1914. Until the 1920s, France had no restrictions on immigration. Numbers for the 1930s vary. Johanna Linsler estimates that between 65,000 and 200,000 German-speaking Jewish immigrants came to France from 1933 to 1939, but for many of these France was only a stopover, so that during those years some 25,000 to 35,000 were in France at one time. Johanna Linsler, "Réfugiés juifs en provenance du Reich allemand," in *Terre d'exil, terre d'asile: Migrations juives en France aux XIXe et XXe siècles* (Paris: Éditions de l'Éclat, 2009), 32.

19. Even in the Jewish scouting movement, which was one of the first arenas for integration, the movement's leaders described themselves as taking an interest in "les sales Juifs" because if left to their fate, they would only contribute to antisemitism. *Lumière*, July 1933, nos. 4, 5.

20. In this regard it was the Jewish youth movements that led the way. The Éclaireurs is-raélites de France introduced a Zionist badge in 1928 and collaborated on summer programs with the International Zionist youth group HaShomer HaTzair. At first the consistory, which was their sponsor, vocally opposed this inclusion. See Alain Michel, "Qu'est-ce qu'un scout juif?" *Archives Juives*, 2002, nos. 35, 78. For a broader argument about the influence of the scouting movement on Jewish pluralism in France, see Paula Hyman, *From Dreyfus to Vichy* (New York: Columbia University Press, 1979), 115–52.

21. For an account of the influence of Lithuanians on French Jewish thought, see Fried-lander, *Vilna on the Seine*. There is no satisfactory account yet of Chouchani, but Salomon Malka's *Monsieur Chouchani*: L'énigme d'un maître du XXe siècle (Paris: J. C. Lattès, 1994) is a helpful beginning.

22. See Alain Michel, *Les Éclaireurs israélites de France pendant la Seconde Guerre mondiale, septembre 1939–septembre 1944: Action et évolution* (Paris: Édition des E. I. F., 1984); Fréderic Chi-mon Hammel, *Souviens-toi d'Amalek: Témoignage sur la lutte des Juifs en France, 1938–1944* (Paris: C. L. K. H., 1982); Renée Poznanski, *Jews in France during World War II* (Hanover, NH: University Press of New England, 2001); Catherine Lewertowski, *Morts ou Juifs: La Maison de Moissac 1939-1945* (Paris: Flammarion, 2003).

23. For a discussion of the discrepancy, see Hannah Arendt, *Eichmann in Jerusalem* (New York: Penguin, 2006), 163–65. Arendt uses the case of France to argue that the Nazis "pos-sessed neither the manpower nor the will power to remain 'tough' when they met deter-mined opposition." On the resistance movement itself, especially the Jewish branches, see Lazare, *Rescue as Resistance*.

24. Paxton, *Vichy France*, 174.

25. Elaine Amado Lévy-Valensi and Jean Halperin, eds., *La conscience juive, données et débats* (Paris: Presses universitaires de France, 1963), v.

26. Emmanuel Levinas, "La renaissance culturelle juive en Europe continentale," in *Le renouveau de la culture juive* (Brussels: Editions de l'Institut de Sociologie de l'Université Libre de Bruxelles, 1968), 21, 23, 25.

27. Michael Abitbol, "The Integration of North African Jews in France," *Yale French Studies*, 1994, no. 85, 248-61.

28. See, e.g., Jeffrey Goldberg, "Is It Time for the Jews to Leave Europe?" *The Atlantic*, April 2015.

29. James Darmesteter, *Les prophètes d'Israël* (Paris: Calmann Lévy, 1892).

30. Joseph Salvador, *Paris, Rome, Jérusalem* (Paris: M. Levy, 1860).

31. For a comparison between the French and German approaches, see Perrine Simon-Nahum, "Wissenschaft des Judentums in Germany and the Science of Judaism in France in the Nineteenth Century: Tradition and Modernity in Jewish Scholarship," in Michael Brenner, Vicki Caron, and Uri R. Kaufmann, eds., *Jewish Emancipation Reconsidered* (Tübingen: Mohr Siebeck, 2003), 39–54.

32. See Levinas, *Difficult Freedom*, 43; Léon Brunschvicg, "Religion et philosophie de l'es-prit," *Écrits philosophiques III* (1958), 209–19.

33. It is also perhaps apparent in his refusal to accept the exemption from antisemitic legislation offered him by the Vichy government.

34. Edmond Fleg, *Pourquoi je suis juif* (Paris: Les Belles Lettres, 2008).

35. Some of the key contributors to that conversation were not included in the volume, such as Wladimir Rabinovitch, known as Rabi, an essayist and playwright considered the colloquium's contentious gadfly, who staunchly resisted the increasing tendency toward Zionism among its participants, and Élaine Amado Levi-Valensi, a psychoanalyst, philosopher, and devoted participant of the meetings, a student of Vladimir Jankélévitch, who, like Neher, veered further toward religious Zionism over the course of her years participating in the colloquium.

There were many others outside the colloquium whose voices also contributed to the postwar political conversation in significant ways. One was Jean-Paul Sartre's assistant Benny Levy, who was a Maoist until May 1968 and then had a radical transformation toward Judaism, became a devoted student of Levinas, but ultimately criticized him for maintaining a universalist stance in his treatment of Judaism. Another was Benjamin Gross, a student of Neher's who was a postwar leader of the Strasbourg Jewish community and helped orient French Jewish thought toward certain strands of the Jewish tradition less popular in its German counterpart, such as the thought of the Maharal of Prague.

36. Glatzer's postwar contributors include Europeans, such as Fackenheim and Wiesel, but all writing from the other side of the Atlantic.

37. Arnold Mandel, "Jerusalem 5728, le Messie va-t-il arriver?" *L'Arche*, October 25, 1967, 30. Quoted in Ariel Danan, *Les Juifs de France et l'État d'Israël* (Paris: Honoré Champion, 2014), 298.

# 1 | The *Israélite* of the Republic

The event at the heart of part 1 is the Dreyfus Affair—the scandal surrounding the trial of the Jewish army captain framed for treason, which embroiled the nation of France in a battle over its identity and placed the Jewish question at the battle's center. The documents included here showcase nineteenth-century scholarly attempts to align the Jewish tradition with the values of postrevolutionary France. They reveal how French Jewish institutions such as the consistory system and the Alliance israélite universelle developed as reflections of Republican ideals; the selections follow the refractions of the affair across these structures and consider the affair's role in recasting expressions of Jewish identity that resisted assimilation.

The first two essays, by Joseph Salvador and James Darmesteter, can be situated within the earliest layers of the French academic attempts at Jewish studies. *La science du judaïsme*, the French rendering of the German *Wissenschaft des Judentums*, was a direct import from Germany, though its character clearly shifted in translation. The German movement can be dated to 1819, when a group of philology and philosophy students at the University of Berlin inaugurated the Verein für Cultur und Wissenschaft der Juden (the Society for Culture and Science among the Jews). While the French version never had the institutional cohesion of its German counterpart, and many of its French practitioners were Orientalists with interests beyond Judaism, it shared some general contours with its German parent. Both instantiations aimed to use the tools of philology, philosophy, and historical inquiry to objectively elucidate the history of Judaism. Out of these aims came some important French achievements: the first critical work on Jewish mysticism by Adolphe Frank (1809–1893), Solomon Munk's extensive scholarship on medieval Jewish thought, including the critical edition of the Arabic text of Maimonides' *Guide for the Perplexed*, and its translation, annotation, and introduction in French, Frank and Munk's joint edition of the Hebrew Bible, and Moïse Schwab's eleven-volume translation of the Jerusalem Talmud, to name a few. Despite stated objective goals, these achievements were not in fact divorced from political and apologetic purposes. Both French and German Jewish scholars wanted to bring Judaism into the sphere of the university, in order to accord it its place in the modern West, to provide Jews with a new means to relate to their culture, one that would replace ritual observance.[1] It is perhaps in the details of the expression of the tension between these two aims, objectivity on the one hand and apologetics on the other, that one best discerns the differences between the French and German movements as they developed in the mid-nineteenth century. In both cases Judaism needed to be defined and comprehended in relation to its host. In the German provinces this entailed understanding Judaism according to an account of historical development, the emergence of its Idea.[2] In France the task was to relate Judaism to the tradition of French humanism and universalism, to show that French Republicanism represented the reemergence of a vision that was originally Hebraic.

By the 1889 centenary of the Revolution, efforts to align Republican and Jewish values had been so successful that paradoxically the association between Judaism and the Republic was cemented enough in the minds of the French that it could be exploited by such right-wing thinkers as Édouard Drumont to stir up anti-Jewish sentiment. In his massive bestseller *La France juive*, Drumont claimed, in fact, that "the only one who profits from the Revolution is the Jew. All of it comes from the Jew; all of it returns to the Jew."[3] In his centenary address, France's chief rabbi Zadoc Kahn still lauded the association, and even in 1932 the Alliance israélite universelle prided itself on spreading Republican values to Jewish communities across the globe.

At the same time, the Dreyfus Affair and the nascent Zionist movement inaugurated a new approach to conceptualizing the relation between Judaism and France. From the 1890s to the 1930s a movement of Jewish national pride developed among some Jewish intellectuals, for whom the very drive to French assimilation among bourgeois French Jews became suspect. In the work of André Spire and Bernard Lazare the French *Israélite* is thus contrasted with the proletarian Jew, the Eastern European immigrant unspoiled

1. Simon-Nahum, *La cité investie*, 13–14.

2. Thus as a counternarrative to the one prevalent among nineteenth-century German thinkers, who understood the persistence of Judaism in history only as a deadened remnant or parasitical plant. One finds variations on this depiction in Hegel, Schleiermacher, and Herder among others.

3. Cited in Zeev Sternhell, *La droite révolutionnaire, 1885–1914* (Paris: Seuil, 1978), 217.

by emancipation. While this was at first a minority position, figures such as Edmond Fleg, who straddled the line between promoting French Judaism in its distinctive form and strong support for the Zionist project, helped steer the Jewish community first toward pluralism, then toward new forms of Jewish expression rooted more in the tradition and less in the perceived alliance between Judaism and French values.

# Joseph Salvador, The People

Joseph Salvador, "Le peuple," Letter 22 in *Paris, Rome, Jérusalem*
(Paris: Michel Lévy Frères, 1860), 360–66.

The son of freethinking revolutionaries, with a Catholic mother and a father who was the descendant of Marranos, and a student of medicine without a traditional Jewish education, Joseph Salvador is an unlikely figure with whom to begin a history of modern French Jewish thought. Yet his influence on its history is undeniable.

Salvador came to Paris in 1817 after having completed his medical studies. In Paris he saw an account on a flyer of the 1819 "Hep Hep" riots in the German provinces, and it changed the course of his scholarship. Haunted by the term and its perceived origins as an acronym for the Latin "Hierosolyma est perdita [Jerusalem is lost]," he began to ask himself the question, If Jerusalem is lost, why does Judaism still exist? The question, he felt, demanded scientific study, and thus the half-Jewish Salvador went on to study with Abraham Hai de Cologna, the chief rabbi of Paris, and to write a series of monographs on Judaism, from its ancient history through its relation to early Christianity and the Roman Empire to its lasting impact on the French Enlightenment and the revolutionary legacy to its potential as a messianic guide for humanity. In the course of his studies Salvador came not only to identify as a Jew but also, as he writes in *Paris, Rome, Jérusalem*, to see Judaism as the rightful guide, over and above Catholicism, to the revolutionary future for humankind. Jerusalem, he predicted, would become the capital of a new world order.

Was Salvador thus a proto-Zionist or an assimilationist calling for the dissolution of Judaism with the emergence of a new universal religion inspired by it? This has been the topic of some debate.[1] Either way it seems clear that Salvador was a scholar in sync with certain post-1848 trends in France, such as Saint Simonism,

---

1. [See in particular Paula Hyman, "Joseph Salvador: Proto-Zionist or Apologist for Assimilation?" *Jewish Social Studies* 34, 1 (1972): 1–22. Hyman sees Salvador as an apologist, and a fairly unimpressive one at that. Graetz, on the other hand, places Salvador at the center of *The Jews in Nineteenth-Century France*, arguing that he represents the means by which the periphery of France's Jewish community influenced its center. Jacques Eladan in *Penseurs juifs de langue française* (Paris: L'Harmattan, 1995) also gives Salvador pride of place, commencing his history of French Jewish thinkers with Salvador.]

which preached a doctrine of progress, universal brotherhood, and peace.[2] He was also among the architects of a particularly French line of Jewish thinking, which aligned the values of the Mosaic faith with those of the 1789 Revolution and insisted on a form of Jewish universalism centered on a missionary logic, according to which the persistence of the Jewish people in the Diaspora served its purpose by preserving Jewish law as a rational religion through the centuries so that it could reemerge in the modern era.

The letter below appears in the last of Salvador's four books, *Paris, Rome, Jérusalem*, which was written in epistolary form to an anonymous recipient. The letter reproduced here considers the importance of Judaism as a national religion and, thus, one suited to be a messianic exemplar for the emergence of democratic national consciousness around the globe. The national consciousness that Salvador imagines here is clearly not one of ethnic nationalism but rather one that is covenantal, producing a people by means of its conformity to the law. The Mosaic covenant would thus itself be the exemplary social contract.

According to textual definitions the name of Israel means the true and strong people, the one which directly sees its source, the Eternal, and which, when necessary, fights hand to hand with God himself rather than letting itself be beaten down by trials or difficulties. [ . . . ]

In terms of social theory, which is the issue here, the intimate correlation of the people with their supreme source, the generator of their unity, is confirmed from the beginning by the lawgiver at Sinai. He makes it known to us above all with the help of a brilliant antithesis whose terms must first be considered separately.

The sacred legislator [Moses] returns more than once to speak about the Unique Being under whose invocation the Promised Land is called to become an exemplary destination of freedom and justice, of productivity and peace. He opposes this true principle, this true God, to narrow, superstitious, vain ideas, to false gods, or, according to the textual expression, to the *non-gods*, who, in general, made of the land . . . a place of oppression, a regime of slavery.

2. [Founded by Claude-Henri de Rouvrou, Comte de Saint-Simon, Saint-Simonism was a radical-Left utopian movement calling for religious and social reform and preaching an immanentist doctrine in sync with positivism and promoting technology. While primarily Christian in origin, it attracted a number of prominent Jews as well. For more on the role of Jews in Saint-Simonism, see Graetz, *The Jews in Nineteenth-Century France*, 110–42.]

The same kind of opposition is inspired by the subject of the people, which he, the lawgiver, gives himself the task of constituting and establishing, a people who must always live in fact and in principle under two conditions: they must live in self-interest and in the interest of universal justice. He does not hold back in characterizing this true people, first conceived in theory, engendered by the power of thought. He distinguishes it from the populations that are physically and morally enslaved, and which he calls false peoples, or, according to the textual expression, *non-peoples*.

In his magnificent speech, one image and the other, one group and the other, are juxtaposed and at the climax the effect is to validate the correlation between the concept, the unity that is God and the concept of the people. "If you irritate me," decries the mouth of his interpreter, the supreme principle personified poetically, "if you irritate me by abandoning me for a non-god *Lo-El*, I will test you and will deliver you to violence and to the lies of a non-people *Lo-Am*."[3]

Many consequences follow for the primitive characters that witness these two opposed states, as in modern revolutions which had and continue to have a providential aim, to substitute one for the other: the state of the non-peoples with that of the true peoples, the state of the sold or enslaved with that of the redeemed or delivered peoples.

To better illuminate the relationship between these principles and their consequences, let's suppose the problem were presented to us today. Let's consider the theoretical and practical steps we would agree to follow with the goal of realizing, incrementally and with order, the long-term promise, the prophetic idea of a universal assembly of peoples.

In order to make a body of a people, let's say that one must begin by creating in our mind's eye a people that is exemplary, educated, and law-abiding. After that, we would consider ourselves pleased to produce this first concept in practice; we would apply our efforts to establishing and preserving this first-born people, who would have a special purpose, a holy mission. This people would be called to serve an experimental teaching, to be its core, and to function as the standard for the other races. We would make it the personification, the figure of the universal gathering to come; we would make it the sign of transition or of passage between the two opposing states defined by the sacred legislator. Finally, to use the expressions of the old books, it must be that this messianic people, that this standard-bearing people, would carry within itself all of the

3. [Seems to be a reference to Deut. 32:21.]

distinctive natures without which the collective unity, the fertile personification, the human people, the human nation, would not have an actual existence.

History, in effect, attests to this, and all our modern revolutions have come more than ever to support it; a people is not put on this earth fully formed. A mere multitude of men, as impressive as they may be, is not sufficient to be called a people. A true people is a living edifice, composed of intelligent and living building blocks. The nature of a people implies joining a mind to a body, an eye toward its future. In order to be a people, they must have a name, a law, and a word; they must show themselves capable of resisting more than a storm, of staying firm in the good and the bad times.

Thus what would seem to be indispensable today, if the problem were posed to us, is this same thing that gave force and grandeur to the Jewish spirit from the beginning. Consult all your books, plumb the depths of your memory, you will be able to cite no one, in the north or to the south, to the east or to the west, who raised up the name and the principle of a people higher than the lawgiver at Sinai; you will find no voice that linked this term to a more intimate and certain nobility, to a more durable legitimacy.

Here resides the sensible distinction separating the universal and unfolding plan of messianism according to ancient Jerusalem, from both the Catholic work of messianism according to the Roman spirit, and from the no less universal or messianic projects of the Islamic prophet. By nature, by essence, the universality of the Roman Church constituted and continues to constitute an assembly, a body of which the essential members are individuals, believers dedicated to the authority of the faith, the faithful. The universality of Mohamed or of Mecca is also founded on an assembly, on a body composed first of all of individuals, believers. But the idea takes a different form in Jewish messianism or universalism; Judaism is always aiming to form an assembly, a great church, of which the constituting members will be the true people, collectivities formed with freedom and originality in the image and likeness of the principle of Israel.

Every other detail seems superfluous to me, your own reflections will do the rest. I only offer and recommend a final image to you. In a church made simply of believing and faithful individuals, there needs to be a believer par excellence, a pontiff, or an ancient sage from whose heart springs the blessing of faith, hope and love, and who casts it over all the followers like millions of rays emanating from a single lamp.

Let's transport ourselves to the [future] epoch when all populations will be raised up to the rank of true people, to the era when they will have acquired full awareness of this way of being. In order to establish the church of churches, the assembly, the universal Jerusalem of nations, in order to satisfy the wish of the first proclaimer of this great messianic body, will there not be a corresponding necessity? Won't it be necessary to return to an ancient and pontifical people, to a people who never let lapse either its will or its law, who were tested more than all the others by hardship and tears? Won't it be necessary to turn to a people whose genealogical nobility and antiquity uncontestably do not depend on the nobility and antiquity of a royal family, or on a single great race; to a people, finally, that possesses the only legitimate legitimacy, that of the law, and that would be in a position to spread its ancient legislator's inspiration and native priestly sanctity to all the other attending peoples, to all its brothers and their newly formed peers?

If supreme decrees and circumstances never bring about the event to which I make allusion, search for it at your leisure. Where else will you encounter this cultivated and proven seed, this principle of a people, this pontifical law, whom will you pardon, I wonder, for having fallen, sword in hand and in its proper form of nationhood, on the battlefields where more than once the brave and the strong from all the countries have preferred to die rather than to surrender?

But whatever the future direction of our new era may be, what spirit would want to affirm that for the morality and good of humanity, the original and universal mission of the ancient people had been definitively completed?

*Translated by Beatrice Bourgogne
and Sarah Hammerschlag*

# James Darmesteter, Preface, The Prophets of Israel

James Darmesteter, excerpt from *Les prophètes d'Israël*
(Paris: Calmann Lévy, 1892).

James Darmesteter (1849–1894) was an Orientalist and a philologist whose research focused on Persia and India. Both he and his older brother Arsène Darmesteter held positions at the École des hautes études. They were among the second generation of Jewish scholars in France, including Salomon and Théodore Reinach, as well as Michel Bréal, to study the history of Judaism as an academic subject. Whereas the first generation was largely made up of scholars trained in Germany, this generation was formed in France, and their political and scholarly concerns tended to reflect the values of the Third Republic and to make a claim for Judaism as fully consonant with its values. As Perrine Simon-Nahum has written, "With them philology becomes political."[1]

The brothers were born in Château-Salins in Lorraine; their father was a poor Jewish bookbinder. Both were given a traditional Jewish education, and in 1852 the family moved to Paris to expand the sons' educational opportunities. James began as a scholar of Zoroastrianism and published a seminal translation of the *Zend-Avesta*. He later turned his attention to Sanskrit. Darmesteter's scholarship, like that of his mentor Michel Bréal, even when focused on the minutiae of grammar and text editing, was never at a complete remove from the broader questions of cultural comparison that were crucial to his day, particularly the debates surrounding Semitic and Aryan races and languages, which laid the groundwork for modern antisemitism.

What appears here is a slightly edited translation of the preface to James Darmesteter's essay collection *The Prophets of Israel* (1892). The essays themselves had been published in journals over the previous eleven years. They begin from the premise that the crisis of belief that Darmesteter discerned in the writings of the prophets, which he analyzes in detail and at great length in his essays, found its parallel in France's postrevolutionary culture in the nineteenth century. The great innovation of the prophets, in his view, was a thinking founded in reason that

---

1. [Simon-Nahum, *La cité investie*, 81.]

abides by a moral God who demands of his people justice and righteousness, an innovation that sets the tradition apart from other surrounding cultures. The prophetic message, he suggests, is the birth of the possibility of religion distinct from race, concomitant with the possibility of conversion.

The time had come, Darmesteter contends in this preface, for a reaffirmation of the prophetic message. Science had revealed itself as incapable of serving as a true arbiter of judgment.

As is clear from the excerpt below, in publishing these essays Darmesteter did not intend to advocate for Judaism, but rather to claim the prophetic tradition as the rightful source of Catholic renewal.

I

For close to a century now France and Europe have been in search of a new god and looking to the four winds for the echo of good news to come. They need this good news not only because humanity needs faith, but above all because it needs a rule of life. Every religion that is engulfed, though it may be ultimately in favor of a better faith, brings morality into the abyss for a time. The modern conscience, in uprooting Christianity, uproots itself.

Thus emerges the cry that fills our age, the cry of the orphan who no longer has a heavenly father who speaks to him or guides him. It runs from one end to the other of the century, under the noise of wars and revolutions, under the triumphant cheers of science, under the sarcasm of egoism and skepticism, under the eternal noise of life running its course. At the dawn of the century René heard it in the forests of the new world;[2] Rolla received it on his bed of debauchery;[3] it ennobles all the poetry of the first half of the century; it penetrated even across the dried-out literature of the Second Empire and the vulgar literature of the Third Republic. And now this century, at its close, begins to whisper words of faith, goes in search of a revelation, from Ibsen to Tolstoy, from Bouddha Gaya to Fiesole. In a magnificent crisis, it greets an amorphous god who does not arrive and tries to join its hands for a creed in which it no longer believes.

Twenty-six centuries ago in a similar crisis that shook the conscience of a small tribe of half savages in Judea, a voice was recorded "Behold the days come,

2. [A reference to François-René de Chateaubriand's *Voyage en Amérique*, 1826.]

3. [A reference to the poem *Rolla* by Alfred de Musset, 1833; Rolla kills himself after having spent all his money in a night of orgies.]

says the Lord, that I will send a famine in the land, not a famine of bread, nor a thirst for water, but of hearing the words of the Lord. And they shall wander from sea to sea, and from the North even to the East; they shall run to and fro to seek the word of the Lord, and shall not find it. In that day shall the fair virgins and the young men. . . ."[4]

And today too the fair virgins and the young men search in vain from sea to sea; the source does not burst forth from any rock or quench the thirst of the soul; the divine word is not in Ibsen or even in Tolstoy, and the light comes forth neither from the North nor from the East.

II

Religion is or ought to be the highest expression of science and the human consciousness. That was the case originally, in the form of myth and its divine symbolism: but as it is constitutive of religion to fix and freeze itself once it is organized into dogma and priesthood, there comes a time when science and the divine conscience that it incarnates and establishes are in contradiction with science and the human conscience that changes and progresses. This is what happened to Catholicism over the course of the last centuries, and what makes it at present a force of resistance and no longer a force of action and progress. . . .

III

As long as the fire of the fight endures, science—free thought, philosophy, or whatever name one gives it—presumes, once victorious, to replace its rival. But even before the victory is complete, disillusion has already set in.

Science equips man but it does not guide him: it illuminates the world for him up to the final limit of the stars, but it leaves night in his heart; it is invincible, and indifferent, neutral, immoral.

Let us leave aside practical science, which clearly is only an instrument, and, as with every neutral instrument, good and evil follow from the hand that manipulates it. It works for the demon as for God, discovers melinite[5] as well as the vaccine, provokes war as it does peace, destroys and creates, changes the

4. Amos 8:11–13.
5. [An explosive chemical.]

quantity of good and of evil, but not their proportion. But the other science, the true, the great, which does not work for compensation but is an end in itself, which enlarges the soul to the measure of God, which ennobles it with all the beauty of the universe, pacifies it with the silence of the infinite, what does it say to man when he comes to ask of it how to live his life? Science believed that it was the queen of the world, but when the de-Christianized Christian comes to it and says, "You breathed on my Christ and reduced him to dust; you closed off the way to heaven; you made life for me a thing without object and issue; replace what you have taken from me; tell me what I should do with my life; I will obey you blindly, command me!"—she [science] is troubled, stammers, and recognizes with confusion and terror that the only thing she has to say, her great discovery, her last word on human destiny, is the same statement hovering over religion, which she had condemned: "This world isn't worth the trouble." To command humanity! She doesn't know how, she can't, she doesn't dare; to do so would be lying. What orders could she even give? In the name of what power? From what incoercible necessity? Her kingdom is not of this world. Hers is that of raptures where the infinity of spaces and time meet, where the eternal flow of the forms of ephemeral life pass by; that blossoming of great nature which she adores in passing before it falls into the eternal nothing. And when humanity throws itself at the feet of the scholar and cries: "It is you who are the oracle of God, the priest of new times! Speak, what should I do?"—he can only cast out waves of bitterness and renunciation for a humanity that nevertheless does not want to die, or indeed he responds with irony and the contempt for advice of the sybarite to the distressed cry of the simple folk, who are better than he; or feeling the impotence and fragility of all his unaided science, he strikes his own heart in silence.

And as a consequence of this omnipotence and impotence of science, the entire moral order falls apart around it. All the principles by which man and society live are called upon to justify their validity by demonstrative reason, and, as they do not rest on demonstrative reason, they are condemned and sink. For science, in the hands of those without conscience, all that is explicated is justified, and man, emerging from the brute, is pardoned when he turns back into one. Consequently, the idea of law is obliterated. The appetite then sets the measure of right between men, classes, people; everywhere self-fulfillment, bestial or smug, predominates; literature falls into these ruts; and the extreme refinement of intelligence leads by every means toward the unbridling of the human beast.

IV

Yet this unbridling cannot endure, as everyone is aware. The modern soul is better than its doctrine and, under the foam on the surface, the font of the ideal flows as deeply as ever. The soul knows well that this cannot be the last word of thought and that there is in all this a sophism that dishonors it and kills it. The impulse that leads a portion of the young people toward mysticism is itself a first reaction of conscience, searching out a means toward pure air; a sterile response, because mysticism is the death of the soul, but the forerunner of fruitful revolt. Turning back, bending once again under the yoke that it had broken, the modern soul wants the impossible. It knows that it cannot deny science; and it knows also that it can be saved only by an affirmation of conscience that science cannot dictate and which must impose itself on science.

Now the truths that would save us are not to be newly discovered. They are prevalent, but anemic and bloodless. For living triumphant realities to be rediscovered, they need only be rendered by a voice that speaks with authority. Those that came eighteen hundred years ago [with Christianity] remain silent, because a portion of their words are abrogated: words spoken to aid a world of the dying, not that of the living, and they are weak in a world starved for justice, life and light. Now behold how humanity without realizing it ascends again toward the highest source, toward those who were the misunderstood masters of Christianity, "whose disciples we are, all of us who search for a God without prayer, a revelation without prophets, a covenant written in the heart."[6]

In turning again toward them, one does not have to retreat back twenty-six centuries. It was they who were twenty-six centuries ahead: humanity was too young to read them and they could fearlessly wait, sure of the immortality of their word and sure that humanity, in its march toward the future, would be forced to pass again by the mountain and to ascend Golgotha toward Zion.

V

Propheticism will come neither to found a new religion nor to convert the world to Judaism. How could a faith that wanted to teach man to forsake altars, rites, and myths raise up new altars, new rituals, and new myths? As for Judaism, if it had a right and reasons to endure, it was as a depository and guardian

6. Renan, *Histoire du peuple d'Israël*, vol. iii, 340.

of the Bible. It is a positive religion, closed by rite, and which cannot endure if it renounces rite, nor propagate if it conserves it.

The role and mission of propheticism is thus not to add to the number of religions and priesthoods; it is to animate the two religions that in fact today are in dispute in France and tomorrow will be shared in peace: that of science and that of Christ. For it matters little to the future if there is unity of forms and creeds. This unity is nothing but the dream of idiotic advocates of external conformity, the Torquemadas or the Pobiedonosefs.[7] But for peace and the work of the world, there must be a communion of spirit under the free and picturesque opposition of forms, so that the churches may no longer be separated by anathema, but march under their various flags for the conquest of misery, vice, and sadness.

Of all the forces bequeathed to us by the past, propheticism is the only one that can appeal to both religions, making two sects of the same religion of progress. It alone can restore to the church the breath of the future, by returning to it the meaning of the expressions out of which it arose: and only it can give to science the power of moral expression that it lacks. For the letter of the prophets is in the church and their spirit is in science.

## VI

The spirit of the prophets is in the modern soul. It matters little that they spoke in the name of a God, Jehovah, and that the modern age speaks in the name of human thought: for their Jehovah was only the apotheosis of the human soul, their own proper conscience projected onto heaven. They loved all that we love, and nothing of their ideal is at the expense of reason or conscience. They set a god in the heavens who wanted neither altars nor burnt offerings nor hymns, "but that justice rolls down like water and righteousness like an ever-flowing stream."[8] They made of righteousness a force; they made of the idea a fact before which everything else would tremble; through belief in justice, they gave it a role in history. They had a cry of pity for all the unfortunate, of vengeance for all the oppressors, of peace and alliance for all the peoples. They did not say to man: this world does not have value. They said to them: the world is good; and so are

7. Tomás de Torquemada was the first Grand Inquisitor in Spain during the fifteenth century.
8. Amos 5:24.

you. Be good, be just, be pure. They said to the rich: do not hold onto the salary of the worker; to the judge: you will strike without humiliating; to the sage: you are responsible for the soul of the people; and they instructed more than one to live and die for righteousness without hope of the Elysian Fields. They taught the people that without an ideal "the future hangs in front of you in tatters"; the ideal alone produces life, and the ideal consists not in the glory of conquering or wealth or power, but in erecting, as a light for the nations, the example of better laws and the most elevated soul. Finally, over the future, above the storms of the present, they spread the arc of peace, of an immense hope: a radiant vision of a better humanity, freer from evil and death, which will no longer know war or iniquitous judges; where divine science will fill the earth like the waters filling the depths of the ocean and where mothers no longer die in childbirth. Dreams of visionaries, today dreams of scholars.

The spirit of propheticism is in science but is concealed and without voice; that is why in the interregnum of the Word, anarchy reigned; for the spirit only is and operates by the magic of the speech that expresses it: in the beginning is always the Word. As the word of these old prophets is at once the most ancient and the youngest, the new age has not yet found words that have a magic power like theirs, neither in its philosophers nor in its moralists, neither in its poets nor in its manuals of civic virtue; for they have concentrated in them all the tyranny of conscience and of the ideal.


VII

The day the Catholic Church puts the word of the prophet in the mouth of Christ, by an act of audacity to which it is entitled, without a renunciation, because it is only a matter of returning to its source, it will have a new lease on life and will easily be able to lead human society. Even as life seems to be retreating from it, it is still the only organized force of the West, the heart whose beat would be felt to the edges of the world if rejuvenated blood came to beat there. Even today in a hostile and disabused society when a word of goodwill comes down from this unique center, a shiver of filial waiting runs across all of Europe —Catholic, Protestant, infidel. Since there is no longer a pope-king, the bare papacy becomes in a more striking way the ideal and immaterial center. The intangible Rome of the great Catholic empire—the only intangible Rome, because it is the impalpable Rome—seems to sense that in the obstinacy of nations and classes humanity awaits an arbiter. Already it tries timidly to raise its voice in the conflict of classes, but the fatality of its traditions, stronger than its instinct, encloses it in a circle of expressions which are powerless and do not penetrate. Without changing dogma, rite, or gesture of prayer, the necessary revolution would change the spirit of Christianity, would give Europe a center, an arbiter, a guide. It would make the church, which has become an obstacle, a force of life. Perhaps it is necessary to have a disastrous schism to accomplish this, maybe the genius of a monk Hildebrand would suffice.[9]

Christianity received the expressions of the prophets, but reduced them to metaphors: does it know how to recover their meaning? You came to fulfill the prophets: fulfill!

If in the name of an immutability—which is only a fiction of dogma that all of its history contradicts from its first hour—if the church misses its chance in a *nonpossumus*, and opposes the summons of the future, the necessary work will be done otherwise but with more difficulty. The profit that the spirit of the future could achieve from this admirable instrument of unity and propaganda will be lost, and the scientific sect will be the only one to take charge of the world.

*Translated by Beatrice Bourgogne*
*and Sarah Hammerschlag*

9. [Also known as Pope Gregory VII, 1015–1085, famous as a reformer and in particular for his role challenging monarchs in the Investiture Controversy.]

**Zadoc Kahn, Speech on the acceptance of his position as chief rabbi of France**

Benjamin Moussé, ed., *La Révolution française et le rabbinat français* (Paris, 1890), 249–73.

As chief rabbi of the Paris Consistory from 1869 to 1889 and head of the Central Consistory from 1889 to 1905, Zadoc Kahn (1839–1905) was a leader of France's Jewish community during one of its most trying periods: from the celebration of the centenary of the Revolution, an occasion of great festivity for the French Jewish community, through the Dreyfus Affair and until 1905, the year of Zadoc Kahn's demise and France's institution of *laïcité*, the official separation of church and state, a policy whose impact is still felt today. Over the course of nearly thirty-six years, from the time he was twenty-nine until his death, his contributions to the history of Judaism in France were manifold and had lasting institutional impact. He created the first French organization for scholars of Jewish studies, the Société des études juives in 1880, which helped coordinate and promote the academic study of religion in France. He organized the relief movement for Jews expelled from Russia, served as honorary president of the Alliance israélite universelle, whose educational work in the Mediterranean he strongly promoted, organized homes and schools for abandoned children, and was a scholar in his own right, publishing a book on slavery in the Hebrew Bible and the Talmud and directing a French translation of the Bible as well as a version for children.

The speech included here was written as his acceptance speech on the inauguration of his tenure as France's chief rabbi and was included in a collection of sermons from rabbis across the country commemorating the centenary of the Revolution. Like many of the sermons included in that volume, it celebrates the consonance of Jewish and French Republican values. It also provides an overarching view of how Judaism adapted to its emancipated role in French society, what it preserved and what it discarded. In retrospect, Zadoc Kahn's optimism is striking. Only three years earlier Édouard Drumont had published his vituperative attack on France's Jews, *La France juive*, which sold more than a hundred thousand copies in its first year and was reprinted more than a hundred times. Less than three years later he would found the antisemitic newspaper *La Libre Parole*. If Zadoc Kahn was aware of the rising tide of French antisemitism in 1889, he does not mention it here. By 1894, however, he had helped establish the Committee of Defense against Antisemitism, though it did not have the support to act publicly.[1] By 1896, the emergence of the Dreyfus Affair would bring the issue to the fore. While Zadoc Kahn continued to express his optimism about the fundamental nature of the nation of France and his belief that "it would not let itself be overtaken by unhealthy sophisms" and would "remain faithful to its most glorious traditions," the affair no doubt hit close to home.[2] Zadoc Kahn had himself performed Dreyfus's wedding ceremony in Paris and was close to the family. While one prominent account of the Jewish establishment's response to the affair highlighted its acceptance of Dreyfus's guilt and its passivity in the face of the accusation, historical evidence clearly indicates that Zadoc Kahn was deeply involved in the fight to redeem Dreyfus, even as his position as chief rabbi of the Central Consistory made him an international representative of Judaism and thus a prime target and symbol in the affair itself. Certainly from 1896 onward, France's Jewish community could no longer ignore the threat of antisemitism, even as many, including Zadoc Kahn, maintained their faith in the ideal of France as a symbol of Jewish emancipation and a harbinger of moral greatness in the world.

[ . . . ] Everything that remains of my force and capacity for action belongs to our beloved religion. I will consider that my life has not been misspent, if it is given to me—with the support of God, acting in concert with my colleagues of the rabbinate and with my honored friends of the Central Consistory [ . . . ] to add a worthy page of value to the history of Judaism in our country.

This history can be measured only in years, because French Judaism, such as it is constituted today only goes back a century; but short as it may be, it was rich enough to prove at every stage the vitality of our faith, its beautiful vision and powerful creativity. It deserves, I daresay, to occupy the attention of this impressive assembly. We will find in it great subjects of satisfaction, motives for hope and, at the same time, a useful teaching.

My Brothers,
Already during the Middle Ages, French Judaism existed, extended throughout all of the provinces in France, and was well known beyond its borders. When

1. [Hyman, *The Jews of Modern France*, 108.]
2. [Zadoc Kahn, "Discours prononcé lors de l'installation du grand rabbin d'Épinal," *L'Univers Israélite*, 16 octobre 1896. Cited in Michael R. Marrus, *Les Juifs de France à l'époque de l'affaire Dreyfus* (Paris: Calmann-Lévy, 1972), 169.]

we read writings left by the indefatigable pen of our ancient authors, we encounter in each instance the mention of Paris, Orleans, Tours, Troyes, Montpellier, Marseille: the list could go on for a long while. It was not, though, for us to be permitted to cooperate, without interruption, in the greatness of France and to share, over the centuries, its entire destiny. Alas, the movements of the times decided otherwise. We still regret the sad exodus that was imposed on our ancestors and what was, for them, another exile from Babylon. However, let us not be too severe about these errors from the past. We were not the only ones to suffer during these times when people were tried and tested by such calamity. Furthermore, there would be some injustice in judging with our present-day sentiments the sins committed by men of another time. It took many centuries of moral labor, repeated efforts by great thinkers, to bring to triumph the very simple idea that the conscience is a sacred domain, that there are imprescriptible rights that cannot be violated without committing an attack against God and against humanity, and that diversity of belief is not an obstacle to the peace and prosperity of people. It will be an everlasting point of pride for France, once this truth is acclaimed, to have been the foundation of this public right. The ancient injustice was repaired. All those who had formerly suffered for their beliefs were respected in their faith. French Judaism, legally recognized, renewed the chain of its history; the old communities situated on the opposite sides of the country that had escaped disaster, like the new ones that formed rapidly, could breathe and develop in the fertile breath of liberty.

However, my brothers, prejudices amassed through the centuries do not disappear in an instant. Judaism had the singular destiny to be a victim of every misjudgment. It has every right to merit the recognition of humanity, and it has exhausted all the bitterness of ingratitude! It should not be surprising if, in the beginning, it had to defend itself against the return of hostility, against the prejudices that would not die. And that is when the man of genius, whose magic name dominated the beginning of this century, had the thought, for which French Judaism can rejoice, to call upon all the regions of its vast empire and reunite in solemn gathering all that our religion counted among its bright and enlightened minds, to ask them about our beliefs, about our tendencies, about our moral laws, and our principles. The Sanhedrin could not but be inspired by the old spirit of Judaism, by our most constant traditions, to proclaim in the face of the watchful world, that Judaism, which adores a God of goodness, of justice and holiness, cannot but be a religion of peace, of integrity, of love and of universal brotherhood, that it preaches to its followers the purest and most demanding moral doctrine, which is the most representative of true humanity, which encourages what gives strength and health to societies, and, lastly, which puts love of the fatherland and absolute respect of the law above all. None of that was new in either our words or our behavior. It is fortunate nevertheless that our modern history begins with this noble declaration.

The effects were immediate. The first official organization of our religion in France dates back to this era, an organization wisely conceived, from which the great lines did not sway and that should, from the center to the periphery, bring with it everywhere life, order and the spirit of harmony, while at the same time connecting Judaism, by close ties, to the government of our country. The state understood, and that brought to it a great honor, that all religions worthy of the name are moral forces united for the public good, and that they have equal rights to be protected, as well as the obligation to accept its [the state's] authority and to submit before this majestic thing called the Law.

A great task then begins, from top to bottom, for the Jewish governance. This task was admirably constituted. Do you know how it is defined and what encapsulates it? By this simple motto: Fatherland, Religion. I recall with great emotion having read, in my early childhood, these two words on the badges worn by the religious followers of the old synagogue of Strasbourg. In these days, I saw again the same words on the seal that the Central Consistory placed on its official declarations. One could not describe more clearly the spirit that animates French Judaism.

It was not difficult, my brothers, for our forefathers to accomplish the first part of their mission. A magnificent momentum, indeed, was driving the souls toward service, I daresay, toward loyalty to the fatherland. Just as out of the heavy rest of winter, into the warm rays of the springtime sun, the forces of nature are born again, a bountiful sap overflowing everywhere, so the sons of Israel, freed from the ties that were opposing their activity and subduing the beating of their hearts, developed the long-suppressed abilities and devotion to the French fatherland, with their enthusiastic love and their immense gratitude, the energy of their will, the reserves of their intelligence, all this treasure trove of qualities that create or fortify from lasting suffering and that remained without use. The transformation is quick, profound, and surpasses the most optimistic of hopes. Oh! The robust hearts, so happy, so proud to be free citizens of a country like France! Their sentiments rise to the height of their condition; they apply themselves to effacing the last vestiges of an odious past and engage themselves with an incredible enthusiasm in every direction where one can make oneself useful to one's country. How many among us, for example, from the first years of the century, have enlisted in the ranks of the army and shown ourselves worthy of passing through this school of courage, of honor, of abnegation, and patriotism!

The administrators [of the consistory], for their part, have not remained inactive. They received the mandate to awaken inside their souls the love of the fatherland, and they do not forget it for an instant. The books of religious and moral guidance written for our children tell of all the sanctity of this work, all the gentleness of this sentiment. The preaching, which now uses the national language to teach and edify the faithful, returns incessantly to this crucial theme. Each noteworthy event provides an opportunity to remind everyone how dear France is to us. And we do not limit ourselves to words; our consistories, at the price of often painful sacrifice, expand the schools, in order to give France enlightened citizens, citizens who feel their dignity and are fully capable of fulfilling their obligations. The manual trades, much respected in ancient Judaism, are made accessible again to our youth. Organizations for encouraging work are being founded in our larger communities. Metz began the trend; Strasbourg and Mulhouse (how these names sound painful to our ears!) are building trade schools, from which hundreds of skilled, honest, and industrious workers graduate.[3] Paris is not falling behind, and with the abundance of its resources and its limitless charity, competes effectively in this social endeavor. Are we not authorized to conclude that French Judaism has honored its debt to the fatherland?

Today, after one hundred years of faithful efforts, I would not say that our patriotic task is achieved: the achievements of mankind incline toward perpetual progress; but the demonstration is complete, strong like the truth, bright as the day. France, in following the aspirations of its noble genius, in making a work of reparation and justice, has not compromised on its interests and has served them all. We have nothing to learn from others where patriotism and civic virtue is concerned. And I want no other proof, my brothers, than the certainty that we have, we, the representatives of the religion, of awakening a long and powerful echo in your souls each time that we happen to speak to you, from the top of the pulpit, of the fatherland, of its glory, and its setbacks, its hopes, and the right that it has to reclaim our love, our devotion and our sacrifices.

My brothers, if the first part of the task of French Judaism, that which con-

3. [An allusion to the Franco-Prussian War, which resulted in the Treaty of Frankfurt in 1871 and the annexing by Germany of Alsace-Lorraine, which included a number of France's most prominent Jewish communities.]

cerns the word of the fatherland, was accepted with honor and full of joyous zeal, that which defines the word "religion," posed a more difficult problem for the great minds [of the Sanhedrin] and created palpable alarm. We were entering a new world, where we found ourselves battling against the unaccounted-for necessities of preceding generations. After having lived a life of isolation for centuries, when religion commanded only in order to be obeyed, it had to reckon with the demands, each day more imperious, of a society that tries to take up all of mankind in its entirety. Ah! The poignant doubts, the anxieties that strike Jewish souls before this simple question: Religion, which had been the great sympathizer, the supreme good, the certain refuge in times of hardship, which had traversed with great strength the most violent tempests, could it withstand with the same success the trial of freedom? Without a doubt we did not fear for the faith itself, for the eternal truths that have their expression in Judaism and that we consider as our raison d'être in the history of humanity: set in stone by the hand of the Divine Architect, they are sheltered from the wind. And if once in a while a breath of madness seems to pass over the world, troubling minds, shaking beliefs and obscuring the view of the heavens, this is only for a time. No fraction of humanity will resign itself to seeing extinguished the flame that warms and illuminates us. But it was otherwise for our devout customs, our ceremonies, for those external forms that multiplied over the course of centuries, for the ritual practice that dominated all of existence, but that was nonetheless so rich in charm and poetry. Was Jewish life, with its religious instruction that regulates, so to speak, each movement, still possible in the face of the obligations and developments of social life? In the face of a conflict, who would have the last word?

My brothers, we know it all too well; these fears were not imaginary. We sorrowfully observe that our homes, by the fault of circumstances more than the fault of men, no longer represent, as in the past, that sanctuary of God where the religion, through its continuous presence and its perpetual intervention in all acts of life, elevated the hearts, purified feelings and comforted sadness. There are exceptions, and—thank God!—these aren't lacking. We kneel with respect and gratitude before the courageous faithfulness that does not find it to be too heavy of a sacrifice to ally the obligations of the present with the devout traditions of the past. Let us not leave off from citing those of our brothers who too easily take part in what is truly moral impoverishment. However, let us not condemn, let us not offend anyone. There are many ways to serve God, and religion knows more than one way to enter the soul.

Those who were concerned for the religious interests of Judaism during this century did not experience it this way. What was lost on one side, they took to heart to win back on the other. The public religion, whose action can be so powerful and so advantageous, precisely enlivened their solicitude. Beautiful and imposing synagogues, worthy of a country of religious liberty and a faith for which the search for beauty is a holy obligation, are rising up everywhere, and, usually, with the liberal consent of the municipalities and the state. Religious ceremonies take on a more noble and harmonious character with the demands of taste. As for the old hackneyed forms, they are substituted with new ones that are more lively and efficacious. Having become the principle center of religious life, our temples hear resonating under their arches the sacred songs that even the highest standard-bearers of art can endorse and the male accents of an eloquence that preaches the highest truths. The youth, initiated to the spirit of Judaism, its rich history, and its beautiful traditions by a methodical teaching, find sustenance for their religious needs in its religious structures. Our women, in learning custom and prayer willingly, having rendered them accessible to their heart and soul. They thus procure for themselves the sweet pleasures of a satisfying faith. Certainly some of the innovations introduced in the religion give rise occasionally to sharp criticism. Currently, there are those who challenge the right to alter any established usages from times past. But, let this speak to the glory of French Judaism, for if the differences of opinion have produced animated conflicts whose echo reaches us through our periodicals—which themselves also occupy an important place in our history—never have these conflicts caused irreversible divisions, and our communities have nearly always benefited from that precious good, which is one of the essential conditions for all society: peace. One can think differently about matters of religion, but we meet back together in equal love for Judaism.

Our Rabbinical School, in existence today for sixty years, was a happy creation and a great opportunity for French Judaism. There, young people, urged by a devout calling, could prepare themselves for the work of the ministry in the silence of a rigorous solitude, drinking from the sources of modern culture, all while nourishing themselves out of the sources of Judaism. There, they learned all together to take into account the necessities of their time and to attend to the maintenance of ancient piety. Thus, they successively trained several generations of pastors, united in their views, animated by the same spirit of progress, rich in their work, roused by the of grandeur their mission and full of reverence before their masters for the science that illuminates and the dedication that acts.[4] Ah! All those should be blessed in their graves, already numerous, who have alas disappeared after having served Judaism with all of the force of their hearts and their intelligence! And you, my beloved colleagues, who cultivate the vine of the lord with such faithfulness and consciousness, and you, young friends, who have been touched by a beam from on high and strive to enter in your turn into the sacred profession, allow me to express to you our gratitude for the past and our confidence in the future. Following the ancient method so dear to us, you still unite science and action, devotion and charity.

The Science of Judaism, my brothers, the study deepened by our past, so rich in its diverse manifestations, could not grow weak among us without immediately impoverishing the living source that bathes and fortifies the same roots as religious sentiment. This is why we have promised infinite gratitude to those of our brothers who, without belonging to the rabbinate, have examined the problems of our history and shed light on its obscurities. What illustrious names among the dead and the living come to mind? I don't need to name them; they are and will remain inscribed in the faithful memory of Judaism, and will be retained by posterity. These were, nonetheless, isolated efforts. For a long time in French Judaism, all connection was lacking between researchers curious about the past, and guided at the same time by the passion for truth and love of their religion. Today this bond exists. The Société des études juives already has some records of service distinct enough for it to count among its achievements some of the most beautiful creations that honor French Judaism and to recall with devotion its principle promoter, the young scholar whose name is so loved and so respected among us, who had only to follow the traditions of his family to evoke and encourage everything that can elevate our religion in the eyes of the public.[5]

Sadly, my brothers, I would not be a proper historian if I did not cast a shadow over the tableau that I just placed before your eyes, if, besides progress achieved, I did not recall the loss that we have endured. We have cried over the tragedy of France that took place nearly twenty years ago, but to our patriotic regret,

---

4. [The term "science" refers here to the scholarly study of Judaism. As in the case of the German *Wissenschaft des Judentums,* in the nineteenth century France developed its own branch of Jewish studies, *la science de judaïsme.*]

5. [Refers most likely to Baron James de Rothschild, who convened the society's founding meeting in 1879 and was its first president. See *Revue des Études Juives,* juillet–septembre 1880, no. 1. Zadoc Kahn was also one of the founding members, and Rothschild credits him as the impetus for the creation of the society.]

are added religious regrets. France was mutilated, French Judaism was equally! How could our heart not be touched on this day, at the memory of those old and beautiful communities that belonged to our patrimony, which were a force for us in the present and a precious reserve for the future? How many among us left behind there, with their childhood memories, a part of their soul! If something can, not console, but soften our pain, it's the thought that a great number of our brothers from the East, in order not to cease loving France freely, preferred to abandon their homes and come to enlarge our ranks and to bring extra strength to our French communities. This is also the thought of this new France that extends, in its picturesque beauty, from the other side of the Mediterranean. Can Jewish Algeria continue to follow the path of social progress on which it has so firmly begun, to take on the obligations tied to the honor of calling oneself a French citizen more and more each day, and to oppose all those attacks, all these affronts that only dishonor those who launch them; can it develop the conscience that comes from duty fulfilled and the decided will to do what is right? This is our wish and our firm hope.

My brothers, those who are familiar with the spirit of Judaism, who know what there is in its laws and in its teaching of humanity and out of tender devotion for those who suffer, will not be surprised if I say that French Judaism proves its creative force as much in the domain of charity as in that of religion. It has married without hesitation all the contemporary aspirations. Don't be fooled, indeed, this infinite sympathy for misery in all its so sadly varied forms will be the distinctive and glorious mark of the century in which we live. There will come a time when all things will be put in their rightful place, when our pointless quarrels will be forgotten, when we will come to pity the crazy passions that are agitated on the surface of our society, but when the depths of the French character will appear in its true light. We will then say: This century was a great century, because it was touched by every suffering; it created wonders to lighten the weight of pain, to protect the youth without support, the old without resources, to give a helping hand to those who have fallen and to introduce more justice, equality, and love in an inevitably imperfect world. Judaism, be sure of it, will gather its share of justified praise: because for a hundred years, it has brought charitable institutions into existence! Is there a Jewish community that hasn't heard the cry of hunger, of disease, of moral or material misery and done everything to come to the aid of victims in this life? It pleases me to see this assembly where I recognize so many good men, so many noble women of Israel, for whom the devotions of charity are a joy and a need. Their active kindness doesn't halt at the limits of their religion, and we know for sure that the holy army of the good does not have more energetic and tenacious combatants.

There is more, my brothers. Our beloved France, among so many high and generous qualities that it has received from heaven, is blessed with the power of expansion. It has always made its moral conquests radiate outward; the work it has accomplished for itself, often at the price of cruel hardship, has benefited all people. French Judaism has shown that it possesses something of this providential gift. Free and prosperous, alive and growing under the protection of law, we have not forgotten that thousands of our brothers have merely heard of the good deeds of civilization, that for them there is neither security nor instruction nor guarantee. Laws that condemn the modern consciousness block them from every route and enclose them as if in a prison without air and without daylight. We have heard their harrowing calls; those that have the power and the heart have been searching for a long time to remedy such desperate calamities. Others have united their efforts, and thus was born on the soil of France, like a native product, the Alliance israélite, one of the most beautiful manifestations of the Jewish genius, which pursues as its singular goal: relieving from undeserved decay populations meriting every sympathy, and employing as its sole means: school and workshop, instruction and work.

Here you have it, my brothers, how French Judaism, to which we have the honor to belong, has appeared to us: as a strong organization that binds our communities into a single network and that, without hindering anywhere the spirit of initiative, so necessary to life and to progress toward the good, is the powerful safeguard of our unity; at the summit, a Central Consistory, composed of distinguished men and which is itself the emanation of Judaism in our country; regional consistories, whose authority is so well respected that it has the endorsement of all, and which, I know through a twenty-year collaboration, is founded on piety, devotion and the perfect knowledge of the interests of our religion; underneath, the administration invested by a freely accepted mandate filled with dignity; a rabbinic body that steeps itself strictly in the cycle of its work and upholds honor in neglecting nothing; everywhere peace and harmony in the emulation of efforts and, despite the sometimes lively battle of opinions, no rupture between hearts; a public religion that tends without ceasing toward purifying and ennobling itself; a magnificent blossoming of charity; respect for the old Jewish solidarity allied to a patriotism that expresses itself with radiance in everyday life; a zealous care not to create difficulties for the government of our country, which in return provides a goodwill and fairness that touches us deeply, and of which we have a precious testimony even today; finally, neighborly relations and mutual respect with other religions, that preach as we do the love of God, love of men, cult of work, and devotion to the fatherland. We could not, at the dawning of this century, conceive for Judaism a more beautiful destiny: it has made promises to the country, and it has kept them; it has received duties from the past that were a sacred legacy, and it has not betrayed them!

My brothers, what have I wanted in tracing this brief history of a recent past? To give you a feeling of pride in your souls? To inspire in you the blissful satisfaction that believes that everything is done and there is nothing left to do? That doesn't please God! We are surrounded by enough difficulties, obsessed by enough sadness, to be inclined to modesty. And so, we don't neglect that life, for individuals as for societies, is a battle of every moment, a fight against blind forces, a fight against outside hostilities, a fight against internal weaknesses.

What I wanted, my brothers, is above all to thank God, who has kept watch over our fate since the beginning of our history until this day; to express our recognition of France, that made itself, in our eyes, the charitable instrument of the Divine Providence; and at last, to pay homage to our precursors, who have had enough resolution in their mind to understand their work, and enough rigor in their character to fulfill it. For this triply paid debt, let's resolve to continue the work that their hands passed down to us, to maintain in our souls the religious faith that animated them, and to devote ourselves, as they have done, to the interests of the religion, the homeland, and humanity.

Let's be inspired by the past to work for the future. Let's raise our children steeped in the feelings of piety, of virtue, and moral austerity such that one day they can take our place as we have taken those of our predecessors and perpetuate, across the ages, the tradition of Judaism, that is of loving God in heaven, and of serving the sacred causes of the good, justice and truth on earth.

Lord, how could we not raise our thoughts and our prayers towards you in circumstances as serious as these? Our destiny is in your hands, and it's your holy will that prescribes our task. We must be inclined before this will and then do our best in order not to neglect the law of our life. But, in your infinite kindness, you come to the aid of our weakness; by a special grace, you gage our strength to the burden you have imposed on us.

How we must be given to one another to carry the weight of our task without weakening, so that we may be worthy to garner with the avowal of our conscience, your divine approbation. That is the true, ultimate blessing!

My brothers and sisters, be blessed!

Amen

*Translated by Beatrice Bourgogne*
*and Sarah Hammerschlag*

# 4

# Bernard Lazare, Judaism's Conception of the Social and the Jewish People; Jewish Capitalism and Democracy

The following two essays appeared in Bernard Lazare, *Juifs et antisémites* (Paris: Alia, 1992), later republished under the title *La question juive*. The footnotes from that collection are included here. Both essays were originally published in periodicals of the day.

Bernard Lazare, excerpt from "La conception sociale du judaïsme et le peuple juif," *La Grande Revue*, September 1899.

Bernard Lazare, excerpt from "Capitalisme juif et démocratie," *L'Aurore*, May 20, 1901.

Bernard Lazare is a pivotal figure in the modern history of Jews in France. Best known for his public defense of Alfred Dreyfus, the Jewish army captain famously accused of treason, Lazare was the author of one of the first books by a Jew on antisemitism, and a prominent figure in the early Zionist movement. He played a number of important roles in framing and describing the Jewish Question in France, but was hardly a consistent advocate for his people.

He was born Lazare Manassé in 1865 in the town of Nîmes. His family could trace its French Jewish roots back two thousand years. In his earliest writings on Jews in *Le miroir des légendes* (1892), he uncritically accepted the medieval Christian depiction of the Jew as a traitor to Christ. He went on to write the first systematic treatment of antisemitism, which allowed him to understand Jewish history beyond the Christian depiction. Yet Lazare's *Antisemitism: Its History and Causes* is hardly a book defending Judaism against the accusations of antisemites. It claims, in fact, that given the diversity of Judaism's enemies culturally and historically, the causes of the phenomenon had to reside "in Israel itself, and not in those who antagonized it."[1]

Reading his early work alongside his most mature essays is a study in contrasts. In the early work, Lazare seeks a solution to antisemitism in assimilation, and point-

---

1. [Bernard Lazare, *Antisemitism: Its History and Causes* (Lincoln: University of Nebraska Press, 1995).]

edly distinguishes *les Israélites* from their eastern counterparts, the "Jews" whom he consistently refers to in the third person and describes in terms borrowed from the antisemites. In later essays, quite to the contrary, he champions the cause of the Jewish proletariat over against "Jewish capitalists," arguing that antisemitism has lost sight of the plight of the majority of the world's Jews, whose suffering outstrips that of any other nation. The shift was impelled by his involvement in the Dreyfus Affair. Asked to write a defense of Dreyfus by the Dreyfus family, Lazare found himself speaking not only for Alfred Dreyfus but for the Jewish people as well. This involvement inaugurated a new phase in his thinking, one that can be characterized as socialist Zionism.[2] Instead of advocating assimilation, Lazare made it his mission to reveal the "moral ghetto" in Paris, the invisible social barriers that separated Jews from their Christian neighbors. Concomitant with this new attitude came a reversal in his understanding of the plight of the Jews and *les Israélites*. As both essays below illustrate, Lazare never relinquished the distinction between the Jew and the *Israélite*, but the latter was now cast in the role of traitor for having developed a slavish devotion to Christian society from which acceptance was sought in vain.

As a figure remembered in history, Bernard Lazare's legacy is largely mediated by two influential accounts, those of the poet, essayist, and mystic Charles Péguy and the political philosopher Hannah Arendt. Péguy and Lazare met in the context of the Dreyfus Affair and developed a strong bond. When Lazare died in 1903 at the age of thirty-eight, Péguy made it his mission to propagate his memory, describing him as a kind of latter-day prophet, a martyr who had lived and died for his people, a hero fighting for the persecuted who had died unrecognized. Whereas Péguy's portrait provides a distinctly Christian perspective on the Jewish figure, Arendt's depiction helped make him a representative of a new way of being Jewish. As Arendt herself came to reject an assimilationist model of Jewish and Christian coexistence in the 1930s, she saw in Lazare a model of a pariah-type Jewish identity. By claiming the pariah role, Jews could take pride in their marginal status, in being "the ever ancient stiff-necked people, the unruly and rebel nation."[3] While some French Jewish thinkers and writers, such as André Spire and Edmond Fleg, followed suit in developing stronger characterizations of French Jewish identity,

2. [Arthur Hertzberg, *The Zionist Idea* (Philadelphia: Jewish Publication Society, 1997), 470.]

3. [Bernard Lazare, "Le nationalisme et l'émancipation juive," *La question juive* (Paris: Allia, 2012), 158.]

the kind of pride in difference that Lazare pioneered began to develop as a cultural movement in France only after the Second World War.

The two essays included here represent the later stage of Lazare's thinking on the Jewish Question. In the first, he addresses a form of antisemitism that infected both the Right and the Left, the association between Jews and capital, and in the process highlights a concept of Jewish nationalism that located the soul of the people in its proletariat. In the second, he attacks in the person of Arthur Meyer, Jewish convert to Catholicism and director of the right-wing royalist newspaper *Le Gaulois*, the class of assimilated French Jews who chose to protect their own social standing even in the face of antisemitism. Here Lazare's portrait of Jewish capitalism draws quite close to the very economic antisemitism that he critiques in the first essay, but with a very different explanation for it and a solution for it very different from that of his adversaries.

## JUDAISM'S CONCEPT OF THE SOCIAL AND THE JEWISH PEOPLE

For two thousand years the Jews have been scattered among the nations and have partitioned off their life; for centuries they have been in constant contact with the Christian peoples, and yet their customs, their spirit, the teachings of their sacred books, even the teachings of their philosophers, are less known than the habits of the Dahomans or the Lapps.[4] In appraising their role, their activity, and their intellect, one consistently makes use of a certain number of given formulas, the same baggage of ancient prejudice that possesses no other merit than an undeniable antiquity.

In the eyes of the world, the Jews were a group of usurers in times past, trained by the Talmud in the most subtle impostures, brought up in the art of garnering the maximum amount of gold. Today they are acknowledged outright for having marvelous qualities as siphons and traders of capital, but one can go further, and if one grants the Jews these gifts, it is by virtue of an alleged social concept that is supposedly characteristic of them. It is not necessary to believe that this is solely an antisemitic view; it would then not deserve the trouble of being opposed, or even discussed; it is likewise the view of men who would vehemently protest were you to attribute to them the least hint of prejudice; it is the view of

4. Dahomans are a West African people, the Lapps an ethnic group of indigenous Arctic dwellers.

intellectuals enlightened in all things save this, it is even the view of some socialists, notably Jaurès, and that is why it must be answered.[5]

For those whom I have just mentioned, the social concept of the Jews is an essentially mercantile concept; in this manner they think as do the antisemites, but they confine themselves to expressing their thought in a different fashion; they present it with a scientific apparatus and a kind of economic dogmatism, yet basically they end up with the same result. They regard capitalism as a Jewish creation, and just as Drumont after Gougenot des Mousseaux, so does Jaurès after Marx speak of the Judaization of the Christian peoples.[6]

[ . . . ]

How can such theories be justified? By producing written documents from Jewish sources that work out an apologetics for mercantilism, by showing within Israel a continuous tradition suited to the development of the idea and practice of trade and, finally, by establishing through facts that the constant concern of Judaism has been commerce.

Let us limit ourselves for a moment to the written sources. Where might we turn to find the social concept of the Jews? To the Bible, to the Talmud, and finally to the philosophers and the economists coming from this nation. Let us examine the political economy of the biblical writers—chroniclers, moralists, and prophets, that of the Talmudists and the teachers of the Middle Ages, that of the philosophers and the theoreticians. Then let us see whether there is any trace of their teachings among non-Jews.

"For our part," wrote Flavius Josephus, "we do not live in a coastal region, we have little liking for commerce. Our cities are far from the sea, and our occupations consist in tilling the fine land which we inhabit."

The biblical authors did not know of a condition for man other than agriculture. [ . . . ] All of the maxims from the Bible are agrarian. . . . As for commerce,

5. [Jean Jaurès was a prominent socialist leader who became one of the most vocal Dreyfusards, though not until 1898. While never an antisemite, he had referenced the role of Jewish financiers in a number of international affairs and associated these actions with capitalist ethics, occasionally using the term "Jew" as a metonym for capitalist. See Harvey Goldberg, "Jean Jaurès and the Jewish Question: The Evolution of a Position," *Jewish Social Studies* 20, 2 (1958): 67–94; Marrus, *The Politics of Assimilation*, 133n.]

6. [Gougenot des Mousseaux was the author of *Le Juif, le judaïsme et la judaïsation des peuples chrétiens* [The Jew, Judaism and the Judaization of the Christian People] (Paris: Plon, 1868). The book's thesis, for which the author received a congratulatory note from Pope Pius IX, is that the Jews and their Franco-Mason allies are the agents of the Antichrist.]

the Bible ignores and scorns it. [ . . . ] It is not in the Talmud or among Jewish teachers and theologians that we finally discover this "Jewish concept" based on trade. Quite the opposite; and the Christian Church was heir to this Jewish antimercantilism. The Church's stricture against usury was that of the Talmud; surely she never acquired it from the Greeks or from the Romans, trading peoples, but from Israel, an agricultural people among whom such theories were naturally bound to develop. [ . . . ] In our time it is the antisemites who represent, theoretically, the antitrade and antiusury concept of the Bible and the Talmud. According to the idea they have of society, the antisemites can, without any paradox, be viewed as intransigent Jews. [ . . . ]

Where shall we then find any trace of this "Jewish social system based on trafficking"? Let us listen to Marx: "It is not," he says, "in the Pentateuch or in the Talmud but in contemporary society that we find the essence of the contemporary Jew; we find it there not as an *abstract* essence, but as an essence as *empirical* as it can be." This amounts to saying that the Jew puts into practical effect, in the society within which he lives, a concept based on trade, and that he has always done so. Stripped of all logomachy, this means that the Jew since his entrance into the Christian world has been suited only to trade, and here is assuredly what we find at the root of all argumentations, of all theories against the Jews, or of the theories that presume to explain the Jew socially. What remains to be explained is how it has been possible for such a mistake to gain currency, how it can have been accepted by informed and open minds.

Let us consider a historian who, in studying a people, in finding out that which is characteristic of it, its philosophy and its ideal, limits himself to considering only one of the classes composing that people. If he examines only the proletariat, he might conclude that this people has a social concept based on antimercantilism and on labor. If, on the contrary, he concentrates solely on the financial, industrial, and commercial bourgeoisie, he will with equal justice assert that this people's social concept is based on trade. No nation on earth could escape the consequences of such a method of writing history.

This is what has happened to the Jews, and they have been considered under the aspect of trade not only by the antisemites, but also by the Jews themselves, when they have undertaken to write their own history. [ . . . ] It is the Jewish bourgeoisie who became traders and money-handlers, and not "the Jews." The Jewish historians, however, [ . . . ] have dealt only with the history of the Jewish bourgeoisie [ . . . ] and turned their backs on the people and refused to look at it. Their history being also an apologetic history of the Jews in relation to the

Christians, a history composed with an eye to show the progressive efforts of the Jews toward assimilation—not a proper purpose—they had one constant preoccupation: to avoid writing the history of the Jews as a nation.[7]

As a matter of fact, their history is not understandable in any other terms. The Jew has never ceased to be a people. If there are among them various types, that is, if, as they exist today, they are not descended from a single human couple, it is nonetheless true that these ethnographic types, different among themselves belong only to the Jews. They have a like mentality. I speak generally, for were I studying the English mentality I should not take as specimens for my examination the sons of naturalized Englishmen living in France. In like manner, when I speak of the Jews, I refer to the mass of Galician, Romanian, Russian, and Oriental Jews, and not the occasional Christianized and Hellenized Jews of the West —although the better sort among the latter have nonetheless preserved their Jewish characteristics. Among this group a special intellectuality derives from a similar education, a like way of life, in material, religious and moral terms. From the threefold ethnological, ethical, and intellectual point of view, the Jews are undeniably a people, among whom single individuals, as among all peoples, are perfectly able to acquire another nationality. If we look upon the Jews from the economic point of view, we find them divided into classes, like any other nation, and it has always been thus. There has always existed among them a financial upper class—whose role, however, has been overemphasized—and an intellectual or trading class. It has not been adequately noted that the economic history of the Jews is not the history of the struggles between Christian and Jewish manipulators of money, but of struggles between petty bourgeois traders, Christian and Jewish. Finally, there has always been among the Jews a vast proletariat. [ ... ]

All the Jewish communities were constituted as follows: a nucleus of rich men, a group of traders engaged in small business, a great number of artisans, and finally a whole gens of poor people centered on the synagogue and subsisting on the pious alms and the assessments made by the managers of the community about the incomes of those who could contribute to the support of the religious services and the upkeep of the indigent.[8] In the charters and in the cartularies, these artisans and poor folk do not appear; they had no dealings

7. [A reference to the *Wissenschaft des Judentums*.]

8. [A gens was a Roman clan descending from the same male ancestor and sharing the same name.]

with the cities and with the religious communities, neither to obtain real estate nor to win commercial privileges; nor do they appear on the lists of those who paid taxes; it was the community that supported them, for its managers were the ones held responsible. On the other hand, there are those chroniclers and historians who incidentally speak of the Jews by speaking in the same way as the antisemites, and one is as well educated by reading them as one would be [ . . . ] by reading Drumont, who without batting an eyelash writes that the Jew is not a worker. Writers such as Ajobard and Rigord see in the Jew only one who practices lending with interest or the operations of the bank.[9] It is when you compare the number of those who paid taxes with the total of the Jewish population that you discover the poor and petty artisans. As for the documentation, it is to be found in the writings of many travelers who visited Jewish communities, such as Benjamin of Tudela [twelfth century] or Petachia of Ratisbon [twelfth century], who, like Jean Belon and others, found Jewish workers everywhere.[10] The Jewish chronicles, moreover, furnish sufficient precise information in the accounts of the popular disturbances or the discussions that everywhere preceded expulsions of the Jews. [ . . . ] Finally, the tombstones of Jewish cemeteries and the archives of the communities, or documents emanating from them, supply us with valuable facts and hints. From their study, one not only may learn the history of the classes among the Jews, but can see as well that the class struggle has always been lively within these communities. [ . . . ]

One will discover as well that no other people has ever had so great a number of poor as the Jewish people. In the first place, since war was held in horror by Israel, the desirable state of being was that of the poor or the doctor of the law. The rich felt honored in having a numerous clientele of poor people and of more or less destitute scholars. [ . . . ] Circumstances, however, greatly contributed to creating this vast class of the destitute. Farmers at home, on their own soil, traders after the dispersion, some of the Jews became the intermediaries within Christian nations between Europe and the East. After the great economic movement of the Crusades, the Catholic middle class took steps to protect its own

9. [Agobard of Lyons (779–840) was a Spanish chronicler and archbishop of Lyon who wrote "On the Insolence of the Jews"; Rigord (1150–1207) was a French chronicler who, in his "Expulsion of the Jews from France" (1182), justified the Jews' expulsion from France in 1182 as punishment not only for their usury, but also for their supposed desecration of Christian ritual objects and accused them of conducting secret killings of Christians during the week of the Passion.]

10. [Jean Belon (1834–1906) was a French parliamentarian during the Third Republic.]

trade and closed to the Jews—besides also having massacred them—the road to the Orient, reducing them to internal traffic with the peasantry, and thus relegated them in large part to the petty bourgeoisie. At the same time, the guilds were taking shape on a religious and Christian basis and drove out the Jewish artisan, forcing him into lesser trades; they made it necessary that he should work almost entirely for his Jewish brethren and thus helped create in every Jewish community a considerable category of unemployed. [ . . . ]

The Jews' economic situation has not changed in our own days. As it was yesterday, as it has always been, class division continues among them: essentially city dwellers, their middle class is almost wholly commercial or industrial, except for a tiny fraction that is made up partly of intellectuals, partly of the financial upper bourgeoisie. As for the vast majority, it is still composed of a proletariat concentrated in Russian territory, in Galicia, Romania, and Bulgaria and in important pockets in London and New York. In these two centers, official inquiries into the sweatshop system have shown that small Jewish bosses heavily oppress the proletariat of their own race. The same is true in the great industrial cities of Russia, for example in Lodz and Berdichev, and in certain districts of Galicia, where periodic strikes bring Jewish bosses and Jewish workers face to face in open strife. But alongside this proletariat that has been able to organize in Holland, England, and America, stagnates a whole unemployed people, a lumpen proletariat, such as exists in no other nation, a mass of paupers, crawling about the steppes of Russia, in Poland, Algeria, and the Orient. [ . . . ] Of all the proletarians, the Jewish proletarian is the most wretched, confronting not only his own rich men but also the rich and poor of the peoples in whose midst he dwells.

Thus the study of the teachings of their books—Bible or Talmud—has not shown us among the Jews a social concept based on trade; study of what Marx called the "empirical essence" of the Jew has not shown it either. One must look elsewhere to explain the development of the system, be it mercantile, industrialist, or capitalist; and it is owing to an inadequate study of the past and present economic position of the Jews that any man could speak as once Jaurès spoke, following Marx, and that any man can think, together with the vast majority of Jewish writers, that this people's enemy is commercial gain and that its masterwork is capitalism—when it is subjected to capitalism and suffers from it in a sharper way, proportionally, than all other peoples. Never has the Jew been studied except in his bourgeoisie; it is time to study him in his proletariat, a mass truly strong and characteristic of the nation.

Great Jewish capitalism has found its prophet. Mr. Arthur Meyer has spoken.[11] Ezekiel would not have wanted to be nourished by these words.[12] The muck of Israel profits. The scoundrel found the discourse necessary to please him, and this is not surprising: don't they have the same soul, the same soul of a sleeping dog, do they not tend with the same joy, the same submissive stance, toward the noble stirrups, the royal boots? In the voice of the one who can no longer be sullied, we felt a rebirth of hope that San Remo's speech had lost.[13] Maybe the days will return when King Philippe will deign to pay his debts through some baron of Hirsch;[14] the neighborhood will come again to sit around the Hebraic tables and eat the truffles that it will vomit on the wall covering of the antechamber, while keeping in its pocket the louis found under the napkin.[15] The richly harnessed Jewish fillies, as Bismarck the cynic said, will be able to remarry again with stallions of the race and the American competition could at least be won.[16] A great hosanna needs to be voiced in the great synagogues. Jehovah be lauded!

11. [Arthur Meyer spoke in two articles published in his newspaper *Gaulois*: "L'union de la défense sociale" and "Ma réponse," which appeared on May 9 and May 15, 1901, respectively. Meyer perfectly fit Lazare's characterization of the rich Jew who wanted to distance himself from his origins. Born into a Jewish family of modest means, he became rich through financial speculation, and in 1901 converted to Catholicism at the age of fifty-seven. Lazare may here be alluding to his conversion. In 1882 Meyer became the director of the right-wing royalist *Le Gaulois*; later he was an avid anti-Dreyfusard. Lazare casts Meyer as attempting to play the role of court Jew, selling out the interests of his people for acceptance in society. He was a fixture in the Paris salons at the turn of the century, and at sixty he married a young woman of noble origin. See Odette Carasso, *Arthur Meyer, directeur du Gaulois* (Paris: Imago, 2003).]

12. [An allusion to Ezek. 3:3, in which God gives Ezekiel a scroll to eat and its words are like honey in the mouth.]

13. [Lazare presumably refers here, with "the one who can no longer be sullied," to the pardoning of Dreyfus on September 19, 1899. With "San Remo's speech," he refers to a speech in February of that year by Prince Philippe, Duke of Orleans (1869–1926), claimant to the French throne, in which he affirmed the seriousness of the Jewish Question in France.]

14. [Refers to a family of Jewish court bankers from which the Baron Maurice de Hirsch (1831-1896) was descended. On Prince Philippe, see note 13.]

15. [A reference perhaps to Philip IV, who, after amassing debts to Jews, expelled them in 1306 and appropriated their property, but also clearly to Prince Philippe (see note 13).]

16. [A reference to Otto von Bismarck, who supported intermarriage and is reported to have said that "Christian stallions should be mated with Jewish mares," in order to over-

[ ... ] Why do we want Jewish capitalism to conduct itself differently from non-Jewish capitalism? It is ready for any alliance, any insincerity to save its coffer, but for this salvation it prefers the cudgel of great power, and it is only in fear that it comes momentarily to hide itself behind a revolutionary militia. True, Christian capitalism doesn't need to employ similar means, but it's just that Christian capitalism is threatened only by revolution; Jewish capitalism is threatened above all by Christian capitalism. Sometimes it searches for a guarantee, but that is only a commercial operation that has nothing to do with its true convictions.

To that, some will respond again: These rich Jews should remember that it's the Revolution that liberated them and permitted them to be what they are. The truth is that hardly two dozen of them remember that. As for the others, they don't even want to be reminded of it, because they only have one preoccupation guiding them: to make others forget they are Jews. This worry is not new; two thousand years ago, the Hellenic Jews, traitors to their race [ ... ] underwent surgery that allowed them to appear in the stadium with the appearance of a foreskin. Today our Jewish bourgeoisie would pay a hefty price to the surgeon who would circumcise their noses. You ask them to recall that they are members of a pariah people. But that is exactly what they want to erase. This is the gnawing cancer that is revived by evoking centuries of insults, suffering and martyrdom, the era that continues still for the true nation of Israel, who agonize in the prisons of Russia, Romania, and Galicia, the nation of poor vagabonds, proletarians, indigents, those subjected to antisemitism from which the rich are able to escape.

And this Jewish bourgeoisie of France is—maybe along with the Italian Jewish bourgeoisie—the worst of all. For one hundred years it's been wallowing in Catholic manure. It wasn't able to do it with impunity, it soiled itself and now it smells stronger than its surroundings. Its soul is dead, that liberated soul, starving for justice and reason, that's the soul of the Jewish people, which evokes so much hate; it is dead and will not be reborn, the Roman virus killed it. None of them were under the illusion that it could be revived, but the antisemites wanted to show it at work in the Dreyfus Affair. What a mistake! These influential people are interested in someone from their caste and not in someone from their race. They were afraid for their own.

---

come the Americans in manufacturing. M. Busch, *Graf Bismarck und seine Leute*, vol. 2, 218, quoted in Maurice Fishberg, *Jews, Race, and Environment* (New Brunswick, NJ: Transaction, 2006), 210.]

A privileged person was attacked, not a poor devil; the privileged shuddered. Those among the Jews who were truly touched forgot that the martyr was this privileged person, and the destitute in the villages of Poland ignored their own pain in order to think of the one who, in one instant and in a striking and symbolic way, embodied them. If the prisoner of *l'Île du Diable* had been one of the humble, who among the fortunate would have lost sleep over his misfortune?[17] I know of one, a Jewish vagabond, who is awaiting death in a cell to which sad human justice condemned him. He's also innocent, a pitiful victim of the most infamous libel that weighs on Israel: the abominable libel of ritual murder. I'm seeking those who stood up for him, among his people. An entire people, however, rushed at Hilsner, the beggar of Polna.[18] They found more false witnesses than the military committee could ever put together against him; they terrorized the judges and the defense. Where are the Jewish capitalists who offered to defend him?

Mr. Arthur Meyer knows all about it. He knows his audience; he is cut from the same cloth. The moment arrived to speak, so he spoke. For the propaganda against the Republic, for the pay of the counterrevolutionary army, gold is needed. Who can afford this? The Congregation or Jewish finance; the Protestant bank has miserly habits that don't allow for much hope. Today, the coffers of the Assumptionists seem temporarily closed—the monks are waiting, they are worried about tomorrow; the militarist and clerical crowd sees the source dry up that for many years replenished it.[19] The despicable Drumont himself holds out his hands.[20] One must thus turn to the Jews. In other times, at crucial moments, when the budgets of the princes didn't balance out, they took some Jews, imprisoned them or lightly grilled them: the system was better than the one that involves establishing and implementing new taxes. The method hasn't changed much. One can no longer as easily burn the Jew, but one can blackmail him, and he'll pay up; he'll pay.

In time, we will see if the plan succeeded. If Arthur keeps quiet, or if he con-

17. [The reference is to Alfred Dreyfus.]

18. [In the 1899 Polna affair, Leopold Hilsner, a poor vagrant Jew, was accused and tried for ritual murder in a case in Bohemia.]

19. [The Assumptionists were a congregation of Catholic brothers founded in Nîmes —Lazare's hometown—in 1845.]

20. [Drumont and Meyer had a duel over insulting remarks Drumont made about Meyer in his book *La France juive*. Nonetheless, by 1911 they had reconciled. Meyer attended Drumont's funeral in 1917 and even provided support for his widow.]

gratulates his peers, we will know that, thank Judas, the church can be saved and the situation will be cleared up; it will then be up to the Jews who are not rich to speak up. Will they?

Among no other people does one find as much servility toward the rich; however, no people hated them so much; scourged them so by the voice of their prophets or the poets in the psalms. Centuries of oppression have changed that. The spirit and the soul have been diminished, the stiff-necked tribe became a tribe of slaves who suffer in silence through the misdeeds of the powerful whom for many years they've allowed to control them. Nonetheless, an awakening appears to be occurring among the petit bourgeoisie, the proletariat, the unemployed, and the beggars. They understand the drawbacks of being united with the people who reject them and their solidarity. Until now the proletariat had a shadow of a reason not to fight against them: they thought they were Jews. But here we have it: they've become antisemites. What are they waiting for in order to push back and act against them? Those involved in Judeo-antisemite finance and industry were able to reassure themselves these past few years by sending in bands of propagandists, and the anti-Jewish criminal underworld pounced on the merchants of the Rue des Rosiers, on the hatmakers, the tailors, and the cabinetmakers in the Bastille district. They must have known that a betrayal would not save them and that if their gold buys reaction, the workers, the democrats, and the Jewish revolutionaries will know not to spare them and might compel them to march for liberty. The greatest homage that these "penniless ones" can render the revolution is to revolutionize themselves. Let's hope they do.

*Translated by Beatrice Bourgogne*
*and Sarah Hammerschlag*

# 5

**André Spire, Preface (1959) to Jewish Poems; Prologue (1919) to Jewish Poems; Jewish Dreams**

André Spire, *Poèmes juifs* (Paris: Albin Michel, 1959), 9–22, 31–33.

The Dreyfus Affair was a dramatic turning point for the poet and essayist André Spire (1868–1966). He was a law student before the affair, which then impelled him into the political fray, introduced him to socialism and, as with Bernard Lazare, ultimately to a new kind of Judaism. The transformation was cemented during travels to London for the French Office of Labor when he came into contact with a Jewish world very different from the Jewish-bourgeois milieu of Paris, which he contrasts with the Jewish proletariat in the poem "Jewish Dreams." As he reports in the 1959 preface to his *Jewish Poems*, the other major influence on him at the time was Israel Zangwill's "Chad Gadya," a short story about an estranged Jew returning home to Venice for Passover, for whom the song brings the double realization of his own Jewishness and of his exclusion from the tradition as a consequence of his own loss of faith, leading to his suicide; he drowns in the canal with the words of the Shema on his lips. Spire's reading of the story provided the occasion for his own awakening to a new form of cultural identity. It stirred his sense of belonging to his past and to his people. By 1920 not only had André Spire published his first edition of *Jewish Poems*, but he had also written a book on Zionism, *Le mouvement sioniste, 1894–1918*, and made his first voyage to Palestine. As he makes quite clear in both the preface and the earlier prologue to *Jewish Poems*, his poetic activity could not be separated from his politics.

Spire was not alone in his Zionism, but he was among the earliest French Jews to publicly assert his support for the movement. Zadoc Kahn expressed sympathy for the Zionist dream, while keeping his distance from the Herzlian version, and never indicated any desire of his own to be part of the movement, seeing it instead as an opportunity for those Jews who had not had the chance to benefit from the emancipation. For most French Jews, the early years of the movement were what Michel Abitbol has called "le temps du mépris" (the time of contempt). The situation began to change only after the First World War, and Spire led the charge. In 1923 the general assembly of the Association of French Rabbis issued its first official resolution on the topic, recognizing "the moral value and ideal" of Zionism "for millions" of their "brethren."[1]

## PREFACE (1959) TO *JEWISH POEMS*

[ . . . ]

My youth was spent in a Jewish family from Lorraine that could be traced back to the first half of the seventeenth century. They were Jewish peasants who had cultivated their land since the French Revolution recognized their right to possess it. It was a happy, athletic youth of long treks with a knapsack on my back, horseback riding, hunting, fishing, a life spent under a tent at the water's edge of my limpid Meurthe and Moselle,[2] which the capitalism of the metal and chemical industries had not yet poisoned.

But 1886! Drumont published his *La France juive*. Nationalism created a furor in Nancy. Barrès, whom I had admired, launched his lackeys against my father's friends, against my father himself.[3] Brawls, injuries, fistfights, duels. In Paris where I was taking courses at Sciences Politiques, Drumont founded *La Libre Parole* in 1892. [ . . . ]

I took my meals on Rue Serpente, at the famous pension Laveur, on whose long tables for 21 or 27 sous per day one could eat a modest but abundant meal, and where, consequently, there gathered a large number of students from the Grandes Écoles, law students, often from Lorraine, who had become part of Barrès's group, as well as attorneys from the Court of Appeal, the Court of Auditors, or the Council of State. Among these young men who came from what were still called "the good families," I felt the seeds dropped from the pages of *La France juive* inflate and expand at the hands of the article writers and polemical editors of *La Libre Parole*, and more than once I had to employ threats or force to ram down their throats opinions that I was not seen as having the right to assert. After two years the virus had spread, the poison was common. On November 1, 1894, *La Libre Parole* announced the arrest of Captain Alfred Dreyfus. On January

1. [Cited in Abitbol, *Les deux terres promises*, 88.]
2. [Rivers in Lorraine.]
3. [Maurice Barrès (1862–1923) was a prominent nineteenth-century writer associated with right-wing French nationalism. He played a leading role among the anti-Dreyfusards, elevating the stakes of the affair and making it a platform for political debate about the nature of Frenchness, and for promoting nationalism.]

14, 1895, eighteen days after the condemnation, ten days after the degradation of Dreyfus, an article appeared in *La Libre Parole* accusing David Raynal, minister of the interior in the cabinet of Casimir Périer (1893–1894) of corruption, and casting aspersions on the Jewish members of the Council of State, of which I had been a member since the beginning of 1894.

Disdain in exchange for insolence. To those who sent me Drumont's lackey, his valet of the pen and sword, I offer no excuses. A duel followed in which I had the luck of being struck only on my forearm. And from then on I was in the fray along with Bernard Lazare, Clemenceau, Jaurès, Lucien Herr,[4] liberal Catholics, Protestants, observant Jews and freethinkers, militant workers, socialists, and members of the Republican old guard, united for ten years in order to deliver the innocent victim of a military conspiracy. [ . . . ] It was an exultant period for many of us during which, out of enthusiasm or perhaps wisdom, many of the values that had provided our reason to live, but had inhibited our actions, were revised.

Thus a kind of revolution was produced inside me; more than that, a transformation. The Athens-Jerusalem problem, as it had imposed itself more than a century ago on Heinrich Heine, dominated me.

[ . . . ]

Soon after, [in] October 1904, [Charles] Péguy published the translation by a Jewish academic, Mathilde Salomon, of "Chad Gadya" by the great Jewish English romantic poet Israel Zangwill.

I recount elsewhere the kind of shock that I felt in encountering this sublime portrait of an imaginary character, an assimilated Jew, who was perhaps only a projection of myself.[5]

In my spirit, strained to the limit by this battle that was not finished, and that had forced me to look into the depths of myself, my past and that of my race, "Chad Gadya" revealed a throng of images that put me in a web of innumerable associations. It played in me the role of a crystal in an oversaturated solution, acting in the manner of a return, of a conversion: upheaval, crisis of tears, direction of life suddenly changed, beginning of a vocation. Had I rediscovered faith? No, but rather my ancestors, my race, the Judaism of my early childhood. I had become Jewish once again with a capital J. And, French poet, Jewish poet also.

4. [These were all prominent anti-Dreyfusards. For more on Lazare, see the preceding selection. Georges Clemenceau was the political editor of *L'Aurore*; Jean Jaurès was a Republican and then a socialist politician; Lucien Herr was the librarian of the École Normale.]

5. [An allusion to Spire's essay collection *Quelques Juifs et demi-Juifs*.]

## PROLOGUE (1919) TO *JEWISH POEMS*

Our poems are Jewish poems. Don't look here, however, for biblical or post-bibilical subjects. We have no taste for pastiche, archaism, the faux-naïf, romance, apology or edification, and the brief verse toward which our preferences tend fits poorly into the epic mode.

Our poems thus are not Jewish by subject: they are [Jewish] by sentiment. They try to express the reaction to the modern world of a man who does not have a single truly Jewish belief, but who was born to Jewish parents, descending themselves from a long line of French Jews, who passed all of his youth in a province of the East of France where there is still a somewhat strong Jewish tradition, whose Jewish milieu has not deteriorated too much, then in Paris all of a sudden found himself plunged into a non-Jewish environment.

Perhaps we will be appreciated for having dared to express this particular quality of feeling from 1905, that is to say, in a time when the majority of Jewish writers were trying to excuse their origin by stifling that which was deepest in them, and maybe that which was best, and letting resonate only that film of Frenchness set over their hearts by years of classical studies and Parisian chatter.


### JEWISH DREAMS

What ash have they thrown in your eyes
Your detestable books!
I come in, my hands full of flowers for your room,
You don't smile; you don't embrace me.

This evening your flowers will be wilted.

I am going to preserve their long stems
In my precious crystal vases.

Look at these carnation stems in this clear water,
These bathed leaves, these reflections, these lights.

My beloved, how fragile are your vases!

Look at these heavy tulips
Leaning toward the etchings.
And these purple anemones
Enhancing this old table.

Your etchings will be pockmarked and your tables will crack.
What veiled pupils, what heavy eyelids
They have imposed on your sad eyes
Your blind ancestors!
Let me love these transient things.

—Destroy them, break them. They govern our souls.
Our fettered thoughts
Don't even know where to set down our enchained dreams.
Snatch them, destroy them, burn these things that possess us;
So our walls would be gray
So our walls would be nude
Like the canvas of a nomadic tent.

You believed you loved them, these things of an instant,
Before, at the hour of your great distress,
When desperate about the people tearing at you
You came to kiss my hands, you came to beg them
To gather up, against the lazy complaints of men
The wall of my ribbons and my flowers.
And so you have destroyed our defense!
Listen anew to their lamentations
Even now mounting.

Open your piano, let your soul flow;
Play these high, insistent chords, these sobs.
By the purest of my senses take my body,
take my soul.

Your hands tremble, stop.
You quiet.
Press those low chords, which ring like bells.

—Oh! My dear, open your eyes!
Our room is full of a sad crowd
Look at these somber eyes, these defeated faces,
These skinny, feverish hands.
They enter, one by one, and their heads bow.
They cry; they listen, they listen like you;

They are sad; they are proud; they come from everywhere;
Some of them are well dressed; others are poor;
But none of them seems to be master of the others.

Oh my brothers, oh my equals, oh my friends.
People without rights, people without land;
Nation, cut off from all other nations,
They took the place of the fatherland.
No refuge can bar me from you.
It is not you that one calms in showing in the streets
The powerful in their finery;
It is not you that one intoxicates by lighting up the banisters
On the friezes of the palace, where others go to dance.
It is not you, prideful people, that one quiets
By sending you by horseback messenger
Theater tickets, or violet ribbons.
With you I am strong, I am sure with you.
Take me, let us dream together, speak together
Of the destroyed temple that we love always.
So let us protest, across worlds full of flesh,
Our uncrushable hope in this infidel God
Whom we have so betrayed that we no longer believe.

*Translated by Sarah Hammerschlag*

# 6

Sylvain Lévi, Alliance israélite universelle

Sylvain Lévi, excerpt from "L'Alliance israélite universelle,"
in *La Voix d'Israël*, 1932, 140–49.

Sylvain Lévi (1863–1935) is perhaps best remembered as a scholar of Eastern languages and religion. His dissertation on Indian theater remains a standard in the
field, and he wrote numerous treatises on Buddhism, Sanskrit, and Indian religion.
He taught Sanskrit at the École des hautes études and held a named chair in the
field at the Collège de France. While his scholarly interests inclined him toward
the East, he remained actively invested in Jewish affairs of the West through his
involvement with the Alliance israélite universelle, a connection originally forged
through his close relationship with Rabbi Zadoc Kahn. As Lévi describes below, the
mission of this organization, as devoted to promoting French values as it was to
improving the welfare of Jews worldwide, provided many prominent French Jews,
distant in belief and lifestyle from traditional Jewish practice, an affiliation with a
Jewish cause that itself promoted assimilation.

Lévi served as president of the Alliance israélite universelle from 1920 to 1935.
He is included here less as a Jewish thinker in his own right and more as a representative of the Alliance. It played a crucial role in the history of French Judaism, both
through the concrete work of building schools and training Jewish leaders and also
by instantiating a model of Jewish universalism, which, like Darmesteter's, posited a
consonance between Jewish propheticism and the French Enlightenment tradition
actualized by the Revolution. Given this understanding of Judaism, it is perhaps
not surprising that the Alliance was distinctly ambivalent about Zionism as a form
of Jewish nationalism until the Second World War. Even as it had devoted considerable energy and resources to building schools in Palestine, the organization saw its
message as sharply distinct from the one proclaimed in the Balfour Declaration. Judaism, Lévi wrote after his visit to Palestine as an envoy in 1918, has two tendencies,
one toward ethnic isolation and the multiplication of barriers, the other "to reach
a fraternal hand toward humanity." According to Lévi, "the French genius with its
passion for universal humanity . . . is the closest parent of the messianic spirit; it is
its natural safeguard against the sectarians who have never given up stifling it."[1]

1. [*Le Temps*, July 28–30, 1918, quoted in Abitbol, *Les deux terres promises*, 72. Abitbol notes

He no doubt feared that the French would lose their influence over Palestine and thus over its development toward a more universalistic model of Judaism.

Until his death in 1935, Lévi maintained his faith in the universalist, assimilationist model of Judaism, even as he lived to see the darkening of the European landscape. "The path of a universal Judaism," he insisted, was to oppose this darkness "in the language of reason and clarity that is the language of our gentle [*douce*] France."[2]

The following text was excerpted from a radio address given by Sylvain Lévi on February 20, 1931, on the weekly show *The Voice of Israel*, which aired on Radio Paris.

### RADIO ADDRESS

[ . . . ] In the month of May in 1860, a group of seventeen young people, all French, reunited in Paris, stirred by an event that had just upset the European world: the violent kidnapping of a Jewish child, little Mortara, seized from his family by the pontifical gendarmes,[3] under the pretext that a nanny had had him baptized surreptitiously. Was one to sit back and watch this violent return of the Middle Ages in the middle of the nineteenth century? The universal conscience had raised in vain a cry of protest. In the face of shared peril, Judaism was obliged to organize itself in order to defend its rights and its threatened existence. French Judaism, which the Revolution had made the first to be called to defend the dignity of the citizen, had been designated to take the initiative. The committee of seventeen that was formed seemed to sum up the society of French *Israélites*: among them were shopkeepers, manufacturers, artists, doctors, teachers; one of them, the poet Eugène Manuel, knew how to translate their emotion into an unforgettable appeal:

If you hate the prejudices we still suffer, the reproaches that are generalized, the lies that are repeated, the slander that is fomented, the denials of justice

---

that the article in which this quote appears was deemed positive enough about Zionism that the League for the Friends of Zionism published it in their brochure.]

2. [*Paix et Droit*, no. 6, June 1934, 12, quoted in André Chouraqui, *L'Alliance israélite universelle et la renaissance juive contemporaine* (Paris: PUF, 1965), 204.]

3. [Lévi is describing here the Mortara case in Bologna, which had far-reaching international consequences in the 1860s and affected the perception of pontifical authority in Italy's remaining papal states. The church's intervention in the life of a child was taken as evidence of the anachronism of the church's power in the regions in which it exercised direct rule until 1870.]

that are tolerated, the persecutions that are justified or excused . . . If you believe that unity is good, that despite different nationalities, you can nonetheless share, outside all [political] parties, your feelings, your desires and your hopes; if you believe that through legal means, through the invincible power of the law of reason, without causing any trouble, without frightening any power, without arousing anger other than that of the ignorant, from bad faith and fanaticism, you can obtain much in order to give a great deal in return through your work and your intelligence . . . If you believe that a great number of your coreligionists, still overwhelmed by twenty centuries of misery, affronts and proscriptions, can recover their dignity, gain the dignity of citizenry . . . If you finally believe that the influence of the principles of 1789 is all powerful in the world, that the law that comes from it is a law of justice and that the example of the people that enjoys absolute equality of religions is a force, come, hear our call. We found the Alliance israélite universelle.

Along with this passionate call, statutes defined the purpose of the work in precise and positive terms: "The society of the Alliance israélite universelle has this mission: First to work everywhere for the emancipation and moral progress of Jews [aux Israélites]; Second to give effective support to those who suffer for being Jewish [Israélite]; Third to encourage all proper publications to bring about this result."

The call found an echo everywhere. Subscriptions started coming in from France, England, Germany, Italy, Poland, Austria, and Hungary. Beginning in 1862, the collected funds allowed a school to open in Tétouan; in 1864, in Tangier; in 1865, in Baghdad; in 1869, in Edirne. Like all strong and profound works of inspiration, the Alliance found passionate apostles from the beginning. The task was not all easy for them. Resistance often came from within their own communities, rooted in their superstitions and their ignorance. Abbé Grégoire, that priest from Emberménil whom the priests of Lorraine sent as representative of the clergy to the Estates General of 1789, this priest to whom the Jews of France owe their emancipation, which was voted by the Constituent Assembly in September 1791, wrote in 1818 about the Jews from Poland: "The physical and moral state of the Jews results from their position among diverse peoples . . . to degrade men, this is the guaranteed way to make them feel useless." The Islamic regime, no less intolerant than Christianity, and less enlightened, had dulled the descendants of these magnificent communities of Spain that had played such a large role in the awakening of the human spirit in the Middle Ages. When one of the great missionaries of the Alliance, Nissim Béhar, who just passed away last month, arrived to open a school in Jerusalem, his birthplace, where his father and his grandfather were well-known rabbis, the sound of the horns was called an anathema, death threats were made, and in front of the door equipment was left for washing and transporting cadavers. He was not shaken. "An obscure instinct," so he wrote to the Alliance, "an obscure instinct informed the poor people that only the school could provide them with salvation." The school opened on April 9, 1882, with a single student and by May 28 there were fifty. In September they had to create a dormitory and establish professional workshops. The pattern was nearly the same everywhere. Thus, today, and for a long time now, it is the Alliance that is approached to open schools, to send over directors. There is no community so humble, so miserable, that it does not agree to self-imposed sacrifices to have their school, a modern school, with the curriculum of the Alliance and under the control of the Alliance. In order to help it manage the constantly heavy burden, the Alliance has earned, among the generations that it has helped raise, recognition for being as effective as it is generous; a patron from Baghdad, a protected Englishman who never failed to express his attachment to France. Sir Ely Kadoorie endowed the Alliance in Baghdad with a girls' school that would have been the most beautiful in the East if only he had never again tried to outdo himself; he built academic structures in Tehran and Mosul; he considered opening other schools elsewhere. Another patron, originally from Baghdad, Shahmoon from Shanghai, donated an école normale for young girls to the Alliance; another donation of funds for the Alliance came for an institution for the deaf and mute in Palestine. And besides the splendid gifts, many modest contributions arrive frequently to show the gratitude of the former students and their appreciation of the education that gave them opportunities.

Thus through these members and donors from around the world, the Alliance israélite universelle still bears the good name that it received at its inauguration. Without a doubt it suffered from the fallout of the tragic ruptures that have shaken Europe since its beginning. In the aftermath of our disasters, after the war of 1870, English Jews [Israélites] claimed their autonomy; they were afraid that a weakened France would no longer allow Jews [les Israélites] from this country the power required to maintain an institution whose value they appreciated. They created the Anglo-Jewish Association, but as a kind of subsidiary in collaboration with the Alliance. A triumphant Germany also wanted to have their own project for assisting the Jews, which had to serve the growing ambitions of the country. In their turn, the English and the Germans founded educational institutions and engineering schools. The Alliance has retained, nonetheless, after seventy years, a privileged role in primary education, to which it was devoted from the first day.

But it is not only to its indisputable birthright that it owes its prestige. Daughter of the French Revolution, of the French fatherland, French culture, and inheritor of Jewish beliefs and the Jewish culture, it was assigned the task of uniting the two magnificent traditions that had inspired it by a common ideal. The prophets of Israel had initiated their people into a brilliant destiny; their dazzling visions revealed to a minuscule nation, squeezed between vast empires, against which it had only to survive, the unity of humanity under the watch of a single God. Against the Baals, the Molochs, and all of the jealous divinities that glorified national pride, they opposed the Sovereign of the Universe, recognized and adored first by a chosen people, but who promised the felicities of the messianic times to all his creatures. Across time and space the affirmation of reason expressed in French literature responds to this affirmation of faith proclaimed in the Hebraic language. Man is one, the human heart and spirit fundamentally identical. Classical theater performs these truths on stage. The Romans or the Spanish of Corneille, the Greeks, the Ottomans of Racine all have the same passions, and all speak the same language. Molière transports the eternal characteristics of human society across social settings. In the name of philosophy and feeling, the eighteenth century continues the project accomplished by the great classics; it transforms their dogma into a principle of action. Voltaire declares war on all of the formalisms that tear apart the unity of the human family; Rousseau celebrates the original purity of primitive man. The French Revolution consecrates this long effort in the Declaration of the Rights of Man. The cause of man has triumphed against the malice of men. France the liberator has given back dignity to the oppressed, the persecuted, and the damaged victims of millennia of prejudice. It rejected with disgust the hatred of race, religion, color—outdated baggage from an abolished past. If temporary crises still arise from time to time and strike by surprise, courageous voices and heightened consciences do not allow it the leisure of giving up. It is not in contemporary France that we have seen bloody pogroms, universities closed to or only half open to Jewish students, boycotts organized as a weapon of war, even the peace of the dead desecrated and their graves violated. Here is what each *Israélite* of France thinks and feels from the bottom of his heart; this is what the schoolmasters trained in France teach in the French language to the forty thousand students of the schools of the Alliance israélite universelle.

On September 27, 1791, after the admirable debates in which Mirabeau, Abbé Gregoire, and the Comte de Clermont-Tonnerre eloquently pleaded the cause of "these people who are always excluded, errant, and vagabond around the world," the Constituent Assembly voted the supreme act: "The National Assembly, considering that the conditions necessary to be a French citizen and to become an active citizen are fixed by the Constitution, and that every man meeting said conditions swears the civic oath and engages himself to fulfill all of the duties that the Constitution imposes, entitles everyone to the advantages that the constitution ensures."

Our fathers took this oath that was demanded of them with an enthusiastic recognition. You just heard what has been accomplished, and what their descendants are still doing. Do you not believe that the sons have kept the promise that their fathers made?

*Translated by Beatrice Bourgogne*
*and Sarah Hammerschlag*

# 7

**Edmond Fleg, Why I Am a Jew**

Edmond Fleg, excerpt from *Why I Am a Jew*, trans.
Louise Waterman Wise (New York: Bloch, 1945), 76–81.

Edmond Fleg (1874–1963) was born into an assimilated family in Geneva. His own journey to understand and learn about his Jewish identity became a guide for multiple generations of French Jews in the twentieth century, as by choice or historical circumstance they came to terms with the ineluctable nature of their own Jewishness.

For Fleg, too, the Dreyfus Affair marked a turning point in his life. He arrived in Paris to attend the l'École normale supérieure in the midst of the affair, but also at the time was captivated by Catholicism. As with his German contemporary Franz Rosenzweig, his earliest investigations into the tradition began out of a desire to understand what he would be leaving behind if he converted. In the process, he came not only to embrace his Jewish identity but also to be among the earliest avowed supporters of Zionism in France. He participated in the Third Zionist Congress in 1899 and visited Palestine in 1931. His life's work, however, was clearly oriented toward reviving French Judaism. Indeed, he played a significant role in many of the initiatives highlighted in this volume. Along with André Spire, Jean-Richard Bloch, and Armand Lunel, he was part of a Jewish literary revival that blossomed in the decades between the Dreyfus Affair and the Second World War. When Robert Gamzon in 1923 proposed the organization of a Jewish scouting movement, Les Éclaireurs israélites de France, Fleg signed on and was its president until 1949, helping shape its inclusive philosophy and openness to Zionists and anti-Zionists alike, Eastern European immigrants, North African Jews, and the most assimilated of French Jews. During the war he gave courses on Judaism to the Jewish scouts, and with Gamzon at his home in Beauvallon, helped run a "camp-school" established to reorient young intellectuals, many of whom had lost their posts at universities and public institutions after the Vichy race laws. Both before and after the war he wrote numerous volumes on Jewish themes and was a collaborator on a number of French Jewish journals. Following the war he was one of the founders of an organization devoted to Judeo-Christian friendship, which organized meetings to promote mutual understanding between the two faiths. Finally, as president of the French section of the World Jewish Congress he was instrumental in the establishment of the Colloque des intellectuels juifs de langue française, presiding over its first meeting.

Among the many books he wrote and edited on Jewish themes, *Why I Am a Jew* helped cement his status as an international luminary. Translated into multiple languages, it summed up a particular moment in the history of Jewish identity when emancipation had borne the fruit of the assimilated Jew, those Jews who knew they were Jewish but had little more than that knowledge to bind them to the tradition. Fleg addressed his book to those on the cusp of abandoning their tradition, particularly to his future grandson, whom he imagined to be even more distant from it than himself. To this imagined interlocutor of the 1950s or 1960s, he posed the question in 1928: Will there be any Jews left when you read this? "I believe there will," he answered, "they have survived the inquisition and assimilation; they will survive the automobile."[1]

## ISRAEL ETERNAL

And now, my child, turn towards the past, look and bethink yourself. There is but one reproach made to the Jews, and despite all the lies and all the martyrdom which accompanies it, this reproach is justified; they will to remain Jews. Does their past give them this right? Does it permit them to be anything else? See the sublime design which is evident from the beginning and which from century to century becomes more apparent. Did the Greeks declare to the world in advance that they would reveal Beauty? The Romans that they would reveal Law? See this people, howsoever wretched and impure, proclaiming what their history is to be, even from the very beginning. See them choose the mission which chose them, and walk with it in the path which they foretold for themselves. See this people of ever-renewed sinfulness, twice exiled and surviving two dispersions, and, as ordained by prophecy, bringing back from its first exile the divine Unity and thru the second exile the Unity of mankind. See it hunted throughout the world, ever nigh to extinction and ever finding some providential shelter which saves it from destruction. See it bearing its truth and, because it wills to keep it pure, spread it throughout the world in flames of light which kindle its own funeral pyres. See it incarnating in its own flesh the two loves which are killing it, even at the moment when it gives itself with them to all the nations of earth. See Israel rebuild the flaming altar of its hope which is the universal hope, so that it yet may survive itself.

1. [Fleg, *Why I Am a Jew*, xv.]

And tell me if in this unique history you do not feel the eternal presence of a mind and a will that have ordained its mission to this people and have made its fulfillment possible, in trying it through suffering, in saving it through trials, in guiding it step by step from its unhappy past to its triumphant future. As for me, my child, who have so long sought for the evidence of the existence of God, I have found it in the existence of Israel.

I am a Jew because born of Israel and having lost it, I felt it revive within me more alive than I am myself.

I am a Jew because born of Israel, and having found it again, I would have it live after me even more alive than it is within me.

I am a Jew because the faith of Israel demands no abdication of my mind.

I am a Jew because the faith of Israel asks every possible sacrifice of my soul.

I am a Jew because in all places where there are tears and suffering the Jew weeps.

I am a Jew because in every age when the cry of despair is heard the Jew hopes.

I am a Jew because the message of Israel is the most ancient and the most modern.

I am a Jew because Israel's promise is a universal promise.

I am a Jew because for Israel the world is not finished; men will complete it.

I am a Jew because for Israel man is not yet created; men are creating him.

I am a Jew because Israel places Man and his Unity above nations and above Israel itself.

I am a Jew because above Man, image of the Divine Unity, Israel places the unity which is divine.

At times, my child, when I go through a museum and stand before the pictures, statues, furniture, arms, crystals, mosaics, vestments, ornaments, coins, jewels, gathered there from all places and all times to hang upon the walls or to place upon pedestals, to be ranged behind barriers and panes of glass, classified, numbered, labeled, I dream that some one of my ancestors may have seen, touched or admired some of these things, in the very place, in the very time, in which they were made for use, for work, for the sorrows or the joys of man.

That door with the gray nails, between two poplars, in the gilded frame, is the door of the Synagogue of Geneva through which my father entered to pray. And there, that bridge of boats on the Rhine over which my grandfather in Hüningen crossed the river. And his grandfather, where did he live? Perhaps while calculating the mystic numbers of the Kabala in his reveries he saw across the pensive panes of his window, the sleds glide over the snow of Germany or of Poland. And the grandfather of the grandfather of his grandfather? Perhaps he was that weigher of gold in the Ghetto of Amsterdam painted by Rembrandt.

One of my ancestors may have drunk from that wine-cup on returning home after listening to the teaching of his master Rashi in the School of Troyes in Champagne; one of my ancestors may have sat in that armchair studded with jade when a Sultan bade him feel his pulse; one of my ancestors may have looked upon a monk in his cowl and carried this cross of Castile while leading him to the auto da fé; one of my ancestors may have seen his children crushed beneath the hoofs of the Crusader's horse, who wore that armor.

These crowns of plumes, were they placed in the hands of another ancestor by an American savage? These African ivories, these silks of China, were they bought by another on the banks of the Congo or of the Amur, to be resold on the shore of the Ganges or on the Venetian lagoons?

One of them tilled the plain of Sharon with that plough hardened through fire; one of them ascended to the Temple to offer his tithe in those woven baskets. When this marble Titus was in the flesh, one of my ancestors, chained to his chariot, followed him with bleeding feet in the triumph of the Forum. This bearded magi, with the fringed garment, between these two winged bulls with human profiles—one of my ancestors breathed the dust of Babylon beneath their feet; this Pharaoh of porphyry, with his two hands on his two flat thighs —one of my ancestors bowed himself before his slightest breath, before girding his loins and taking his staff in hand to follow Moses across the Red Sea; and that idol of Samaria, with spherical eyes and triangular jaws, perhaps that was the idol that Abraham smashed when he left his home in Chaldea to follow the summons of his invisible God.

And I said to myself: from that far distant father to my very own father, all these fathers have transmitted a truth to me, which ran in their blood, which runs in my blood; and must I not transmit it with my blood to those of my blood?

Will you accept it, my child? Will you transmit it? Perhaps you will want to desert it. Then may it be for a greater truth if there be one. I could not then reproach you. It would be my fault; for I could not have handed it on to you as I received it. But whether you abandon it, or whether you treasure it, Israel will march on unto the end of days.

# 11 | The Cataclysm and the Aftermath

With a sizable Jewish community of 340,000, including both Eastern European refugees and natives, and a 75 percent survival rate, the French Jewish community was in the unique position of being able to document its wartime experience, to actively cultivate its memorialization, and to theorize as survivors about the event's postwar impact on French Judaism. Mass roundups, detainments, and deportations to concentration camps in the East began first in the German-occupied North, and hence in Paris, but in the South it was only after the Germans invaded in late 1942 that Jewish lives were in grave danger. The delay made the southern Free Zone a relatively safe locale for the first few years of the war, even as Jews were subject to Vichy's Jewish Statutes, which instituted discrimination against Jews and eliminated their roles in the public sector. These developments left room for many to process the events as they were unfolding and also to prepare strong networks of resistance after the Germans moved south. For some Jews the response to persecution both during and after the war was a stronger commitment to shed the ethnic marks of a Jewish heritage, whether through conversion or name change. But for others the war was the necessary catalyst for a kind of Jewish awakening, either religious, political, or both.

The effects of France's betrayal of its Jews, its enactment of race laws, and the revocation of French citizenship from Jews in Algeria definitively unraveled the strong sense of identification between Judaism and the ideals of France so prevalent in the Third Republic. The effects of this betrayal remain even today. Most profoundly, Judaism is no longer predominantly understood in France in purely confessional terms; instead it is widely understood as an ethnic, religious, and political category. Furthermore, the trepidation about the Zionist project that many felt before the war disappeared after the war, and French Jewish attachment to Israel has only increased with time.

At the same time, despite the presence of so many Jews in postwar France, the standard narrative until recently has been that the decades immediately following the war involved something of a repression of the Shoah that resulted in a failure to translate the tragedy into public memory until the 1960s. Recent accounts, however, have revisited that claim and shown otherwise.[1] Certainly the ground of Holocaust memory and representation in France has been well trodden since the 1960s, if not earlier, and efforts at memorialization have spanned multiple genres—from André Schwarz-Bart's novel *The Last of the Just* (1959) to the work of such historians as Pierre Vidal-Naquet and Annette Wieviorka, filmmaker Claude Lanzmann's *Shoah* (1985), and the philosophical debates about Holocaust representation and revisionism that were prevalent in the 1970s and 1980s, giving rise to works such as Maurice Blanchot's *The Writing of the Disaster* and Jean-François Lyotard's *The Differend*, which explored the question of its representation in philosophical terms.

The essays and excerpts included here begin with the processing of events as they occurred. Simone Weil's letter to the commissioner for Jewish affairs under Vichy was written just after the issuing of the Jewish Statutes, when French Jews had hardly begun to come to terms with these new laws and their political, economic, and social ramifications. Robert Gamzon's essay *Tivliout* or *Harmony* refers to the war with only a brief mention of the parallel between the French scouts and the Jewish slaves of Egypt. Yet the text was first given as a lesson in 1941 in the South of France and completed over the course of the war. Paradoxically for Gamzon and others like him invested in Jewish renewal, the wartime displacement of Jews into new communities in the South provided the opportunity to actualize a new vision for Jewish life. Over time, the ramifications of the events were registered more clearly in the reflections of Jewish thinkers. In 1944 Jacob Gordin was still able to consider Jewish suffering as part of God's plan. Just after the war, writing about his experience in a labor camp for Jewish soldiers protected from the fate of the death camps by their uniforms, Emmanuel Levinas described the Jewish prisoner's state of suspense as akin to Isaac's three-day walk to Mount Moriah. By 1957 Jewish identity, in Jankélévitch's account, had become inextricable from the experience of surviving the war. Finally, with Sarah Kofman in the 1980s, the landscape of memorialization was already in place and the dilemma of its representation had come to the fore.

1. For an account that presumes a delay, see Wieviorka, *The Era of the Witness*; for a different view, see François Azouvi, *Le mythe du grand silence: Auschwitz, les Français, la mémoire* (Paris: Fayard, 2012).

In sum, the goal of this part is not only to provide insight into the French Jewish experience of the Second World War but also to reveal how the issues of the last two parts of the volume—which concern Jewish universalism and particularism, and identification and disidentification—emerged from the Jewish experiences of persecution during the war.

# 8

# Simone Weil, What Is a Jew?

Simone Weil, "What Is a Jew? A Letter to a Minister of Education," *The Simone Weil Reader*, George A. Panchas, ed. (Wakefield, R.I.: Moyer Bell, 2007), 79–81.

As the letter below itself suggests, Simone Weil (1909–1943) would not have been happy about her inclusion in this volume. Although born to parents raised in observant Jewish homes, Weil did not even learn that she was Jewish until the age of ten, her parents having chosen to shield both Simone and her brother André from this knowledge in the hope of sparing them some of the pain of antisemitism. If the family had a religion, it was a religion of pure reason, a faith into which she was inducted very early, particularly in the guise of her brother André's mathematical genius. He was a recognized mathematical prodigy by the age of twelve. Early on Simone also devoted herself to the plight of others, declaring herself a Bolshevik when she was ten. Her fascination with Jesus Christ and the Catholic Church came later, culminating in a mystical spiritual awakening in the late 1930s. She is remembered best as something of a Christian mystic, following in a tradition of women mystics going back at least to Saint Teresa of Avila, though she was never baptized and considered herself "a Christian outside the Church."[1] In letters she expressed a sense of unworthiness that prevented her from being baptized, but the question clearly preoccupied her. And it was not for lack of love of the tradition that she resisted this final move, and certainly not out of loyalty to her Jewish background. In fact, Weil was notoriously negative about Judaism, describing the notion of cosmic justice in the Hebrew Bible as a "view that makes cruelty permissible and indeed indispensable." Nothing in the "Old Testament" could compare to the Greeks; what was good in the Gospels, she claimed, was their Greek heritage, not their Jewish one.

Weil is then something of an anomaly in this volume in her conception of Judaism, but certainly not an anomaly among assimilated French Jews. One could include as well Henri Bergson and Irene Nemirovsky among those who expressed their Jewishness only in the avidness of their criticism of the tradition. The letter below, written in November 1940 and addressed to Xavier Vallat, the commissioner

1. [Francine du Plessix Gray, *Simone Weil* (New York: Viking, 2001).]

for Jewish affairs under the Vichy regime, came only a month after the Jewish Statutes in October, which barred Jews from the civil service and from positions of public influence such as in the military, the press, or the commercial and industrial world. Though clearly not intended for a public audience, the letter has often been republished, presented as an example of the sense of betrayal many French Jews felt when their very French identity was called into question by the statutes. It additionally exemplifies the very riddle of Jewish identity — What makes one a Jew, if not belief or upbringing? — which equally plagued those French Jews who found their way back to the tradition in an effort to solve it.

MONSIEUR LE MINISTRE,

In January, 1938, I took a sick leave, which I renewed in July, 1938, for one year, and again for another year in 1939. When my leave expired last July, I asked for a teaching post, preferably in Algeria. My request was not answered. I very much want to know why.

It occurs to me that the new Statute on Jews, which I have read in the press, is perhaps connected with your failure to reply. So I want to know to whom this Statute applies, so that I may be enlightened as to my own standing. I do not know the definition of the word "Jew"; that subject was not included in my education. The Statute, it is true, defines a Jew as: "a person who has three or more Jewish grandparents." But this simply carries the difficulty two generations farther back.

Does this word designate a religion? I have never been in a synagogue, and have never witnessed a Jewish religious ceremony. As for my grandparents — I remember that my paternal grandmother used to go to the synagogue, and I think I have heard that my paternal grandfather did so likewise. On the other hand, I know definitely that both my maternal grandparents were free-thinkers. Thus if it is a matter of religion, it would appear that I have only two Jewish grandparents, and so am not a Jew according to the Statute.

But perhaps the word designates a race? In that case, I have no reason to believe that I have any link, maternal or paternal, to the people who inhabited Palestine two thousand years ago. When one reads in Josephus how thoroughly Titus exterminated this race, it seems unlikely that they left many descendants ... my father's family, as far back as our memory went, lived in Alsace; no family tradition, so far as I know, said anything about coming there from any other place. My mother's family comes from Slavic lands, and, so far as I know, was composed only of Slavs. But perhaps we must now investigate whether each of them had less than three Jewish grandparents? I think it may be quite difficult to get reliable information on this point.

Finally, the concept of heredity may be applied to a race, but it is difficult to apply it to a religion. I myself, who profess no religion and never have, have certainly inherited nothing from the Jewish religion. Since I practically learned to read from Racine, Pascal, and other French writers of the 17th Century, since my spirit was thus impregnated at an age when I had not even heard talk of "Jews," I would say that if there is a religious tradition which I regard as my patrimony, it is the Catholic tradition.

In short: mine is the Christian, French, Greek tradition. The Hebraic tradition is alien to me, and no Statute can make it otherwise. If, nevertheless, the law insists that I consider the term, "Jew," whose meaning I don't know, as applying to me, I am inclined to submit, as I would to any other law. But I should like to be officially enlightened on this point, since I myself have no criterion by which I may resolve the question.

If the Statute does not apply to me, then I should like to enjoy those rights which I am given by the contract implied in my title of "professor" ["*agrégée*"].

SIMONE WEIL

# 9

# Robert Gamzon, Tivliout

## Harmony

Robert Gamzon, excerpt from *Tivliout: Harmony*
(Paris: Éclaireurs israélites de France, 1945), 33–51.

Robert Gamzon (1905–1961) was the founder of the Éclaireurs israélites de France (EIF) in 1923, a Jewish branch of the French Boy Scouts. Still active today as the EEIF (Éclaireurs, Éclaireuses israélites de France), the French Jewish scouting movement was part of the larger development of youth culture at the beginning of the twentieth century, among Jews and non-Jews alike. Like most French Jews in the first decades of the century, the EIF was keen to represent Judaism as a religion rather than a national identity and thus did not see the movement's Jewish character as in conflict with one's French identity. Members of the movement expressed the same nostalgia for rural life, the same critiques of contemporary Jewish culture as their counterparts in Germany and Poland, and in some cases were strongly Zionist. The EIF shared the Zionist emphasis on nature, manual labor, and cultivation of the land, without adopting as doctrine that the end goal was to transplant the Jews to Palestine. Instead, the renewal of Judaism that Gamzon envisioned, at least until the end of the war, was largely a renewal of Jewish life and values on French soil.

Composed during the war, *Tivliout*, meaning "harmony" in Hebrew, was Gamzon's expression of the movement's philosophy. While the vision itself may not have had a lasting impact on modern Jewish thought, the impact of the scouting movement on young Jews in wartime France is hard to underestimate. Gamzon first presented his vision in draft form in 1941 at Beauvallon, the home of Edmond Fleg, at a "camp-school" organized to help reorient young Jewish intellectuals who had lost their positions at universities or in public professions as a consequence of the Vichy regime's Jewish Statutes issued in October 1940. Soon after the camp was held, the regime established the Union générale des Juifs de France (UGIF) as an umbrella organization to handle Jewish affairs. Under the law that created the association, membership was compulsory for all Jews, both citizens and alien residents in France, and all Jewish organizations, excluding the consistory, were dissolved and their functions turned over to the UGIF. In January 1942 Gamzon became minister of the UGIF's youth division, thus officially making him responsible for all Jewish youth in the unoccupied zone. During the war Gamzon supervised a number of farm schools, and the association maintained numerous children's homes for orphans and children separated from their parents by the war.

The world of these farms and the world envisioned by Gamzon in the treatise below seem unimaginably distant from the descriptions of Jewish wartime suffering that predominate in our collective memory. They were places of hardship and sacrifice, but also of great joy, where Jewish festivals were celebrated with intense devotion and, for some, Jewish life was experienced for the first time. An experiment in collective living, the farm schools gave Gamzon an opportunity to actualize his vision of Jewish life, one that curiously was not at odds with the Vichy regime's emphasis on renewing the culture of manual labor and pastoral life among its citizens.[1]

After the war Gamzon established the École Gilbert Bloch in the Parisian suburb of Orsay. This provided him an opportunity to implement his philosophy in peacetime. In 1949 Gamzon and his wife made aliyah and established a short-lived kibbutz. Meanwhile the École Gilbert Bloch continued its work until 1970 under the leadership of Léon Ashkénazi and others.


I. THE PEOPLE OF ISRAEL

It is not enough to understand and to feel unity and harmony with the entire world; men must undertake for themselves to bring about a harmonious and unified society, and each man should achieve this unity within himself.

We are going to see how Israel wants to establish harmony among men and among the [earth's] people. But first, what is a people?

I think that the best way to understand this is by returning to the biblical concept. The people of Israel (*bnei Israel*, sons of Israel) refers to all of the descendants of Israel. There is clearly here a notion of family, of kinship.

Within this family are created traditions, familial ideas, something analogous to the traditions of certain older aristocratic lineages.

And even if this community continues through generations and through alliances ("your children will be as numerous as the grains of the sand upon the seashore"),[2] it continues to maintain its own character. And from generation to generation, these qualities take shape and are passed on.

1. [See Lee, *Pétain's Jewish Children.*]
2. [Paraphrased from Gen. 22:17.]

The people not only is the assemblage of men of which it is composed for a given era, but exists across many eras and ages; it is a great living body [that evolves and has a soul].

An individual is created through a very great number of cells that are born, grow, multiply, and then die.

Despite the constant regeneration of cells, man keeps his physical and moral personality; however, every generation of cells counts in a man's life, because a sickness, or an accident, whether happy or sad, can sometimes change him for life.

The same is true for a people. Individuals grow, reproduce, and die, but a people maintains its personality, which is its very consciousness.

A shock experienced in youth leaves a mark for life, like a cellular change. This is why each one of us can say truthfully, "That is what the Lord did for me, when he took me out of Egypt."[3]

The body is practically eternal compared to the lifespan of a cell.

A people is practically eternal compared to the lifespan of a single man.

The individual is the sum of all of his cells in space and time.

A people is the sum of all of its children in space and time.

In turn, humanity is a great body whose organs are the peoples.

The Jewish belief is that humanity, this great body that suffers and hopes, can and must evolve toward harmony and peace, and thus draw closer to God.

This belief in the necessity and above all in the possibility of humanity's progress (despite all its oscillations and regressions) is the condition itself of all progress.

How can we act on men and people to put this conviction in practice and bring them into harmony?

Not by the sword, nor by words, but *by example*. It is here that the notion of "the exemplary people," of the chosen people emerges, whose mission is to make men progress toward harmony.

Already in Exodus, the idea of an exemplary people appears clearly:

Now therefore if you will indeed obey my voice and keep my covenant, you shall be my treasured possession among all peoples, for all the earth is mine; and you shall be to me my kingdom of priests and a holy nation. These are the words you shall speak to the people of Israel.

(Exod. 19:5–6)

3. [Exod. 13:8, in the context of the commandment to eat unleavened bread during Passover.]

Later, with the prophets, this belief in the election and the purpose of Israel is further clarified and becomes the mainstay that will allow Israel to cope with poverty and persecutions with an unwavering confidence and optimism.

> And it shall come to pass in the last days, that the mountain of the Lord's house shall be established in the top of the mountains, and shall be exalted above the hills; and all nations shall flow unto it. And many nations shall come, and say, Come, and let us go up to the mountain of the Lord, and to the house of the God of Jacob; and he will teach us of his ways, and we will walk in his paths: for the law shall go forth of Zion, and the word of the Lord from Jerusalem. And he shall judge among the nations, and shall rebuke many people: and they shall beat their swords into plowshares, and their spears into pruning hooks: nation shall not lift up sword against nation, neither shall they learn war any more.

> (Isa. 11:2–4)

But before studying the purpose and the doctrine that Israel must, by its example, radiate out into the world, the question arises: Why Israel more than any other people? Were they the most evolved, the most powerful, or the most numerous people? By no means; they were a small tribe reduced to slavery by powerful Egypt.

It was from this tribe of slaves that God was going to create his people, the chosen people. There is in this contrast a profound meaning: this tribe's *coming out of slavery* will [be able to] bring the concept of human freedom to the world, for only one who has suffered in his flesh will suffer in the flesh for another.

Coming out of slavery and witnessing the devouring of the strongest army of its era, this tribe knows, *from experience*, that the strength of an army is not everything and that the spirit is more powerful.

And escaping from a flourishing Egypt overflowing with countless gods, gold, and pleasures, the people of Israel will be able to hear the voice of the ONE God in the desert that belongs to everyone and no one.

This voice will dictate a law that only Israel will gladly follow. The tradition recounts that the law was pronounced in seventy languages at once so that the seventy peoples of the earth could understand it, but only Israel would consider itself "charged with a mission" until the messianic era.

> And Moses came and told the people all the words of the Lord, and all the judgments: and all of the people answered with one voice, and said, all the words which the Lord hath said will we do.

> (Exod. 24:3)

Robert Gamzon | 69

In Jewish thought, "all of the people" means: all in space and all in time, in the present and in the future. Even children who were not yet born, says the Talmud, will respond with their fathers, in a single voice: We will do all that the Lord has said.

This definitive and complete promise is again recalled by Moses before entering the Promised Land:

And the Lord has today declared you his people.

(Deut. 26:28)

But the entrance into the Promised Land was possible only after a period of ordeals, struggles and the purification of forty years, in the course of which the entire generation of the Golden Calf passed away.

This too has an equally profound symbolic value.

Just as each one of us, in each generation, must escape from his own servitude, the Egypt of his passions, in the same way, before entering into the Promised Land of absolute freedom and service to the Eternal, we must make an effort toward purification, self-examination, and abandoning idolatry in the desert of our tribulations.

## II. THE SOCIAL LAWS OF MOSES

As we have seen in the first part [of the text], man is one, flesh and spirit. God does not ask man to kill his flesh out of love for him, but to *live as man, in order to love him*. It is in this that Judaism departs from Christian asceticism, and from disembodied Hindu ecstasy, without, for all that, getting caught up in "sordid materialism."

Man is a social being. Thus this one life, in which flesh and spirit will both be satisfied, will be possible only in a harmonious and unified society guided by laws that will bring or facilitate this harmony.

In particular, and in the first place, if work is necessary for man to provide himself with material subsistence, rest is indispensable for his material and *spiritual* liberation.

Rest is indispensable to all, to all who live and work; and the first and fundamental social law of Moses is *the institution of mandatory weekly rest*:

Observe the Sabbath day by keeping it holy, as the Lord your God has commanded you. Six days you shall labor and do all your work, but the seventh day is a Sabbath to the Lord your God. On it you shall not do any work, neither you, nor your son or daughter, nor your male or female servant, nor your ox, your donkey or any of your animals, nor any foreigner residing in your towns, so that your male and female servants may rest, as you do. Remember that you were slaves in Egypt and that the Lord your God brought you out of there with a mighty hand and an outstretched arm. Therefore the Lord your God has commanded you to observe the Sabbath day.

(Deut. 5:12-15)

This law introduced the notion of rhythm into the life of man, a notion essential to the continuation of effort as well (everything is rhythmic in physical nature: respiration, circulation). It is also, through its universal value (even for animals), a law *of universal liberation from slavery* and from matter, and this is why it is associated with the idea of the liberation from Egypt.

The notion of liberation is so anchored in the Jewish soul that it should not be surprising to see so many revolutionaries among the Jews.

But a revolutionary can be driven, either by an idealistic feeling for social and human progress and the rejection of slavery, or, sometimes, we should admit, by one of the basest of human sentiments: envy. Social peace will never be possible, *whatever the adopted regime might be*, if envy persists in the heart of man.

This is why the Decalogue places murder, theft, and adultery on the same level as the Tenth Commandment, the foundation of a harmonious society,

Neither shalt thou desire thy neighbor's wife, neither shalt thou covet thy neighbor's house, his field, or his manservant, or his maidservant, his ox, or his ass, or any thing that is thy neighbor's.

And here again appears this union between matter and spirit that exists in Jewish thought. *All* the articles of the Decalogue, except the tenth, command or forbid *legally* controllable and punishable *acts*; then suddenly the tenth commandment appears, purely moral and volitional, and yet determines the four social commandments that precede it.

We will now examine which technical measures Moses used to realize this "harmonious society" that he was seeking.

Before studying them, we should make a comment concerning the notion of "abundance" in the Bible that seems fundamental to me.

### Biblical Abundance

The society to which the Mosaic laws were applied had to be a society in which *abundance* and even *overproduction* reigned (2,500 years before mechanization); and that is why the study of Mosaic laws seems so fascinating to me, because they were carried out under living conditions that were, roughly, like those before the war, and that will reappear once the reconstruction is finished: conditions of abundance and overproduction.

Palestine was a country that "flowed with milk and honey"; in the era of Isaiah (as in 1938), the prophet could cry out:

> They grope like the blind stumbling at noonday, and in the middle of abundance, men die of hunger (because the Mosaic laws are no longer observed) and the truth stumbles in the public square.[4]

The measures foreseen by the Mosaic code are measures of *limitation and redistribution of wealth, mandatory consumption, periodic repayment of debts, and the liberation of workers.*

Does this not remind you of anything?


### III. SABBATICAL YEAR

This is a year for uncultivated land:

> And six years thou shalt sow thy land, and shalt gather in the fruits thereof: But the seventh year thou shalt let it rest and lie still; that the poor of thy people may eat: and what they leave the beasts of the field shall eat. In like manner thou shalt deal with thy vineyard, and with thy olive yard.
>
> (Exod. 2:10; Lev. 25:3)

Making the land fallow is indeed a current practice, used by all the farmers of the world up until the relatively recent invention of "green manure" (sowing nitrogen-fixing vegetables); it is habitually applied by shifting between sections of the same land (by a cycle of three or four years) and, remarkably, letting the entire land lie fallow at the same time, which is exactly equivalent (particularly Lev. 25:2).

That leads to a one-year paid vacation every seven years for all the agricultural owners and *workers*. Thus it makes possible intellectual development and renewal during this particular year. All those who know the exhaustion that a rural life *without vacation* can bring about will better appreciate the human value of such a measure.

It seemed to us that we could derive (as many others have) very modern appli-

---

4. [This seems to be a loose paraphrase of Isa. 59:10.]

cations from this ancient law, and that is what the Éclaireur israélite movement tried to do for their employees, as we will see later on.

Like the day of the Sabbath, the sabbatical year provides an interruption in the relation between man and the object of his work; further, by doing so, it implies that man is only a day laborer, an "employee" of the Lord, and not the true possessor of the earth or of the product of his work.

Moreover, the sabbatical year can be regarded as a means of *absorbing harvest surpluses*, applicable to the regime of abundance:

> Wherefore ye shall do my statutes. . . . The land shall yield her fruit, and ye shall eat your fill. . . .
>
> (Lev. 25:18–19)

The laws of the *three festivals*, Pesach, Shavuot, and Succot, which brought the peasant crowds to Jerusalem from Palestine, seem to be in the same spirit:

> And thou shalt rejoice before the Lord thy God, thou, and thy son, and thy daughter, and thy manservant, and thy maidservant, and the Levite that is within thy gates, and the stranger, and the fatherless, and the widow, that are among you, in the place which the Lord thy God hath chosen to place his name there. And thou shalt remember that thou wast a bondman in Egypt: and thou shalt observe and do these statutes.
>
> (Deut. 16:11–12)

All of the farming families went up to the great "fair." This was not just a fair, because each had to remember and recognize, in light of the abundance, that they came out of slavery, were liberated by God and his Law, and that the orphan, the widow and the foreigner, these pariahs of ancient society, should be able to enjoy this abundance the same as the principal owner.

Here it is about paid leave again, and also, an *increase in consumption and exchange* to avoid an increase or decrease in price during these fairs. The price being taxed: there is nothing new under the sun. A tenth of the production was required to be consumed (Deut. 14:23) before the Eternal.

## IV. FINANCIAL LAWS

Every seven years, you will make a break. . . . Each creditor who has given a loan to his fellow man will release his claim; he will not pressure his brother to repay the debt.

It is an inner moratorium (Deut. 15:1–2) on debts. It does not seem that it was applied completely in the biblical era; but in fact, very frequently in the contemporary era, in a crisis of overproduction, the burden of debt can end up blocking commerce and exchange.

V

*Laws of limitation, of redistribution of large agricultural properties*

The land shall not be sold forever: for the land is mine; for ye are strangers and sojourners with me. And in all the land of your possession ye shall grant a redemption for the land. . . . But if he be not able to restore it to him, then that which is sold shall remain in the hand of him that hath bought it until the year of jubilee: and in the jubilee it shall go out, and he shall return unto his possession.

(Lev. 25:23–24, 28)

One does not sell the land, only the harvest.

According to the multitude of years thou shalt increase the price thereof, and according to the fewness of years thou shalt diminish the price of it: for according to the number of the years of the fruits doth he sell unto thee.

(Lev. 25:16)

Thanks to these measures, a land "trust" becomes impossible and the property stays within the family and of moderate importance. However, a hardworking man can prosper more than a lazy man.

## VI. LAW FOR THE LIBERATION OF MAN

And when thou sendest him out free from thee, thou shalt not let him go away empty.

(Deut. 15:13)

It is no longer slavery, but actually a rental contract for seven years, analogous to the contract for the modern farmer.

All the Mosaic social laws are inspired by the will to liberate man from the enslavement of other men and from the enslavement of work, in order to produce the harmonious enjoyment of life.

In all the biblical legislation, supposedly so arduous, there appears not only a love of God and of life, but a true human tenderness.

I will merely cite texts; any commentary is unnecessary:

When a man hath taken a new wife, he shall not go out to war, neither shall he be charged with any business: but he shall be free at home one year, and shall cheer up his wife which he hath taken.

(Deut. 24:5)

When thou dost lend thy brother any thing, thou shalt not go into his house to fetch his pledge, Thou shalt stand abroad, and the man to whom thou dost lend shall bring out the pledge abroad unto thee.

And if the man be poor, thou shalt not sleep with his pledge. In any case thou shalt deliver him the pledge again when the sun goeth down, that he may sleep in his own raiment, and bless thee.

(Deut. 24:10–13)

Thou shalt not oppress a hired servant that is poor and needy, whether he be of thy brethren, or of thy strangers that are in thy land within thy gates. At his day thou shalt give him his hire, neither shall the sun go down upon it; for he is poor, and setteth his heart upon it: lest he cry against thee unto the Lord.

(Deut. 24:14–15)

When thou cuttest down thine harvest in thy field, and hast forgot a sheaf in the field, thou shalt not go again to fetch it: it shall be for the stranger, for the fatherless,

and for the widow: that the Lord thy God may bless thee in all the work of thine hands.

When thou beatest thine olive tree, thou shalt not go over the boughs again: it shall be for the stranger, for the fatherless, and for the widow. When thou gatherest the grapes of thy vineyard, thou shalt not glean it afterward: it shall be for the stranger, for the fatherless, and for the widow.

And thou shalt remember that thou wast a bondman in the land of Egypt: therefore I command thee to do this thing.

(Deut. 24:19–24)

All these laws are based on an idea of the harmonious enjoyment of life in trust.

And if ye shall say, What shall we eat the seventh year? behold, we shall not sow, nor gather in our increase. Then I will command my blessing upon you in the sixth year, and it shall bring forth fruit for three years.

(Lev. 25:20–21)

This was possible only thanks to overproduction. But instead of leading to misery and war, as it does in our era of capitalist madness, this overproduction led to a life great in "the Lord."

One left a corner of the field for the poor, did not glean from it . . . did not stock up . . . lived in trust. . . . What a difference from the rough and petty mentality of so many farmers! But they *knew* that if they obeyed the voice of the Lord, they could harvest with joy, would receive the autumn rain. And who knows if the harmonious life, the *"tivli"* life of the biblical farmer did not give him this feeling of being in harmony with nature, this mysterious foresight of the blessed who, like the sense of direction of the swallow, announces whether the spring will be early or late.

The Jewish farmer had the profound feeling of *alliance* between God and man, an alliance symbolized by Shabbat, the sabbatical year, and all the biblical laws. This alliance was repeated every day, as it is now by the Shema, but it was maintained by all the *acts* of life:

If you hear the commandments that I give to you this day: to love the Lord your God and his service with all your heart and all your soul, I will give to you rain on your land when needed, rain in the spring and rain in autumn and you will harvest your wheat, your grapes and your oil and I will give to you feed for your livestock. You will eat and you will be satisfied . . . , so that your days will multiply and the days of your children on earth that the Lord has promised to give to your fathers, as long as the sky is over the land.

## CURRENT APPLICATIONS

And now? We, young Jews, and especially young Jews of France, who also have been slaves, do we not feel committed to a certain mission? Do we not have something to give to the world?

The biblical legislation is a "legislation of happiness," a legislation of abundance, that could certainly bring fertile ideas to modern civilization and to the future; it is up to us to bring about the modern outcome, *to seek to live them and to bring them to the world.* . . .

Translated by Beatrice Bourgogne
and Sarah Hammerschlag

# 10

# Jacob Gordin, The Galuth

Jacob Gordin, "La Galut," in *Aspects du génie d'Israël*
(Paris: Cahiers du Sud, 1950), 105–25.

Despite having published relatively little and dying just as his influence began to take hold, Jacob Gordin (1896–1947) is widely recognized in France as one of the most influential spiritual leaders of the postwar revival of French Judaism. After his early passing, his influence was perpetuated by his students, particularly Léon Ashkénazi, who credited much of his own approach to Judaism to Gordin as his spiritual master.

Born in Dvinsk (now Daugavpils) in 1896, Gordin was in Saint Petersburg in 1917 for the Russian Revolution, in Berlin for Hitler's rise to power, and in Paris when the Nazis invaded in June 1940. In his trajectory from East to West he managed, with the exception of the First World War, to be at the geographical centers of the major, catalyzing European events of the first part of the twentieth century. He also accumulated on this journey a multifaceted approach to Jewish thought inflected by each of these locales. In the Russia of his youth he learned Hebrew, Syriac, and Arabic. In 1917, when the Bolsheviks took power, he found himself on a prolonged stay in the Ukraine when his train ran out of fuel. There he became acquainted with a number of Hasidic communities and with the fundamental texts of the kabbalistic tradition. Having first read the work of the German neo-Kantian Hermann Cohen in Saint Petersburg, during the ten years he spent in Berlin he became a member of the Academy for the Science of Judaism (Akademie für die Wissenschaft des Judentums) and wrote a thesis strongly influenced by Cohen titled "Investigation into the Theory of Infinite Judgment." In 1933, a few months after Hitler was appointed chancellor, Gordin, his wife Rachel, a renowned expert on the Montessori method, and their daughter left for Paris. Gordin had by that point amassed a depth of both traditional and philosophical Jewish learning unparalleled among his French contemporaries. In the years before the war, he gave a course on medieval Jewish philosophy at l'École rabbinique and published in journals on related topics, such as Spinoza and Maimonides. He made his living as the librarian at the Alliance israélite universelle, where he first met Emmanuel Levinas. Despite multiple contacts and prodigious learning, Gordin was virtually unknown until the war, when the family was recruited to one of the children's homes run by the Éclaireurs israélites de France in Beaulieu because of his wife's specialization in early education. There Gordin began his encounter with a generation of young Jews for whom the war was a fundamental turning point, a time of intense self-questioning and curiosity about the tradition to which, they now realized, they were irrevocably linked.

Thus, stories abound about the discovery of Gordin's great learning and its impact on a group of scholars and thinkers who would lead the renaissance of Judaism in postwar Paris. Georges Hertz, the director of the children's home in Beaulieu, describes Gordin asking to attend one of his courses on Judaism for young scout leaders, only to discover after a few questions that he and Gordin needed to change places; it was for Hertz to sit at the feet of such a learned scholar.[1] At the end of the war, when the children's homes had been disbanded, Gordin gave what have been remembered as legendary courses in an abandoned house in Chaumargeis that came to be known as the school of the prophets. His courses, students report, often lasted four or five hours without breaks and synthesized Jewish mysticism and neo-Kantianism into a particular teaching about Jewish election and the nature of man, the course of history, and the symbolic interpretation of the patriarchs. In the years immediately following the war he taught a generation of young enthusiasts, including André Neher and Léon Ashkénazi, both at scout camps and at Gamzon's École Gilbert Bloch (in its first year of existence) until pulmonary illness made teaching too difficult. The reports of these courses describe Gordin as tireless, a teacher of inexhaustible knowledge and deep mysticism. According to André and Renée Neher, one of his favorite expressions was "There is brokenness [la casse] in the world." "Sometimes," they recall, "we had the impression that it was he who was breaking open the world before us, the false world, the parodies, the hypocrisies, as Abraham had once broken the idols."[2]

The text published here is a transcription by Georges Levitte of a course that Gordin gave at the end of the war. One has to imagine Gordin's students gathered around him. Not only had many of them first learned the history and rituals of Judaism during the war, but they had been driven by a desire to understand the history of Jewish suffering and their own role in that story. What they heard was this cosmic interpretation of Jewish dispersion infused with the teachings of

---

1. [Georges Hertz, "Le mystique venu d'octobre," *Tribune Juive*, September 16, 1977.]

2. [André and Renée Neher, "Les trois exils d'une vie," *L'Arche*, no. 188, October–November 1972, 50–51. Reprinted in Jacob Gordin, *Écrits: Le renouveau de la pensée* (Paris: Albin Michel, 1995), 297–303.]

Lurianic Kabbalah, but reminiscent as well of Hermann Cohen's theory of the role of the Jewish people in history. It is difficult not to read it as a theodicy, that is to say, a justification of Jewish suffering.

The galuth (Diaspora, exile) makes sense only in relation to the movement of return, freedom, the *geulah* (redemption). The three terms: galuth, *eretz* (land), *geulah*, are closely related. The Jewish people will have to live in this world on one foot, and outside this world on the other. This will be a nomadic people.

The mission of Abraham begins only with the *Lekh lekha*, the "Go forth" (Gen. 12:1). God orders Abraham to sever the material links with his country and with the cosmic order: "Put at least one of your feet outside this world, outside this universe." To be nomadic is to be outside the world, while yet staying within the world: such is the problem of Judaism.

Cain is sedentary; he is a farmer; he brings the fruits of the earth. Abel is a shepherd, but his sacrifice is not bloody: he has sheared his sheep, and it is the wool he offers; he is the ancestor of the Jewish people.

Adam. Feminine: *adamah* (earth, land); it [earth] is his mother.

The individual man, the human soul, is in exile, like the people of Israel. The earth, connected to man, is also in exile. The weight of exile weighs on the earth as well (Cain's mistake—sacrificing the fruits of the earth). The nomadic people can only become settled on *its* land, the Land. If man is in galuth, the earth is in galuth, and so are the people and the entire cosmos.

The sin of Adam is the foundation of the galuth of the individual and of the people. But even before man appeared, the earth had committed a sin, it had produced an *etz-peri* (a fruit tree) and it had produced a tree that, instead of being entirely fruit, only carried fruit; the fruit is preceded by trunk, by branches, by wood, by bark, all opaque material. The entire cosmos is in a state of sin; all of nature is full of opaque, impenetrable, dead places. The holy sparks are dispersed in the world of opaque material; the fruits are hidden by bark.

Thus, we ask ourselves: why did the family of Jacob enter Egypt? (Note that the portion Miketz [at the end] [Gen. 41:1] is read during the winter solstice, at the time when light is at its lowest point in the world, when warmth diminishes, when man asks himself if the warmth, if the light, will ever return to him.)

"Because there is grain in Egypt" (Gen. 42:2). We translate the Hebrew *shever* with "grain," but the root of the word means "to break, to shatter" (in order to use the grain, one must break the wheat, separate it, crush it, knead it—farming operations similar to the creation and the separation between light and darkness).

Jacob noticed that there was "damage" (*shever*) in Egypt (Gen. 42:2). The verse can be understood to mean "Let us go to Egypt because there is 'damage' there, the remains of the broken world," because holy sparks are hidden there in obscurity, because the sparks of the broken world are concentrated in Egypt, nakedness of the earth.

"Let us go under the bark to look for the sparks." Cf. the idea of debris of the sacred vessels—sparks of light—imprisoned in the bark or rind (*kelipot*). Likewise with the operation of the grain, all that separates us from the edible and digestible bread is chaff.

Exile carries an element of punishment: the First Temple was destroyed because of the nonobservance of the Torah (murder, transgression of sexual laws, absence of pity); the Second Temple was destroyed because of disagreements and disputes.

But why exile, why leave the country? Couldn't the punishment and purification have occurred in the land itself?

But the Holy Land, the center of the terrestrial globe, made from a light and subtle material, sensitive to human actions, does not tolerate sin on its soil: it vomits up sinners. Other peoples, living farther from the center, on a more "material" land, can be punished in their own country ([by] war [or] epidemics).

Purification through suffering is indeed one of the meanings of galuth, purification of the Jewish being and, through him, that of the human being and that of the earth. In effect, each time that a member of the community of Israel is purified, the dissemination is spread to all humanity and through all the cosmos.

But, once again, could not this purification have been accomplished in the Holy Land? As Rabbi Nachman of Bratzlav said: "If, at the site of their true life, of their sanctification, the evil spirit overcame them, could one hope that they would be purified outside the land, in those degraded places, where even the atmosphere is impure?" Here the meaning of punishment (purification) is purely negative, but we should not allow ourselves to be foreclosed by it. The promise remains; let us not forget that *galuth* is incomprehensible without its complement, *geulah*, freedom.

It is written: "With a mighty hand they will be driven from the Pharaoh's country" (Exod. 6:1). Why *expel* a slave, and with a mighty hand? It is not enough to say to the slave: "You are free." There are some slaves who, during the sabbatical year, no longer realize what slavery is, who have lost the dream of freedom, the worst form of slavery. The Midrash tells us that Moses understood that Israel wallowed in exile ("When we ate bread to fullness," Exod. 16:3 and passim). The Hebrews did not *deserve* to leave Egypt; the stars were not aligned; the people were not ready. Exit was possible only by the merit of women and the grace of God.

Abraham and Jacob were also in Egypt, [for them it involves] voluntary acts and has a positive sense: to gather up the holy sparks, to liberate the sparks, to collect the debris of the holy vessels, to defeat evil (on the level of the human *and* the cosmos). Through suffering, we atone and we purify ourselves, but we also liberate. Atonement leads to purification that leads to redemption, to *geulah*; through it, we become a *goel*: redeemer, liberator.

The galuth is thus also a work of redemption. The galuth man must also be a *goel*, redeemer. Cf. the Book of Ruth, read at Shavuot ("Pentecost," feast of the giving of the Torah): the *goel*, the "purchaser," is Boaz (in himself the force); it is he who liberates Ruth (Ruth 2:20, 3:12, etc.).

One must be strong enough to become a liberator. Thanks to the redemptive action of Israel, the damage of the world is repaired; evil is defeated in each of us, for humankind and the cosmos.

How could a people born on the delicate and tender land be transplanted to lands where everything is mixed, where orientation itself is perverted, where the North-South axis and the preeminence of the cold North have replaced the East-West axis that oriented us toward the East?

In the desert (*midbar* in Hebrew, that is, "place of the Word"), the people of Israel walked enshrouded, protected, clothed in the cloud of the Shechinah, the spirit of God. But here, in our galuth, in our northern desert, who protects us? Here equally, we are accompanied by the Shechinah, which is exiled with us and protects us.

When Israel leaves exile, another galuth begins: the exile of the Shechinah, the exile of the Divine Presence (the Divine Name is divided because of the presence of evil). It is the Shechinah that permits us to guide ourselves in this life that would be unbearable to us without it.

We carry our motherland by the soles of our shoes.

Nomadic peoples can, sporadically, dedicate themselves to agriculture, stop for the time of one or several harvests. In the desert, Israel had sojourns of longer and shorter periods. But that takes nothing away from Israel's *destiny* as nomad, from the principle of its nomadism. The travels of the three patriarchs, the pilgrimage in the desert after leaving Egypt, determined the ulterior destiny of the Jewish people and their constant displacement.

The settled people create cities. Cain, the farmer, was the builder of the first city (Gen. 4:17), and it was also the settled Cain who materialized original sin in the first murder.

The shepherd Abel travels the earth, while Cain grows his roots as a plant incapable of moving. Detached, Cain becomes "errant and a vagabond."

Nomadic Israel is destined to enter the Promised Land. Galuth is only a temporary situation; Israel is heading toward the Promised Land, toward freedom, *geulah*. The link persists between Israel and Zion.

Israel must create the synthesis (the reconciliation) between Abel and Cain. Nonetheless it must not create an urban civilization that would be founded on murder and slavery (the city-man becomes the slave of his work).

But Israel did not achieve the "kingdom of priests" (Exod. 19:6 and *passim*), did not observe the sabbatical year. Israel did not give the earth rest, and the earth spewed out the people, in order to be able to rest after its departure.

One must not confuse "being a nomad" and "not being connected to the land." Even though nomadic, Israel keeps its connection to the land in every possible way: in psychological, spiritual, and material ties. But this link is not automatic, it can always be broken, and cannot be reduced to a simple territorial possession.

Why does the Torah commence, "In the beginning"? Rashi responds: Because the nations could say: You are thieves, you took possession of a territory that was not yours. But all the earth belongs to God and he gives it to those who are just in his eyes. He first gave the earth to the nations, but in light of their injustice, he took it away from them to give it to us. The Torah begins, "In the beginning" to affirm to us that all the earth belongs to God.

And on Holy Land we built the civilization of Cain and not that of Abel; the civilization of Ishmael and not that of Isaac; the civilization of Esau and not that of Jacob.

And each one of us, in his individual life, relives the entire sacred history; the individual vicissitudes correspond to the vicissitudes of the Jewish people. Each one of us carries Cain and Abel in himself; the human soul is woven from this fundamental contradiction. The individual is neither absolutely good nor absolutely evil: in Cain, there is more evil; in Abel, more good.

And the entire biblical text is a long essay of synthesis between Cain and Abel that culminates with the marriage of Moses (Abel) with Tziporah, daughter of Jethro (Cain) (Exod. 2:21).

Always remember that galuth blossoms in *geulah* and never basks in galuth; never accept galuth in itself, but fill it with meaning.

*Purification-suffering*: we must go through trial by fire. Abraham (according to the Midrash) went through the furnace; the Hebrews through the suffering of Egypt. The Havdalah, the selecting, becomes reality, and as in agriculture, we separate the grain. The purification of the soul and of the flesh is obtained by the crossing of the fire, the passage through suffering.

We have learned that only suffering moves us closer to *geulah*. The Midrash teaches us that God showed four things to Abraham: the Torah, the Temple, Gehenna. and galuth, and said to him: "If your descendants occupy themselves with the Torah and the service of the Temple, they will be liberated from Gehenna and from galuth." God asked the sons of Abraham, upon their having sinned: "Which punishment do you choose for your descendants? Will I judge them by hell or by the power of nations?" Abraham chose galuth. (According to another tradition, he first chose Gehenna, but even God himself recommended the other punishment.)

According to Rabbi Simeon bar Yohai, God offered three gifts to Israel: the Torah, the earth, and the future world; but they are obtained only through suffering: through the suffering of the body, the human soul achieves its destiny.

Abraham, having seen all the promises fulfilled, must sacrifice his son. Isaac, the tradition tells us, was thirty-eight years old; he was a man; he would have been able to resist. The Midrash tells us, besides, that Satan, during the trip to Mount Moriah, revealed to him the goal of the journey. (Cf. also the discussion between Ishmael and Isaac about the redemption of the world: Ishmael was circumcised as a man, in suffering; but Isaac left himself tied to the altar.) So Isaac accepted it thus, climbing the altar, knowing that he would be sacrificed; and he was returned to his father.

Life in galuth is life on the altar of sacrifice. To take pleasure in suffering is morbid; but if we do not lose sight of the fact that the term *galuth* is *geulah*, we take on galuth with joy (joy not from galuth itself, but from *geulah*).

According to Rabbi Levy Itzhak of Berdichev, "The true meaning of exile is joy." We must not suffer, nor tolerate galuth, but fill it with its true meaning, which is joy, giving it a positive meaning, which is *geulah*.

If we have not thoroughly anchored the link galuth-*geulah*, joy-suffering, in ourselves, if we do not assume galuth voluntarily, we are lost; from nomads, we become errant. Consider this Hasidic tale: the son of the king behaves badly; his father drives him out, but, in his exile, he continues to behave badly. His father, however, does not abandon him, and sends him a messenger who finds the prince in a cabaret, drunk and naked. "What should I say to your father, the king?—That he should send me money, shoes, and beautiful clothing." He does not even think of asking for his father's forgiveness; he no longer even hopes to return to the kingdom of his father; could it be that he wallows in his exile? Well! Then he should stay!

The Gypsies are there to give us a warning, a living example of an errant people. They also are dispersed; they also were persecuted by Hitler; but they do not have a country to regain, a law to keep, they do not have hope of the *geulah*. (Cf. also the false messiahs who recommend passing through all the religions in order to pick up the holy sparks.)

The great danger for the Jewish people in galuth is to become the opposite of itself, its own caricature, to no longer be a nomad except like Cain, in erring.


In order to survive, in order to feed ourselves, we cause suffering. In turn, man suffers; but Israel suffers more than anyone. Having received more, Israel suffers more: more is asked of it than of anyone else; it has less of a right to sin than anyone else.

But the other peoples, they also have sinned; but they are not punished with the interminable suffering that is galuth. The punishment is not a sufficient reason; the punishment would be too great!

Rabbi Yohanan ben Zakkai says: "You are happy, Israel, when you accomplish the will of the Lord, no one can defeat you. But when you do not follow his ways, you are given to the nations of the world, and even to their slaves, and even to the animals of their slaves." There is no mean for Israel, no mediocrity.

Because there is a positive meaning to suffering, a joyful meaning. As long as evil exists in the world, Israel cannot sleep quietly. The suffering of Israel is its own purification, our individual purification; but at the same time, it is the purification of its environment, of humanity. Through his suffering, Israel also purifies the other peoples.

Each Jew is responsible for other Jews (as long as a single Jew does not observe the Sabbath, the Messiah cannot come) and for all of man. Each member of Israel is responsible for the suffering in this world, for the reign of evil in this world. To be the "Heart of the World" is to take part in all of the suffering in this world. Cf. Isaiah 53:

He had no form or beauty....
He was despised, shunned by men,

A man of suffering, familiar with disease
. . . Yet it was our sickness that he was bearing,
Our suffering that he endured.
We accounted him plagued,
Smitten and afflicted by God;
But he was wounded because of our sins.
Crushed because of our iniquities.
He bore the chastisement that made us whole,
And by his bruises we were healed.[3]

The Christian exegesis applies this chapter to Jesus, but Rashi and all Jewish exegesis applies it to the holy community of Israel, which is the Messiah of the nations of the world, the Redeemer.

Every periphery has its center, every fruit its rind and its pulp; the profane days have a Shabbat that illuminates them from the inside; the heart animates the living being. To become a man, to become oneself, requires orienting oneself, centering oneself, choosing. In our sacred geography, the center is the Holy Land; in the plan of sacred history, the center is Israel.

The *choice* of Israel introduces the notion of individuality into the world and guides history, gives it meaning. Without Israel, there would not be history, there would only be an unformed, moving mass of peoples without direction or center. Israel is the center of a system of coordinates along which we orient history; Israel introduces a notion of *quality*, guarantees the existence of values in the world, of the individuality of each person and of each nation, and of the originality proper to each one, proper to man's existence.

Israel is the cornerstone of humanity.

Just as the Shabbat transforms the week, the nations benefit from the presence of Israel, this center without limits. We do not know where it begins or where it ends, dispersed everywhere, to all the corners of the world, without which the world would not have its proper originality, would not survive as a "holy place."

Thus new perspectives open to us on galuth: on the apparent paradox of this universal people of acute particularism; separated from the other peoples (as the light from the darkness) and yet united with the seventy nations, identified as all humanity.

The separation into seventy nations dates from the Tower of Babel. The Mi-

3. [The French follows the Louis Segond 1910 French translation. We have followed the JPS translation.]

drash tells us that at the tip of the tower there was an angel (Jupiter), holding the sword of Tubal-Cain, symbol of blood that will reign over the diversified nations, divided (by war, prisons, police, tyranny . . .).[4] And each nation has its particular mission, possesses its own melody that is sung before the Divine Throne by the angel (the *sar*) of this nation. Because each nation has its *sar* above that guides it (cf. the *Volksgeist*, spirit of nations, of Hegel).[5]

But the people of Israel is led by God himself. When the family of Jacob entered into Egypt, beginning thus the world's advancement toward salvation, it was composed of seventy members; the structure of the body of Israel is based on the structure of the entirety of humanity.[6] The Sanhedrin also was composed of seventy members, each one having his own specificity, each one "affected" by one of the seventy nations, having to speak the language, knowing the music, the interior melody, so that Israel, in its isolation, holds contact with the entire world (and the cosmos), identifies itself with the world.

To be chosen means to identify oneself with the entire world; such is galuth, which sings the seventy languages. (The day of the translation of the Septuagint —the Tenth of Shevat—is a day of mourning, because the translation of the Bible is an entry into galuth.) But galuth will not last forever; from the four corners of the world the people will be reassembled, after having been disseminated everywhere, to the ends of the earth: because the center is no longer perceptible anywhere, it must be everywhere.

Let us see how the Jewish tradition concretizes this situation, crystallizes these ideas. We have seen Cain and Abel; we have said that with their own nuances, Isaac and Ishmael, Jacob and Esau repeat history.

The birth of Jacob, of the House of Jacob, of Israel, of the people of Israel: "The children struggled in her womb" (Gen. 25:22). Even before birth, the twins Jacob and Esau struggled with each other; these two principles are incompatible if one

4. [Tubal-Cain is mentioned in Gen. 4:22 as the one "who forged all implements of copper and iron."]

5. [Gordin is suggesting that there is a parallel between the rabbinic image and Hegel's notion that each culture has a spirit or *Volksgeist* particular to it. See Hegel, *Philosophy of Right*, para. 340. Most see the notion as not original to Hegel, attributable as well to Herder and Montesquieu.]

6. [The nations of the world are numbered as seventy by rabbinic sources, following from the list of Noah's descendants in Gen. 10.]

wants to bring them up in the same geographical space, on the same histori-cal plane.

A midrash says: When Rebecca went before a pagan temple, Esau wanted to come out; when she went before a synagogue, it was Jacob who wanted to come out.

Another midrash (battle for preeminence): "I will be the first to come out."

"No, it's me."

"If you don't let me be the first," says Esau, "I will kill my mother."

"That's malicious," says Jacob, "even before your birth you want to spill blood," and he gave in, thus also leaving political supremacy to Esau.

Another midrash: While they shared the world with each other, Esau chose this world, Jacob the world to come. Jacob takes pride in the *Malchut Shamayim*, in the Kingdom of Heaven; Esau prefers earthly, immediate royalty, history. Nei-ther of them can coexist on the same plane. Rome and Jerusalem are incompat-ible; Rome stands tall, while Jerusalem is in ruins, but when Jerusalem is rebuilt, Rome will be in ruins. "Two nations are in your womb, and two separate peoples shall issue from your body" (Gen. 25:23). We can read the following: "will sub-ject" or "will be subjected," according to whether Israel deserves or does not de-serve the Kingdom of Heaven.[7]

Esau is born red (ibid., 25), the color of blood, and he will make blood flow throughout the world; he demands the plate of *red* lentils (same root as *adamah*, earth, land [*glèbe*]: this world)[8] in exchange for spiritual benediction (the world to come). "The voice of Jacob and the hands of Esau" (Gen. 27:22). The hand, the strength, the sword of Esau builds this world; but the voice, the faith, the prayer in the world belongs to Jacob and ensures the world to come. "Go before the bar-racks of legionnaires, then before the house of prayer, and you will understand why the two cannot be on the same plane."

As soon as Jacob has received the blessing of Isaac, he has to go into exile in the desert, to the place of the Word; it is there that the prophetic vision of the ladder with the angels that ascend and descend intervenes; note that the angels

7. [Gordin is referring to the end of Gen. 25:23, which continues, "One people shall be mightier than the other, and the older shall serve the younger." The Hebrew verb trans-lated here as "serve" is *ya'avod*.]

8. [Gordin is referencing Genesis 25:30 here, where Esau refers to the stew as *ha-adom*, the red [stuff]. This is also connected to his association with Edom. These two words have the same root—aleph, daleth, mem—which is also the root for earth (*adamah*) and for man (*ha-adam*).]

ascend and then descend (Gen. 28:12). They do not come from heaven; they go there. The Midrash tells us that [the verse] is about angelic princes from the nations of the world. According to a midrash, the ladder has forty rungs; God first shows Jacob the *sar* (angelic prince) of Babylon who ascends, then descends; then the prince from Persia ascends and descends; then the one from Greece ascends and descends; finally the *sar* of Edom, from the Rome of Caesars and popes, ascends but does not descend. Jacob asks: "Why does he not descend?" God says: "Remain calm, my chosen son. Even if he ascends up to heaven, he will descend again when I want him to." As space knows its four dimensions, history knows its four seasons, its four kingdoms of galuth: the angels who ascend and descend Jacob's ladder.

Another midrash: God says, "Since you are afraid he will not return, go up yourself." Jacob is full of dread and afraid that if he ascends he will come crashing down. Despite the invitation from God, Israel is afraid to trust the hand of the divine. Fear, lack of trust, lack of faith; Jacob did not climb up and Edom dominates. But the invitation remains and the Messiah awaits our act of faith.

In other circumstances the people were also afraid: the incident of the guides sent by Moses into Canaan; they return on the Ninth of Av (day of mourning, day of the destruction of the Temple), and the entire people cries in despair while waiting for their report; Israel cries all night, this first night of galuth; it weeps and does not enter. It did not yet have a genuine connection with the earth, and thus the refusal of the guides in this night sets in place the entire galuth.

God says: "This time, you have lamented for no reason, because the land is good; but I will give you the Ninth of Av, then you will know why you weep!"

Similarly, when Jacob leaves the earth, night falls.

When Jacob saw the four eras of the world, night came, the great nightfall of galuth. And Jacob fought with the angel—the *sar*—from Edom. On the spiritual level, Jacob is stronger. He attains victory and the angel demands of him: "Let me leave, because even though Edom, I am an angel of God, and the hour has come when I must participate in prayer in Heaven." In effect, the *red* disk of the sun, the star of Edom, rises, introducing the "great army of Edom." But the spiritual victory is heavily paid: Jacob, hit in the sciatic nerve, remains weak. The *white* moon is weak and cannot catch the sun; the Virgin of Israel comes alive only at night, because Israel is in exile. But there will come a day when "the moon will shine like the sun" (Isa. 30:26), when the encounter, the reconciliation of Jacob and of Esau, will take place.

According to the Midrash, God sits on his Throne for the whole night and roars like a lion. The night is made of three parts:

that in which the donkey cries out

that in which the dog barks

that in which the child takes the breast of his mother and the husband speaks to his wife.

Thus, the galuth

of Babel, where Israel is regarded as a donkey that has to be commanded;

of the Maccabees, of the persecutions, when the dog bays at the dead;

of Rome, which drinks from Israel and when dialogue is still possible;

But in this last period they are all encompassed by the complete night, in the total darkness, which concentrates the qualities of all the galuth; sometimes the dog barks, sometimes the husband speaks with the spouse. The reason this last period, when Edom encompasses everything, is so long is that in the fourth phase of galuth, Israel is scattered everywhere, and the light of the *geulah*, of liberation, thus illuminates the night of humanity's galuth.

Man ignores two "ends": the end of his life and the end of galuth. But he knows that he is not alone, that the Shechinah accompanies him, encompasses him, and protects him; that the Ninth of Av will shine with the sun of freedom; and that the Shechinah, the Divine Presence, the Sukkat Shalom (Tent of Peace), protects us today as it did in the desert.

But the higher plan of galuth and its completion remains. The mission of Israel is embroiled in it, half-consenting, half-forced into the Diaspora, the dispersion.

The Midrash says that God imposed three oaths, two concerning Israel: that it will not isolate itself in a fortress and that it will not rebel against the nations of the world.

The third concerns the nations: that they swear not to suppress Israel beyond a foreseen limit. Whichever attempts to make Israel disappear will itself disappear from the arena of nations.

According to others, Israel took three more oaths: not to reveal the end, even if the prophets know it; not to tamper with the end by precipitating it through an external means; and not to reveal the mystery of Israel to the nations.

However, the *tzadik*, the just, the wise, can break one or more of these oaths under certain circumstances, to force the hand of nature, and even of God.

What does it mean "not to reveal the mystery of Israel to the nations"? What is the mystery that history itself reveals about the destiny of Israel?

We are indeed in a situation where the mystery, the veil of the world, is lifted partway. The Tradition (Kabbalah) had remained secret, known only in small circles (the *Sefer Yetsirah*, *Zohar*, etc.) until the 13th century, when it began to spread toward the approach of a new turn in universal history (the expulsion from Spain, the discovery of America, etc.). The nations even begin to read and translate our secret texts. (It is worth noting that the *Zohar* is written in Aramaic, so that the angels, who speak only the sacred language, could not understand it themselves.)

But the nations who can read the words of our texts cannot grasp the meaning; behind the letters hides the deep significance. The entire Torah is nothing more than a series of divine names.

Above all there remains the problem of the *real action* of the people. How to be an *actor* of the world, how to assume one's full role, how to seek out the holy sparks everywhere they can be found, how to translate galuth through joy?

The word "galuth" has as its root GLH [gimel, lamed, he], which means both "to reveal" and "to exile." There is an intimate relation between Exile and Revelation.

By creating, the Creator reveals himself, but through this, in some way, he stops being alone; he exiles himself in the creature.

Israel is the premise of the world, the true center of creation; it realizes the intimate link between Exile and Revelation: to be dispersed, to be everywhere, this is to really carry out the act of revelation of the Divine Glory. As soon as Abraham appears, the nations of the world are no longer punished except for the transgression of the limits of oppression (cf. the highest midrash).

From creation onward, the problem of galuth is posed. It is posed again on the eve of the Exodus from Egypt. Cf. the burning bush: "I will be (present with you in this galuth) as I will be (with you in the galuyoth to come)." This announcement [ ... ] seems so terrible to Moses that he refuses to deliver it to the people and receives permission to deliver only the beginning: "I will be."

We have already seen that it is insufficient to take the meaning of *galuth* as suffering and purification, purification for Israel and all humanity. What is the real positive sense of exile?

We can find one of the keys to the mystery in Jacob's exclamation: "There is 'damage' in Egypt" (cf. supra), and with that Israel (seventy people of the House of Jacob) goes into exile. They leave in part by necessity, impelled by famine (there is wheat in Egypt), in part voluntarily, by their own decision to repair the "damage" and to search for the holy sparks (*the true* galuth still involves an element of necessity, but also a considerable element of decision, of will).

It is known that the "sense of *galuth* is to find (recover, retrieve, rediscover), to make reemerge, the holy sparks that fell into opaque matter because of original sin. Israel will suffer galuth until the holy sparks are all gathered; until the opaque matter has lost its only support and dissolves." As soon as the Havdalah (separation, sorting) is done, evil evaporates; as soon as good is isolated, evil disappears. Satan can exist only by imitating good.

Such is also the meaning of the spoils that the Hebrews take in leaving Egypt (Exod. 12:35). According to the Midrash, they signify the holy sparks that Israel brings back from Egypt, and consequently Egypt no longer exists for Israel. "You will never come back to Egypt," because holiness is removed from it. Jeremiah, for example, did not want to set foot there (according to rabbinic law, a temporary stay is allowed).

In fact, what is this all about?

The existence of Israel in galuth has a salutary sense, a lifesaving action for the nations of the world. Nothing is more in its place in this world; the community of Israel is the "housekeeper of the world."

The midrash of Rabbi Nachman: A kingdom is in ruins. A young prince goes to the palace and simply moves the furniture into place. The kingdom flourishes again.

Israel repairs the broken, displaced, cracked world, the kingdom of absolute misery. "You will be a kingdom of *kohanim* (priests)" (Exod. 29:6). The *kohen* is in fact a "repairer." In order to repair the broken and deprived world, the Tent of Meeting is built, then the Temple. The structure of the Temple is the very structure of the world.

We have already seen how the menorah, the seven-piece candelabra, answers to the seven planets, just as the symbolism of the colors of the walls answers to the floors (QRSH, flooring = SHQR, lie), etc.[9]

The act of the sacrifice takes place in the center of the Temple. The ruined Temple is spread throughout the entire world, and the people of Israel are the altar of the sacrifices.

The restorative act (*tikkun*) is the act of priesthood. It is the action of Israel in the world. The meticulous and ordered camp of Hebrews in the desert had the same function; galuth expands the camp up to the edges of the earth.

---

9. [Gordin is using a method here called Gematria and referring to the numerical values of the words, which are equal to each other, so that in some way the words are conceptually linked. Here the letters of the words are actually the same but in different orders.]

The mistake of emancipation: the people of the Bible have to preach (morals) to the world; the mission of Israel is to prophesize, to proclaim the Ten Commandments and the Jewish ethical code. It is a naïve and bookish concept to believe that it will be enough to have the Bible in hand and speak about it to justify the existence of Israel and its presence in galuth. These are childish ideas from writers who write articles in their studies. It is the church and Mohammed who have translated and spread the Bible to the extent that the word is now accessible.

According to others, Israel is an example for the world. There is an element of truth there. Israel is intimately linked to the Torah; but can we really claim to be examples of purity and mercy? No, this figuring of Israel is somewhat academic. We can benefit from a gymnastics or swimming instructor if he does his job well. But we, are we doing ours well? We obviously know what true purity and true mercy are, but we have lost so much, we accomplish the mitzvoth (commandments) so little, that we no longer live by example.

And besides, once again, history is not a school. Israel is not a teacher, who is more or less competent.

No, despite their grammarians and their dictionaries, the nations of the world cannot understand the essential contents of the Book, this long sequence of Divine Names. To live the Book, one must be a son of the Divine Name (*Shem*).

The relationship between Israel and the nations is not posed in theoretical terms. It is in reality a matter of that which is in the center and that which is at the periphery. The *real* action of Israel occurs by its natural presence, by the naked presence of Israel among the nations, such is the element of salvation for the fallen world.

Such is the Alliance of Salt. When Saint Paul says to the apostles: "You are the salt of the earth," he takes an old idea that Judaism applies to the twelve tribes. Israel is the salt of the earth, the catalyzer of the world. This is what it must be by its very presence, but it must *realize* its presence, by its action, by its act of Temple sacrifice renewed by prayer.

The salt stops the putrefaction, purifies the atmosphere, it gives a taste to the earth. The Jewish meal, essentially the absorption of the sacrifices, begins with salt, thus an angelic act ("food" and "angel" have the same numerical value). Meat becomes kosher through salt. To eat kosher is to diminish the blood in the world by expelling it, thus reining in the excesses of war; one delivers the meat from the blood. To eat the blood is to acknowledge no limit to the spreading of blood in the world. It is in this way that the reparative practice of the 613 mitzvoth is linked to the problem of man and the Jewish year.

Thus the elements of Jewish life, even in galuth, comprise all these restorative actions. The Shechinah accompanies us in galuth, but we have to replace the presence of the land; this is why we double our holidays—one is for galuth, the other for the Holy Land. And so it is for each rite and each detail.

But all of that cannot be done by some external and automatic means. "We mock the Jews who mumble in prayer," said a rabbi, "but we don't have to make a theatrical act of our prayer. The mother understands the inarticulate stuttering of her child. God understands us, even when we mumble the prayer."

The *kavanah* (intention) illuminates each word in the prayer from within, each gesture gives it a spiritual flame. Everything, each word, each gesture, each piece of clothing, possesses an exterior and interior, a body and a soul. The soul must live in our actions; it must interpenetrate the flesh and the spirit. Such is the accomplishment of the mitzvoth with *kavanah*.

One cannot live only by good intentions; faith alone does not suffice. To possess tzitzit (fringes, Num.15:38) without touching them means nothing; to touch them without intention means nothing. Salvation is in the mind *and* the body. What every person, and the entire cosmos, awaits is the total resurrection of the mind and body. The *kavanah*, the intention, is not transferred through reading; the *kavanah* must be the spiritual flame enlivening the effective accomplishment of the mitzvoth.

The nations know the commandment: "Thou shalt love thy neighbor as thyself" (Lev. 9:18), and apply it in its moral sense. But let us put this phrase back in the context of ritual and sexual law. The text appears in the midst of the laws on forbidden marriages. Because pleasure is solitary, all pleasure being its own proper goal, all pleasure without love is selfish. In order to really think of others, to love others, one must realize in life the accomplishment of the mitzvoth of marriage, which is one of the principal means of repairing the broken world.

The accomplishment of the mitzvoth, repairing the broken world, is the true means to love one's neighbor as oneself, and is the meaning of the mission of "savior of the world."

But why then in the Diaspora?

Because, as Judah Halevi says, one cannot sow the seeds from elsewhere. It is why "my heart is in the East, and my body in the West" (Judah Halevi). From Paris, I cannot sow the seeds in Moissac.[10] The seed must be put in the soil in

10. [Moissac is a town in southern France where the scouts ran a children's home that they maintained even after the war.]

order to sprout and grow. I know today one just throws the seed, but the Jew puts every grain in the soil. Just as the land is transformed, so a new humanity will germinate. If Israel is the scattered center, if it is everywhere and nowhere, the messianic times will fill the entire world.

History teaches us that life in the Land of Israel has not succeeded. Israel has not realized the heavenly kingdom on its soil. Gideon expressed what the kingdom should have been: God alone must reign over the people (Judg. 8:23). Instead, Israel asks for the establishment of the monarchy despite the protests of Samuel (1 Sam. 8); the Midrash teaches us that when Samuel saw David for the first time, he was afraid, because David was redheaded like Esau who lived by the sword (1 Sam. 16:12); the beautiful eyes of David hardly make up for the danger, because the danger comes from the ancestor of David, from the violator, from Perez. The king is always the violator of the Torah (prisons, armies, etc.).

The high priest wore clothing made of eight parts, but to enter the sanctuary, he wore only four. He had to divest himself of the earthly state. In order to reveal oneself, one must remove some clothing, some covering. They would have had to divest themselves of the earthly kingdom to live on the soil of Israel, the heavenly kingdom.

On the other hand, you cannot save yourself alone. No Israelite can save himself outside the holy community and outside the entirety of humanity. This is why the Messiah comes from the line of Tamar; Tamar is not Jewish; we do not know which people she comes from. The Midrash says she is a daughter of Melchizedek, which we know refers to Shem. Similarly, Boaz marries Ruth the Moabite; the woman always comes from the outside, from abroad. And Ruth is the ancestor of David and of the Messiah. Her name lacks only a ה for its letters to be those of the word "Torah." She is the gift that the nations offered so that it [Israel] accepts and takes up the Torah.

Israel will not be saved alone; it receives the Messiah only thanks to the gift of the nations of the world. The missing ה in Ruth (near sanctity) is the sanctity that we must restore to the nature of the world; the nations offer us Ruth so that we can restore the Torah, so that we can repair the world, and so that we can revive all mankind, in body *and* in mind. (It is why, again, the Book of Ruth is read at Shavuot, at the festival of the giving of the Torah.)

As the Gospel of Saint John says, "Salvation comes from the Jews" (4:22). They return holiness to the world, so that it participates in the resurrection in body *and* spirit. The presence of Israel guarantees that, despite the "damage" of the world, the flesh will be transformed by the resurrection.

The body of the world is a social organism. But Israel has no state, no language, no home; our flesh is transformed, reworked. In order to possess this transformed flesh, one must not give in to bloodshed, wars, prison, battles, and nations.

These sociological problems arise only in the profane world. They are not admissible in the interior of the holy community.

But notice that the life of nations is not entirely that of Cain, that of evil; otherwise it would be unlivable. Evidently, from time to time the incarnations of absolute evil appear: Amalek (what is, from this perspective, the exact role of Haman, of Hitler, of the Third Reich?). Here, there is no possible compromise; the name of Amalek must be erased.

This is in no way the case for the nations of the world, even under the form of states. "Don't forget that Edom (Esau) is your brother, and even your twin brother." It is not coincidental that the numerical value of Esau is identical to that of *shalom*, peace.) Through our exile, we are linked to the states; we participate in their conflicts. But as the holy community, as the center of the world, we cannot and we should not make a state (a notion issued from the Tower of Babel and from Cain), because it is exactly what we have shed in order to represent the world to come, the heavenly royalty.

The midrash on the four kingdoms of the galuth presenting themselves before the heavenly court in order to justify themselves: "We have built bridges, wells, thermal baths, arenas where gladiators are killed." God responded: "I don't accept your theaters for my sons, but your baths, I accept them." (Judah HaNasi gave his courses in the hot baths of Tiberias.) Since then, a Jewish community cannot be developed without a synagogue or without baths.

The nations of the world elevate the works of "civilization," but Israel has the voice, the song, and the words. The hands are from Esau, but the voice and the spirit are from Jacob.

Israel promised not to build walls, that is to say, not to isolate itself; however, it must "pitch its tent far from others." We can benefit from bridges, from wells and the thermal baths of nations. Let us not forget, however, that the rain that fills them up is obtained by the prayers of Israel for the preservation of the Holy Land. Let us never forget above all that the nations are our brothers, that Edom is the brother of Jacob.

But "how beautiful your tents are, Jacob" (Num. 24:5). Let us keep our own tents. We cannot wholly identify with the nations, with their lands, with their states. And the nations know this; they learned it from us: the notion of an absolute state, prevailing over all, is not Christian. The body of Jesus is embodied in the Universal Church, and the body of nations in the state. The Jew learns that one can live in the world in a spiritual way: our spiritual homeland is the Holy Land, with its spiritual qualities; it is the real center of the terrestrial globe. Our body is here, in the country where we live, in which we are citizens.

Jacob had two wives: Rachel, wife of the day (visible), and Leah, wife of the night. In life, he preferred Rachel: but at the Cave of Machpelah, he is buried with Leah. Just as each Jew puts in his coffin pieces of *the* land; our visible spouse is our country, our hidden spouse is the Holy Land.

This is not the place to pose the problem of Zionism. As the definitive end of galuth, for Israel and the nations, Zion can rebuild itself neither by technique nor by armies alone, but only through grace: *Tsion behesed yibane*. Zion will be rebuilt by grace. The problem of a "Jewish state" is another problem.

Midrash: On the day when the Second Temple was destroyed, the soul of the Messiah was born. But where? Some say in Rome, others say in Arabia? In the family of Herrari?[11] At the discovery of America, Jews hurried to search for the holy sparks, the soul of the Messiah.

But we cannot unveil everything. The exile of the Jewish people expiates sin (*galuth mekhaper ḥatat*). The Messiah comes from every one of us. The Messiah comes from Israel. The Messiah comes from the nations of the world.

"The hidden things are in the hands of God; the revealed things are in us and in our children" (Deut. 29:28–29.).[12] This marking of this phrase with special points indicates that it can just as well mean the contrary.[13] We possess at least the prescience, the scent of mystery.

11. [Perhaps a reference to Haile Selassie, emperor of Ethiopia from 1930 to 1974. Believed by the Rastafari movement to be the Messiah, he was born in Harar. The family Harrari appears in 2 Samuel 23:11, in the figure of Shammah, as one of David's warriors who routs the Philistines. Thanks to Ryan Coyne for helping me figure out the reference.]

12. [JPS translates this verse: "Concealed acts concern the Lord our God; but with overt acts, it is for us and our children."]

13. [The dots that appear over the words "It is for us and for our children" have been a source of much debate in the Jewish tradition. See BT Sanhedrin 43b; B'Midbar Rabbah 3:13; Avot d'Rabbi Natan 2.37.]

In each breath, in each movement of our body, we feel the mystery and, intuitively, we feel the mystery of the presence of Israel in galuth, among the nations of the world.

*Translated by Beatrice Bourgogne*
*and Sarah Hammerschlag*

# 11

# Emmanuel Levinas, The Jewish Experience of the Prisoner

Emmanuel Levinas, "L'expérience juive du prisonnier," *Carnets de captivité suivi de Écrits sur la captivité et Notes philosophiques diverses*, vol. 1 of *Œuvres completes* (Paris: Grasset, 2009), 209–15.
© Éditions Grasset & Fasquelle 2009.

Born in Kovno, Lithuania, but a naturalized citizen of France by the late 1930s, Emmanuel Levinas (1906–1995) was the most influential French Jewish thinker of the twentieth century and one of France's most significant philosophical voices. His work is often divided into these two genres, though his philosophy and his Jewish thought are closely linked conceptually. The central claim undergirding his most important philosophical works, *Totality and Infinity* (1961) and *Otherwise than Being* (1974), is that the encounter with the other person is the most fundamental event for the human subject. In this encounter, Levinas claims, the other makes on me a nonreciprocal demand that upends my autonomy. Instead, then, of a subject who is first of all free and defined by its rights and duties, for Levinas the subject is first and foremost responsible. Levinas's emphasis on responsibility has led to his having been read as an ethicist. While he is not concerned with formulating a normative system of values, he does maintain that ethics is first philosophy. The model for this form of the subject, Levinas also argues, is already instantiated in the Torah in the person of Abraham, who is not primarily a subject deliberating between choices but one who is called upon, a structure that is manifested in Abraham's response to God: *Hineni*.

Levinas's Jewish writings include occasional essays written for journals, papers written as speeches to Jewish gatherings in his professional capacity first as a clerk for the Alliance israélite universelle and then as the director of the Alliance school, the École normale israélite orientale, and his Talmudic readings presented from 1960 to 1989 at the Colloque des intellectuels juifs de langue française. These writings often reveal how the rabbinic tradition should be understood as an endeavor concerned primarily with the demands of the other. The Jewish tradition, Levinas argued, was the carrier of this prophetic teaching, "a rupture of the natural and historical that are constantly reconstituted and thus a Revelation that is always

forgotten. It is written and it becomes Bible, but the revelation is also continued
. . . produced in the guise of Israel."[1]

The essay printed below was not published in Levinas's lifetime, though it appears to have been given as a radio address on September 25, 1945, on the program *La voix d'Israel*.[2] The essay describes Levinas's experience as a Jewish prisoner of war in a camp near Hanover, Germany. As Levinas notes, his status as a French army officer protected him from the fate of the death camps. As this essay and his journals from the period attest, his time in the camp was also the period of his Jewish awakening, when he began to think of the modality of being-Jewish as itself worthy of phenomenological description. This and other writings collected in the first volume of Levinas's previously unpublished works reveal how the war transformed his outlook, and the role of Judaism in that transformation.

In the drama that European Jewry just experienced, Jewish [*les israélites*] prisoners of war did not play the primary role. They did not live in death camps. Miraculously protected by their uniform, the great majority of them returned from Germany. Admittedly they knew the desolate existence of all prisoners— thankless work, the cursed work of slavery, the monotony of interminable days, months, and years—and the hunger and cold, but this was everybody's lot. And this participation in the general destiny brought the beginnings of consolation. When physical suffering is not mortal, it gives way to moral reason and is compensated by the luxury of reassuring thoughts. In these years of racial distinctions and exclusion, by recognizing in their pain the pain of the whole world, the Jews [*les Israélites*] could rejoin the universal order, could rediscover the dignity of being human.

At the same time, despite all the equality captivity creates, it was at every instant for *l'israélite* an experience of Judaism: this overwhelming thing for which there was no special rubric in any official French registration before the war. The Jew lent his own significance to the sadness that he shared with his non-Jewish comrades, a consciousness of Judaism acute as a spasm.

Early on, news of the persecutions to which Jews were subjected in all the occupied countries reached the camps. Letters addressed to a parent, a wife, a sister returned with the label "no forwarding address." The euphemism was

---

1. [Emmanuel Levinas, *Beyond the Verse* (Bloomington: Indiana University Press, 1994), 4.]
2. [There are no remaining recordings from this program and no published listing. This is, however, the same program from which Sylvain Lévi's essay originated.]

understood. The day of the mailman became a day of anguish. But we knew in Germany even earlier than in France the fate of all those with "no forwarding address." We knew of the mass extermination of Jews in Eastern Europe. We were never disconnected. Before a systematic will to exterminate, which could at that moment of reckoning warrant the Geneva Convention, that mere sheet of paper, Jewish prisoners felt the suspension of death that hung over their work and their laughter like a familiar shadow. In the special work details in which they were placed, often in some lost part of the forest, they found themselves at once separated from other prisoners and from the civil population. Everything happened as if something was being prepared for them, but was always deferred.

The consequence for these little groups dispersed throughout Germany was a moral solitude that lent a special gravity to all our acts and thoughts. Since his bar mitzvah the prisoner had unlearned the religious language and would never have consented to call his existence religious even if it had that character. But in a condition without an outside world, with no connection to the set of rules, fixed customs and recognized leaders that we call civilization, the individual facing a tomorrow full of unknowns and dangers with no human recourse, is this not a solitude with God, even if by pride or prejudice one does not dare pronounce his name?

It was a situation that the prisoners and the deportees had in common; but whereas martyrdom was immediate for the deported, the prisoner had the time to prepare for it. Between the man and his suffering there was an interval that allowed for a consideration of the pain before being seized and destroyed. In this interval reflection slips in. Here spiritual life commences. What I like most in reading the biblical story of Abraham going to sacrifice Isaac is to imagine the three days during which the father and son were en route toward the place indicated by the Lord, when they had the leisure to assess the act in which they were engaged, the silence of these three days, interrupted only in the last stage by the son's question and the father's response with all that this exchange leaves to suggestion. It is by virtue of all these delays on the way that the test is fruitful. It is because of all that was bearable in the misery of the prisoner that this suffering could become a source of Jewish consciousness, a possible seed of a future Jewish life, that which the deported had known as torture, death, and kiddush hashem.

We had thus the time to look into our misery and to interrogate ourselves. Some tried to go further. Driven to their Judaism, they sought refuge in it. Jewish history, Hebrew, the Bible appeared worthy of interest and study and even the performance of religious service became possible.

All of it was often performed with awkwardness, almost always without following up with ideas. But imperfect human undertakings have worth only through the purity of such instants. I want to recount for you a few of the exceptional moments of these services in captivity when all the meaning, all the content of Judaism appeared as in a nutshell.

I will avoid indulging an easy lyricism concerning the ambience of these services: a meeting of ten volunteers amid beds in a bunk room, lit by gas lamps —when there was gas—lit by acetylene lamps when we did not have any. The services could not be too long because the flame of the acetylene lamps burned down quickly, especially in the old bicycle lamps that we used, which were always broken. The end of the service was in darkness. I will not speak much of the sarcastic smiles of those who did not attend out of adherence to their convictions and their sense of belonging to the 20th century. Always the services were held in the evening, because we had to work from dawn. All those evening prayers without a tomorrow. All those Maariv [evening prayers] without Shacharit [morning prayers].

In the rapid recitation of ancient prayers, some of the faithful restored the meaning of these old formulas to their spirit by murmuring them on their lips.

In the period of the great German success—France crushed, England and London under bombs, Yugoslavia and Greece annihilated, Russia invaded all the way to Moscow, force in its most brutal triumph, a triumph that makes one doubt everything that one was ever taught of good and evil, in a world governed by misery, someone said it: One has to believe either that God is not good or that he is not powerful.

And the old liturgical words recount unbelievable stories: God who loved Israel with an eternal love—the God who saved us from the hand of the tyrants —the power of Pharaoh overtaken by floods and the songs of Israel's joy, all those Jewish prayers with their indefatigable repetition of belief in the triumph of the weak. What to think of these out-of-date matters when in 1940 or 1941 one is a Jewish prisoner in Germany and one understands them?

Should one close the prayer book with a scornful air and depart, holding to the blasphemy on the tip of one's tongue? Repeat these things without thinking them, without believing them, with the indulgence that one can have toward the candor of the ancient ages? Think that these things were dead and that we were without truth as without protection and without future? At the bottom of the abyss, to implore the Lord like Jonah? All of this, certainly and in its turn, around and around. But one could climb up, for an instant, a short instant, one level higher and emerge from the magic circle. In the love of God, one could find a terrible confirmation in this pain and doubt. In the total passivity of abandonment, in the detachment from all connections—one could feel as though between the hands of the Lord, feel his presence; in the burning of the suffering, distinguish the flame of the divine kiss. One could discover the mysterious return of that supreme suffering in happiness. What is Judaism, then, in the end? How does it differ from other religions, which are also full of moral teachings and precepts of goodness, having also acceded to the idea of the unity of the divine principle? What is Judaism if not the experience since Isaiah, since Job, of this possible return, before hope—at the depth of despair—of the pain in happiness; the discovery of the signs of election in suffering itself? All of Christianity is already contained in this discovery, which is much earlier than it. Oh, for some among us those instants existed; when the perverse happiness of suffering penetrated at the very moment we were becoming aware of the triumph of force, and our affirmation of the eternal love of the Lord for Israel was no longer a lie or an anachronism.

The same prayers, the same formulas came back to us on other evenings, when the mood was similar.

Then things changed in the world. That which we had hardly even hoped for became a reality. The forces of evil everywhere retreated. The German press reported nothing but defeat: the Allied landing in North Africa, Stalingrad, invasion. And then the evening prayers took on a different meaning. After so many detours, they regained their literal meaning. Yes, God loved Israel with an eternal love, yes, he saved us from the hand of all the tyrants, yes the power of Pharaoh, his chariots and his troops, were at the bottom of the sea. Yes, the protecting wings of God extend over us—yes, the tent of peace extends over us, over all Israel and over Jerusalem. To think that all these words had to be taken as they were said, that they were true in their elementary truth, in their truth for children, academic and secular, in their popular truth, in their vulgar truth. That was a singular emotion!

To read an archaic text and to be able to accept it to the letter without adapting it to an interpretation, without searching for a symbolic or metaphoric truth!

And this truth itself, this truth taught from childhood that the unjust and the strong succumb, that the weak and the poor are saved and triumph, this truth appeared marvelous in its simplicity. After so many years when good and evil changed places and we had begun to get used to it, after years of Wagnerism, Nietzscheanism, Gobinism, by which our very selves had been eaten away, to come back to the truth of its six years, to see it confirmed by the events of the world—that takes your breath away, that takes you by the throat. The Good became good again, the Evil, evil. The dismal masquerade was finished.

Later, disappointments may come to tarnish this joy in the recovered literal sense, in this simple truth regained. One may see the rebirth of evil, the failure of men. All that will begin again. But that will take away nothing from these marvelously incommunicable instants before the truth of a text to which the entire universe brought confirmation in one fell swoop. Before this truth lived with all the acuity of the actual, before this accomplishment that our own eyes witnessed.

The recitation of these prayers of triumph mingled, in the same era, in the same place, with the memory of all the older readings performed in doubt and despair. The events came to crown a painful experience of doubts and despair. They appeared as though fulfilling an expectation. They were a fulfillment. "The election of suffering" of yesteryear appeared like the promise of a glorious and visible fulfillment. Judaism in this privileged instant was lived to its depths. The cycle was closed.

*Translated by Sarah Hammerschlag*

# 12

Vladimir Jankélévitch, Judaism,
an "Internal Problem"

Vladimir Jankélévitch, excerpt from *Sources: Recueil* (Paris: Éditions du Seuil,
1984), 39–51. Originally in Jean Halpérin and E. Amado Lévy-Valensi, eds.,
*La conscience juive, données et débats* (Paris: Presses Universitaires de France,
1963), 54–62.

A French-born son of Russian Jewish immigrants, the philosopher and musicolo-
gist Vladimir Jankélévitch (1903–1985) held the chair in moral philosophy at the
Sorbonne when he gave the following discourse at the first meeting of the Colloque des intellectuels juifs de langue française in 1957. The author of over forty
monographs on topics ranging from death and irony to the ineffable in music,
Jankélévitch was known as a thinker of great conceptual subtlety and rhetorical
flourish. As a student at the École normale supérieure, a disciple of the philosopher
Henri Bergson, and a student of Léon Brunschvicg, Jankélévitch felt little concern
with Judaism before the Second World War. His first fascination was with mysticism and his earliest writings were on Plotinus, Schelling, and then Bergson. It was
the war itself that brought his own Jewish identity to his attention, when in 1940
the October 3 statut des Juifs stripped him of his position on the Faculty of Letters
at the University of Lille because of his Jewish heritage. Before the Armistice of
June 22, 1940, Jankélévitch had been mobilized as a member of the French army
in 1939, and he was injured and hospitalized in 1940. Under occupation, he became
an active member of the Resistance in Toulouse but continued to publish and give
courses at cafés. While he would never intensively study Judaism, the war indelibly
altered his sense of both religious and political identity. He began to turn his attention to Jewish themes such as messianism, and he argued for a prophetic ethic
even in his interpretation of Bergson. Bergson, too, was of Jewish heritage, but
his dichotomy between open and closed morality and dynamic and static religion
tended to favor an ethic of Christian love over Jewish law. It was Edmond Fleg,
the poet, philosopher, and motivating force behind the Colloque des intellectuels
juifs, whom Jankélévitch credited with restoring him to an awareness of his own
Judaism. In the first years of the colloquium he was an active participant. In provid-
ing the closing remarks to the 1960 meeting, which dealt with Jewish morality and
politics, he described the common project as that of survivors: "Everything that is

most common and essential to us, you will admit, is summed up by our being alive. [ . . . ] There has been in our lives a series of horrible tragedies which have forever marked us and set us apart from others."[1]

In a paragraph not included here, Jankélévitch prefaced his comments by describing his own trepidation in discussing the internal dilemma of Jewish identity after returning from his first trip to Israel, where he had witnessed the Jewish Question transformed into practical activity. He had also come into contact with other Jewish intellectuals, whose primary occupation was the study of Jewish texts and history. In the early years of the colloquium, Jankélévitch's voice was often that of the outsider, along with Jean Wahl's, whom he said he felt closest to during the meetings. Both were openly ambivalent about the very fact of being Jewish. In the following essay Jankélévitch compares the experience of being Jewish to sickness. Several of his interlocutors at the meeting responded, including Edmond Fleg who recommended a "homeopathic remedy": "learning [Judaism's] extraordinary history. . . . It is useless to ask what Judaism is, you have a library, take pains to learn and *voilà*, you will be cured."[2]

To tell the truth, the trip that I just took to Israel did not provide a solution to this internal problem; on the contrary, it made it more acute, in the sense that [the state's existence] drives us toward difficult choices.[3] It has created an even greater state of tension among the contradictions I carry within me, for the temporal, secular existence of Israel as a state on the surface of the earth makes keener the dilemma, sharper the choice that each one of us carries inside ourselves. It isn't that the Israelis criticize anyone. For them, there is a solution in action to the problems that we pose to ourselves [in words]. To speak about the difficulties of Kierkegaard, Kafka, or Proust on a kibbutz in the Negev is a bit like going to

1. [Vladimir Jankélévitch, in Élaine Lévy-Valensi and Jean Halpérin, eds., *La conscience juive, données et débats* (Paris: Presses Universitaires de France, 1963), 436. Levinas quotes from these lines of Jankélévitch in his 1961 essay "Jewish Thought Today," collected in *Difficult Freedom*, trans. Sean Hand (Baltimore: Johns Hopkins University Press, 1990), 162; I have used Hand's translation here. Levinas cited these lines again in a 1968 essay, "La Renaissance culturelle juive en Europe continentale," *Le renouveau de la culture juive* (Brussels: Éditions de l'institut de sociologie de l'Université libre de Bruxelles, 1968), 23.]

2. [*La conscience juive*, 67.]

3. [In beginning with this paragraph, we are using the version collected in Vladimir Jankélévitch, *Sources: Recueil* (Paris: Seuil), 1984. The version published in the proceedings from the Colloque des intellectuels juifs de langue française includes one preceding paragraph and discussion of the essay by participants at the conference; see n. 1 above.]

speak on a kolkhoz in Russia about the problems of Alyosha Karamazov or any of the other heroes in Russian literature who deal with metaphysical problems.[4] These problems have something a little contemptible about them.

There is at one and the same time a reality from which we feel relatively estranged, though we have seen it to be the case, and an internal protest that disallows any urge toward denial. And there is moreover something even more subtle, facts that nothing can erase, not stamped paper, nor conversion. To cease to be a Jew it is not sufficient to convert. To cease to be a Russian Jew, it is not sufficient to be a naturalized Frenchman. The fact of being Jewish is a fact that is effaced neither by naturalization nor by conversion. How can we define something whose essence is so indefinable? There is a virtue to this alibi, a constitutional alterity that belongs to Jews. This indeterminate attribute that a Jew has of never being absolutely present, but always absent in some way, is not anything stable or objective. [ . . . ] There is within us this indiscernible evidence that is nonetheless undeniable. It is this alterity that we have to make tangible here.[5]

Obviously every man is other than himself, and is only a man by virtue of this possibility that he has of being outside the self and beyond the self, of not being graspable by definition, and of always overflowing his current state. But the Jew is two times absent from himself, and by virtue of this we could say that he is man par excellence. He is man twice over. By virtue of this ability to be absent from himself and to be something other than himself he is twice as human. Man is only a man because he ceaselessly becomes what he is and consequently he is always another. But in the fact of being Jewish there is a supplementary exponent of alterity that resides in his escaping every definition.

We who claim our Judaism, who attempt to find it within us in its essential dimension, nonetheless object when we are defined by this quality of the Jew and consider it one of the marks of antisemitism to consider the Jew as a Jew

4. [A kolkhoz is a Russian collective farm. Alyosha Karamazov is the protagonist of Fyodor Dostoyevsky's *The Brothers Karamazov*.]

5. [Jankélévitch had already published extensively on the concept of the *tout autre*, and although Levinas is often credited as the philosopher of "the other," it is Jankélévitch whom he often credits with the concept. On the *tout autre* in Jankélévitch, see Daniel Moreau, *La question du rapport à autrui dans la philosophie de Vladimir Jankélévitch* (Quebec: Les Presses de l'Université Lavalle, 2009); Isabelle de Montmolin, *La philosophie de Vladimir Jankélévitch: Sources, sens, enjeux* (Paris: Presses Universitaires de France, 2000). For a concept genealogy of this idea of otherness in Levinas, see Samuel Moyn, *Origins of the Other: Emmanuel Levinas between Revelation and Ethics* (Ithaca, NY: Cornell University Press, 2005).]

and only as such. It is one of the characteristics of antisemitism to want to close the Jew off in his Jewish confines, only defining him by this quality [of his Jewishness]—which for all that, we ourselves claim. How is it that the antisemites who, after all, contribute to our sense of ourselves as Jews, mistake so profoundly the essence of Judaism? They should be our best friends! In this sense Hitler would be a benefactor of the Jewish people: he permitted a great number of us to become conscious of their Jewishness! Nonetheless, the antisemites are deeply, subtly Machiavellian, let's say diabolically antisemitic, in the sense that they deny us the essential mark of the Jewish spirit, which is not only to be Jewish, but to be also something other than oneself. What the antisemites deny us is to be other than ourselves. Their Machiavellian subtlety is in the confinement of the Jew.

But if the mark of antisemitism is defining us only by the quality of our being Jewish, to take no account of this, to act as *if* "it didn't exist," to make "as if it was nothing," to ignore this Jewish quality through modesty or through simple omission, is no less to miss the truth. It is settling for a butchered truth, unjustified modesty, or pure and simple lies! We can't deny the evidence. There is a debate here, or, as Jean Wahl says, a tension between two contradictory elements: an indeterminate something more (*en-plus*) (with a hyphen between *en* and *plus*) and an indiscernible evidence that does not have legal existence but that, nonetheless, is an integral part of our being and our nature. Two incomplete truths send us indefinitely back and forth from one to the other. The fact that we are Jews implies some distinct attributes, but the fact that we are something other than that matters more still; and not to take this into account, to corner us into a preconceived definition, is to lie about our essence.

This unavowable and nonjuridical something-more, overflowing all definition, like the hidden ground of our being, we can hardly call anything other than mystical [*mystique*]. It is something unthinkable and impalpable, which does not have to do with religion—which many do not even practice—nor with race, the existence of which we deny, nor even with nationality. It is a hidden ground that prevents the Jew from being a pure man, in the chemical sense of the word "pure" (as we would say a pure Frenchman, a pure Russian). A secret difference prevents us from belonging completely to our category, without reservation and without ulterior motives. Even those among us who ignore Judaism completely cannot without a certain sense of humor regard themselves as French, indiscernible from others, nor integrate without ulterior motives (or without provoking ulterior motives!) into the milieu in which they live. This hidden ground is first of all a specific complication for the civil state, something suspicious and questionable at first glance. When it is a question of a Frenchman of Dordogne, as much as one might dig, one finds only France, ancestors of France, and even more France. For the Jew, there is something else.

During the war we had several identity cards: two, sometimes three. There were the real cards, and the fake ones, sometimes the real-fakes and the fake-fakes. Three superimposed levels, two clandestine identities, of which one was more clandestine than the next. But naturally this was not connected to our being, but to the chance circumstances in which the war had placed us. Our fundamental complication is more subtle. It is not about having done something, as with criminal records, for example. Imagine an unremarkable man who walks peacefully along the boulevard with a legitimate identity card; and one day you find out that he has a criminal record. But it is because of his acts, of the crime he has committed. The complication arises from his "doing." For the Jew, the complication arises not from "doing" but from "being." It is the complication of his being that prevents him from having an integrated existence, that is to say, from being one hundred percent French or Russian, or even Israeli, and that creates in him this complexity, this additional "impurity."

Lived from the inside, this complication, this intangible and imperceptible evidence, is experienced as an additional difficulty of existence. Someone will object that there is no particular difficulty to existing, that it is simpler than good morning and good evening, simpler than breathing or sleeping. *To be* is the only verb that requires no effort, no difficulty. It's what we share with the animals and plants, with dogs, cats, and vegetation. When we talk about a difficulty of existence, we are aiming not only to exist, but for means of existence, ways of life. And the way of life for the Jew is rougher, riskier, rockier than for others. It is more difficult in the sense that where there is no problem for others, difficulties occur for the Jew, and where there are problems for everyone, the Jew's problems are greater still.

This intangible thing lies first of all in grasping the difficulties we experience. It is a je ne sais quoi that increases the difficulty of existence. Among ourselves we could compare ourselves to the sick. It's the condition that is bad. In a state of precarious health, a cold is worse when we are predisposed to it. Similarly, when one is Jewish, the troubles that can arise are more serious; the "diseases" are exponentially aggravated. And of all the evils, one of the gravest and most heart-rending, and therefore consequently a good touchstone—a logician would say that it is a cross-check [*contre-épreuve*]—is war. Now, war is an evil for everyone:

a universal evil that blindly strikes all men. And this universal evil, painful for all men, proves to be especially painful for Jews.

I don't need to remind you of all the "special difficulties" that we encountered, the memories of which, even when hardly evoked, resurface for each one of us. The Resistance itself was also more difficult for the Jews than for the others, since, before being able to serve our country, a Jew had to expend more effort and show more ingenuity to get himself into a state of relative security, so as to keep loved ones safe. Sometimes it would take so much effort that there was no more left to take on more constructive tasks. Our non-Jewish friends, without this risky condition, did not have to take extra precautions, could devote themselves to more meaningful work than we could. Our field of action is littered with obstacles. We would say, in a theological language (which is not mine), that we are marked by a fatality or a kind of malediction. A cursed man is sick from the beginning, but from a sickness a priori. It's like original sin. The Jew has a disease a priori, handicapped from the beginning. He's had this before coming into contact with others. He was born sick. This difficulty looks to us like a second hereditary fault: not a committed fault, not a sin of omission, but an ontological flaw, a second fall without sin.

It is not vain to recall: we are struck down for who we *are*, even as we are trying to deny our being. It is not even because of the color of our skin, which is just like that of the majority population among whom we live. It is our very being that is in question, and not our acts nor our appearance. The hatred that the Jew inspires, just like the hardship he carries, whether this hardship is accepted or not, bears an ontological complication. The events of the war were for many Jews who did not want to be Jewish the revelation of their own Jewishness. They had always denied it, and this fundamental existence that they carried inside themselves was suddenly revealed to them.

Can we be surprised if this complication, which is so ambiguous, so impalpable and so indefinable, becomes the object in our very own hearts of feelings that themselves are ambiguous, ambivalent, equivocal? Can we be surprised if a suspicious complication engenders suspicious feelings? This ambivalence that we experience along with our difficulty is simultaneously a desire to erase the difference and a desire to maintain it. There is an obscure desire in each of us to level it, to deny this difference, and also a desire to preserve it like a rare flower, like a precious plant that we should cultivate inside ourselves. We want to be like the others, assimilate ourselves, be part of the flock and become invisible and anonymous; the delightful feeling of anonymity and disappearance that exists more or less among all men and is a form of the desire for nothingness, maybe one of the variants of this desire for nothingness experienced in the plenitude of vitality. But we also have the desire to preserve in ourselves the perilous difference of which we are the bearers. We want to be like everyone, and keep this dangerous originality that is ours and in which our dignity possibly resides. The desire to be both same and other is a universally human trait. Every man is first himself and gradually becomes other by the process of becoming, which alters him. But for the Jew, there is not only the becoming that makes the same other common to all men, there is also a simultaneous desire to be the same as the others and different from the others, which is also internalized at the same time in this double quest.

And naturally this warrants reproach. The contradiction we bear makes us suspect for double-dealing. We are accused of seeking out every advantage simultaneously, wanting to have it both ways. And that creates a number of misunderstandings; this is, for example, the case with communist societies in popular democracies. And this misunderstanding, if it is not justified, is nonetheless logical: how is it possible that in a society that wants equality for all men and whose goal is humanism, man as such, independent of his assets, man in his most fundamental being, how is it possible that a certain class of men are not satisfied with this ideal, refuse to bend to it, to let themselves be circumscribed by it? How is it comprehensible that in a communist society men would want *in addition* [*en plus*] to be Jews? Here, two eschatologies, two messianisms, confront one another and there is something paradoxical in the Jew's discontentment. The Jew would be the only one who would remain dissatisfied, even before the tribute paid to man as man in a society without alienation. But within this paradox and the misunderstanding that emanates from it, we might discover a more profound and more metaphysical dimension, a need that even the idea of double nationality could not fulfill.

A man can have two nationalities; legal experts recognize this fact. But when it is a matter of the Jew, it is something else that is in question. To be both French and Jewish makes a demand infinitely more perilous. It is not about belonging to both the French state and the State of Israel, considered as a state among others: this could easily be comprehended. But Judaism complicates it. Judaism is an idea, something beyond the supernatural, an unreasonable demand, that concerns all of one's being. Under these conditions, can I still be French beyond the plane of normal everyday obligations—that which does not have to be called into question? I would still not be at ease if one granted me "dual nationality," if I were permitted to be both at the same time. The idea of a French Jew or a Frenchman of the Israelite faith is a reassuring idea, and I would like to have the serenity that it brings; but we can have it only under the condition of not plumbing its depths. Certainly, when I leave here, I will continue to personify this fiction, to carry it within me in order to live and move about in the streets along with everyone else, among my friends who are a part of the general population and those who are not my friends. But what we have to understand now is the positive side of all of this, which up to this point has appeared as something worrisome and rather negative.

Wherever they are and first and foremost in the country where they live, the Jews embody this principle of " something else." We have tried to define this "something more (en-plus)" as an alibi and an alterity, as the refusal to allow one's self to be circumscribed in a definition. In this sense the Jews are—or should be—the opening onto alterity for others as well. Being other than themselves, they are—for those who are only themselves and who can so easily get in a rut, those who isolate themselves in their aloofness—an invitation to get beyond themselves; they represent a fertile principle of opening and movement. They have as their function notably to arouse concern everywhere for the foreigner. Wherever he is, actually, the Jew has his eyes turned elsewhere; he is interested in something else. This concern for the foreigner is so natural to him that the Jew is often reproached for his cosmopolitanism, without the understanding that this is exactly what preserves all of humanity against the provincialism of the closed City. These Jews who arouse anxiety represent in sum the opening of the city. They embody the "mobilization" of the immobile or, better yet, *motion*, the very shock at the origin of the movement. The Jews who are for themselves the very movement that escapes them, are with regard to the nations the motion that worries them, but that at the same time maintains men in this vital mobility, essential to the human condition.

This characteristic, and this is the other side of our indefinable particularity, has the antisemite's obsession as its repercussion, which itself is a bit mysterious. And antisemitism in turn becomes for the Jew more than an obsession, it is a reason for perpetual bewilderment. I was recently asked to participate in a conference on antisemitism and music. This group of Jewish students asked me if I could speak to them about the antisemitism of Richard Wagner. It wasn't music but antisemitism that interested these young Jews, however liberated and full of the vital plenitude of the State of Israel. I refused, antisemitism being a terrain full of noxious air and sad evocations.

In antisemitism there is something that plays an important role in our own being. First of all, it sets us up to define ourselves negatively, as the mystics defined their God through the means of negative theology. Antisemitism is in some ways the apophatic psychology or philosophy, that is to say negative, of Jews who cannot define themselves positively. At the same time, this explains that antisemitism itself, even for the antisemites, has this elusive, irrational, even in its own way impassioned quality, which is mysterious and somewhat contradictory. Antisemitism is mysterious and our tendency, like that of the Marxists, moreover, is to trivialize it. One appealing proposal is to regard it as a particular case of racism or colonialism. Among the different ways that a man has to hate another man, there are those that are more banal. It would be nice if we could make this unique complex ordinary, if we could present antisemitism as a simple diversion of capitalism that designates a "privileged" people, a representative people to carry the weight of injustice and thus to discharge capital itself of this responsibility. It is understandable that Marxism, the enemy of magic, of every theological interpretation of history, every notion of affliction or blessing, is inclined to see in antisemitism only a deviation of this type. But it is incomprehensible in our case to place the Jew in a general category that would include Arabs, Blacks, Berbers, or others. Even if there are shared issues, to consider antisemitism a common or simple form of colonialism makes no sense.

To be clear, I do not say this out of a patrician concern to distinguish ourselves from other people. This professed privilege is a painful and burdensome one to bear. This is not a noble privilege, even if perhaps, in psychoanalyzing us, one would find at the bottom of our hearts a claim of this order. But there are fundamental differences. In our case, at least until the creation of the State of Israel, it was not a question of a well-defined people, an assembled and organized ethnic group. Instead, we were a people dispersed among nations, everywhere in the minority, living according to the principle of dissemination. Antisemitism is not this sentiment of superiority that the white racist has toward people who are supposedly inferior, in other words for whichever people he pleases, out of hate, to regard as such. Here it is about a complex—complicated as all complexes are—in which both a feeling of superiority and a feeling of inferiority support each other. The feeling of superiority is only a complex because it encompasses a feeling of inferiority. And for non-Jews the feeling of superiority in relation to Jews is only a complex because the contempt masks here a secret feeling of inferiority, a secret jealousy of this new thing of which we are the bearers, this intangible and mobile something that is life itself. Paradoxically, this jealousy is directed at our distress itself, because it happens to be the case that men need distress and claim pain: to have suffered, to have endured pain, isn't this one of the characteristics of our humanity, evidence that we deserve to be called human? The fact that the war made us special victims bestows on us an eminent dignity, a historical dignity.

There is thus a secret jealousy that the people of the majority harbor toward the astute, industrious, hardworking, and unfortunate people. And this jealousy is aimed at misfortune itself. It is composed of a multitude of extremely complex feelings, evanescent in their contradictions. These feelings do not have much in common with the other forms of racist hate, which, to be clear, does not make such hatred any more defensible. But it is a question of a specific complex, unique in its genre, which resembles no other in its content, even if there are analogies on the surface. The feeling of the non-Jew toward the Jew is that toward one who is at the same time both similar and dissimilar. The feeling of the white man toward the black man is a crude, primitive, and simple one that targets those of another skin color. The Jew resembles the non-Jew in the color of his skin, and in nearly all things. Besides certain diacritical marks, the structure of their faces is often completely alike. And for that matter, the Jew is superior in certain aspects. The non-Jew, at least, feels this to be the case: he plays an important role in the elite of occidental peoples, and the antisemite has an obscure feeling that puts him at odds with himself. This is why it is useless to treat antisemitism as banal. On the one hand, with regard to ourselves: the Jewish people are infinitely definable; which is only another way to say indefinable. The idea of a definition implies finitude. On the other hand, in the relationship that binds us to the non-Jew, from our perspective there is something specific, essential in their feelings concerning the feelings of man toward man. At some point if the Jews had not existed, they would have had to be invented; it would have been necessary to fabricate a mysterious people, a people dispersed as we are, with regard to which man could have feelings that do not resemble others, that do not allow for trivialization and that will persist until the end of time.

But as soon as I say this, I think that perhaps a bit of complacency has made its way into these restrictions, and into our remarks themselves, and in the very fact of our uniting and speaking among ourselves, with this more or less explicit presupposition that we constitute a special case, that we are not like the others and that the Jewish people will be different from the others until the end of time, remaining, even with the creation of the State of Israel, the center of a privileged tragedy, that of the minority people. We have to repudiate, maybe, a part of this game. Why did I go to Israel? Why am I here talking about Judaism when, in the activities of my daily life, it plays practically no role and hardly connects at all to my teaching? Is there a part to play for the Jew who is Parisian or French? Hardly have I asked this worrying question before I am reminded of the seriousness of its stakes. First, because certain tragedies date back less than thirteen years. They still linger with us. They ravaged our lives and often our flesh. They haunt our nights and they obligate us to consider this internal problem with profound seriousness, if nothing else. And now to all this is added the temporal evidence and secular and worldly certitude of Israel incarnate, of an incarnate state that we have not spoken about until now.

This state is a state that appears to be like all the others, with a border, a government, a police force, and I wager that among the Israelis there is a certain childish delight in constituting a state "like the others." I imagine that, when the Russians had the revolution of 1918, a similar complex of respectability surfaced among them: to have a flag, a national anthem, a new currency, and embassies in other countries—what satisfaction for the wretched! Well, in Israel, there are also ambassadors, and we have the honor to have here even a cultural official of this state. The State of Israel has all the attributes of sovereignty; it is a part of the elite nations, it is a state like the others. Through certain traits, it recalls for us the eschatological absolutism of popular democracies. The spirit of community, the freedom of man as such, these are also Israeli ideals. But to all this is added something that does not exist in popular democracy, something "more (en-plus)" that comes from another eschatology, that constitutes a messianism above and beyond social messianism, and which is Judaism itself. Everyone agrees, believers and nonbelievers, practicing and nonpracticing, that the word "Judaism" includes a spiritual meaning, the sense of moral messianism, what in Western, rather bourgeois language we would call an ideal. In Judaic thought there is a tension—I come back to this same term—between this state like all the others and yet not at all like the others, and this reality without precedent of a diaspora that is left outside it, and that without a doubt will never be absorbed and that does not look anything like a diaspora that continues outside the home country, like Italian or German emigration. This situation of tension between a state like all the others and an immense and unabsorbable diaspora that maintains throughout and in every locale this unnerving principle of spirituality, of folly, of contradiction, this principle, which we embody right here, is the source of a rich debate. It is unnerving, even when it is no longer on the order of tragedy. It is a solicitation to always look elsewhere, always beyond. It is a creative tension; its solution resides in the infinite. But it also resides in time and movement. It is the cause of a predicament, of an aporia, as Plato would say in Socratic terms. Socrates is honored in Ben-Gurion's kibbutz! Is this because the Jewish "aporia" and the Socratic "aporia" correspond to one another? There is here an infinite perplexity that does not contain an end or a solution. I don't know how to rectify in myself the sum of these contradictions, and the Hegelian synthesis has little attraction for us. Our perplexity will last until the end of time, which has no end.

*Translated by Beatrice Bourgogne*
*and Sarah Hammerschlag*

# 13

# Sarah Kofman, Smothered Words

Sarah Kofman, excerpts from *Smothered Words*, trans. Madeleine Dobie (Evanston, IL: Northwestern University Press, 1998), 7–11, 34–35.

The author of over twenty-five books, Sarah Kofman (1934–1994) was first and foremost a philosopher. She wrote extensively on Freud and Nietzsche, the relationship between art and philosophy, the feminine in the history of philosophy, laughter, irony, antisemitism, and autobiography. In two of her late works, particularly in *Smothered Words*, from which the passages below are excerpted, Kofman not only wrote about autobiography but also intermixed philosophical and literary analysis with details from her own life, addressing for the first time her experience as a Holocaust survivor and the daughter of a Polish rabbi and ritual slaughterer who was killed at Auschwitz. While this text, published in 1987, broaches the subject and announces her intention to write from the subjective stance of a "Jewish woman intellectual," it was not until *Rue Ordener, Rue Labat* (1994) that she told the story of her own wartime experience in hiding, torn between her Jewish mother and the French Catholic woman who maintained them both in Paris during the war. Although the later text is very much a memoir, both books established Kofman as a significant voice in Holocaust studies and French Jewish thought.

The two passages from *Paroles suffoquées* (*Smothered Words*) reproduced below include the most autobiographical sections of the book. The majority of this short work of under one hundred pages provides commentary on Maurice Blanchot's stories and essays and on Robert Antelme's *The Human Race*. The text was originally planned for a volume of *Les cahiers de l'Herne* to be devoted to Blanchot. Although neither Antelme nor Blanchot was Jewish, it was their texts that impelled Kofman to reflect on the nature of being Jewish. It is Blanchot's texts, she writes, "which teach us to remember that which must henceforth be the ground of our memory . . . that which is not measured in terms of power: the infinite distance which never ceases to reaffirm the relation with the infinite of which the Jew, for Blanchot, is the emblematic figure, he who has been able to preserve throughout his history the vocation of foreignness, of exile, of the outside." Kofman's contribution in the work is to provide her own pastiche of Blanchot's late writings on the disaster, to extend his commentary on Antelme in his essay "The Indestructible," and to lend to these texts the layer of her own voice, as one whose life as a Jewish woman was profoundly affected by the event. Kofman's choice to focus her most systematic reflections about Auschwitz on the writings of two non-Jews is significant in two ways. First, it stages an encounter between the figural Jew who emerges from Blanchot's texts, along with his reading of Antelme, and the experience of Kofman, writing as a Jew. Second, her repetition and thus reinscription of these texts brings them into the corpus of Jewish thought. This is particularly noteworthy given the scholarly controversy surrounding the appearance of the trope of the Jew in French writing by non-Jews.[1]

I

If, since Auschwitz, the categorical imperative has become the one which Adorno has formulated in the style of Kant, though ridding it of its abstract and ideal generality, "to arrange one's thoughts and actions so that Auschwitz will not repeat itself, so that nothing similar will happen;"[2] if with Auschwitz, an absolute has been reached before which other rights and other duties must be judged;[3] if Auschwitz is neither a concept nor a pure name, but a name beyond naming (or, in Lyotard's terms[4] a name which designates that which has no name in speculative thought, the name of the anonymous, the name of that which remains without result and without profit for the speculative), it behooves me, as a Jewish woman intellectual who has survived the holocaust, to pay homage to Blanchot for the fragments on Auschwitz scatted throughout his texts: writing of the ashes, writing of the disaster which avoids the trap of complicity with speculative knowledge, with that in it which is tied to power, and thereby complicity with speculative knowledge, with that in it which is tied to power and thereby complicit with the torturers of Auschwitz.

Texts which teach us (without making this the object of a lesson) to remember that which must henceforth constitute the ground of our memory; which teach

1. [See, e.g., Susan Shapiro, "'Écriture judaique': Where Are the Jews in Western Discourse?" in Angelika Bammer, ed., *Displacements: Cultural Identities in Question* (Bloomington: Indiana University Press, 1994); Michael Weingrad, "Jews (in Theory): Representations of Judaism, Anti-Semitism, and the Holocaust in Postmodern French Thought," *Judaism* 45, 1 (Winter 1996): 79–98.]

2. Theodor Adorno, *Negative Dialectics*, trans. E. B. Ashton (New York: Seabury Press, 1979), 365; translation modified.

3. See Blanchot, "Les intellectuels en question," *Le Débat*, no. 29 (March 1984).

4. Jean-François Lyotard, "Phraser après Auschwitz," *Les fins de l'homme* (Paris: Galilée, 1981).

us all, young or old, Jews or non-Jews, if this senseless breaking of the human race into two can, after Auschwitz, still make sense. A break desired by the Anti-Semites and the Nazis so that the Jew would signify repulsion, the Other in all his horror,[5] the abject man who must be kept at a distance, expelled, exiled, exterminated. What the Nazis could not tolerate, what they tried to commit to the invincible power of death, is that which no form of power can overcome, because it does not encounter it, that which is not measured in terms of power: the infinite distance which never ceased to reaffirm the relation with the infinite of which the Jew, for Blanchot[6] (even if he is not only that), is the emblematic figure, he who has been able to preserve throughout his history the vocation of foreignness, of exile, of the outside.

## II

Since Auschwitz all men, Jews (and) non-Jews, die differently: they do not really die; they survive death, because what took place—back there—without taking place, death in Auschwitz, was worse than death:[7] "Humanity as a whole had to die through the trial of some of its members (those who incarnate life itself, almost an entire people, a people that has been promised an eternal presence). This death still endures. And from this comes the obligation never again to die only once, without however allowing repetition to injure us to the always essential ending."[8]

5. See Blanchot, *The Infinite Conversation*, trans. Susan Hanson (Minneapolis: University of Minnesota Press, 1993), 123. A figure of the Other quite different from that of the Greek suppliant who inspires fear because he might possibly mask some divinity brings with him some new truth that must be confronted. The suppliant, though separated from the omnipotent force that welcomes him and offers him hospitality, escapes power's jurisdiction and answers another law, that which affirms his truth as a stranger. Engulfed in misfortune, deprived of everything, he is still able to speak and is therefore still a man.

6. Ibid., 123ff.

7. See Adorno: "The administrative murder of millions made of death a thing one had never yet to fear in just this fashion. . . . The last, the poorest possession left to the individual is expropriated. That in the concentration camp it was no longer an individual who died but a specimen—this is a fact bound to affect the dying of those who escaped administrative measures" (*Negative Dialectics*, 362). "In the camps, death has a novel horror; since Auschwitz, fearing death means fearing worse than death" (371).

8. Blanchot, "After the Fact," afterword to *Vicious Circles*, trans. Paul Auster (Barrytown, NY: Station Hill Press, 1985), 69.

Because he was a Jew, my father died in Auschwitz: How can it not be said? And how can it be said? How can one speak of that before which all possibility of speech ceases? Of this event, my absolute, which communicates with the absolute of history, and which is of interest only for this reason. To speak: it is necessary—*without (the) power*: without allowing language, too powerful, sovereign, to master the most aporetic situation, absolute situation, absolute powerlessness and very distress, to enclose it in the clarity and happiness of daylight. And how can one not speak of it, when the wish of all those who returned—and he did not return—has been to tell, to tell endlessly, as if only an "infinite conversation" could match the infinite privation?

My father: Berek Kofman, born on October 10, 1900 in Sobin (Poland), taken to Drancy on July 16, 1942. Was in convoy no. 12, dated July 29, 1942, a convoy comprising 1,000 deportees, 270 men and 730 women (aged 36 to 54): 270 men registered 54,153 to 54,422; 514 women selected for work, registered 13,320 to 13,833; 216 other women gassed immediately. It is recorded there, in the Serge Klarsfeld Memorial: with its endless columns of names, its lack of pathos, its sobriety, the "neutrality" of its information, this sublime memorial takes your breath away. Its "neutral" voice summons you obliquely; in its extreme restraint, it is the very voice of affliction, of this event in which all possibility vanished, and which inflicted on the whole of humanity "the decisive blow which left nothing intact" (AF, p. 68). This voice leaves you without a voice, makes you doubt your common sense and all sense, makes you suffocate in silence: "silence like a cry without words; mute, although crying endlessly" (SNB, p. 61).[9]

. . .

IV

. . . *Auschwitz*: the impossibility of rest. My father, a rabbi, was killed because he tried to observe the Sabbath in the death camps; buried alive with a shovel for having—or so the witnesses reported—refused to work on that day, in order to celebrate the Sabbath, to pray to God for them all, victims and executioners, reestablishing, in this situation of extreme powerlessness and violence, a rela-

9. See also *Writing the Disaster*, 51: "Like writing . . . the cry tends to exceed all language, even if it lends itself to recuperation as language effect. It is both sudden and patient. . . . The patience of the cry: it does not simply come to a halt, reduced to nonsense, yet it does remain outside of sense—a meaning infinitely suspended, decried, decipherable-indecipherable."

tion beyond all power. And they could not bear that a Jew, that vermin, even in the camps, did not lose faith in God. As he did not lose faith in God on that afternoon of July 16, 1942, when a French policeman came to round him up with a pained smile on his lips, almost as if he, too, were excusing himself. Having gone to warn the Jews of the synagogue to go and hide because he knew there would be a raid, he had returned to the house to pray to God that he be taken, so long as his wife and children were spared. And instead of hiding, he left with the policeman; so that we would not be taken in his place, as hostages, he suffered, like millions of others, the infinite of violence: death in Auschwitz.

In the unnamable "place," he continued to observe Jewish monotheism, if by this, with Blanchot, we understand the revelation of the word as the place in which men maintain a relation to that which excludes all relation: the infinitely Distant, the absolutely Foreign. A relation with the infinite, which no form of power, including that of the executioners of the camps, has been able to master, other than by denying it, burying it in a pit with a shovel, without ever having encountered it.

# III | Universal and Particular
## The Jew and the
## Political Realm

The question of Judaism's universalism and the charge against it of ethnic particularism have been endemic to the history of the Jewish Question in France since at least the debates over Jewish emancipation in the 1780s and 1790s. Thus the desire to portray Judaism as a form of universalism pervades the scholarship and literature of nineteenth- and early twentieth-century French Judaism. Here we treat it in the postwar context because of the shifts in political self-understanding prompted by the war. Additionally significant in shaping French Jewish thought in this period was Israel's Declaration of Independence in May 1948, followed in 1967 by the Six-Day War. During the same period North African colonial conflicts, particularly the Algerian War, led to the mass migration of Jews to the metropole, dramatically altering the demographics of French Jewry.[1] North African Jews had already felt the tenuousness of their French citizenship during the Second World War. The colonial conflict and its accompanying episodes of antisemitic violence cemented as well the alienation of North African Jews from the majority-Muslim culture of the former colonies, further heightening the community's sense of marginalization.

French Jewish thinkers of this period consistently cite the Six-Day War as a turning point in relation to both their French identity and their allegiance to Israel, impelling many to make aliyah. On the one hand, it entailed a sense of helplessness as the fledging state fought for its existence in the face of overwhelming opposition, followed by the experience of miraculous victory and thus the renewed opportunity to be part of the historical drama. At the same time, with Israeli victory came new suspicion by the French establishment,

1. From 1950 to 1970, 220,000 North African Jews resettled in France. Hyman, *The Jews of Modern France*, 194.

including the imposition of an arms embargo on Israel during the war. In November 1967, de Gaulle infamously referred to Israel in a press conference as a "warlike state, resolved to self-aggrandize," and to the Jews as "an elite people, sure of itself and domineering," sparking a backlash from the Jewish community and a renewed sense of betrayal. The prominent Jewish columnist and political scientist Raymond Aron, who had theretofore been somewhat suspicious of Diaspora Jewish allegiance to Israel, asserted that de Gaulle had now, "with some half a dozen words . . . rehabilitated an always latent anti-Semitism."[2]

The 1967 war affected French Jewish political identity in multiple ways, but most clearly insofar as it isolated the concerns and allegiances of French Jews from the majority population. Most notable about all the essays included here is the claim to differentiate a Jewish political ideal from that of the Christian West. Yet the basis of that differentiation varies, from those such as Neher, Atlan, and Trigano who derive their formulation of Jewish politics from the canonical texts themselves to Memmi and Marienstras, for whom it is the contemporary exigency of the postwar world that demands new ways of conceptualizing Jewish political identity. While not all of these essays explicitly take into account Israel's role in shaping French Jewish self-understanding, the stakes of the state's existence are implicit in each of them.

2. Wolf, *Harnessing the Holocaust*, 48. See also Raymond Aron, *De Gaulle, Israel and the Jews*, trans. John Sturrock (New York: Praeger, 1969).

# 14

Albert Memmi, The Jew, the Nation and History

Albert Memmi, "The Jew, the Nation and History," *Portrait of a Jew*,
trans. Elisabeth Abbott (New York: Orion, 1963), 195–205
(plunkettlakepress.com/poaj).

Born in Tunisia, raised in a poor Jewish family that spoke Arabic, and educated at a school run by the Alliance israélite orientale, Albert Memmi (1920– ) became a sociologist, novelist, essayist, and poet as well as an international voice on racism and colonialism. As an adolescent, despite religious doubts, Memmi felt a strong sense of belonging to the Jewish community and was an early supporter of Zionism when the state was only aspirational, long before the mass migration of North African Jews in the 1950s and 1960s. As a lycée student and then at the University of Algiers, he strongly identified with the universalism of France and its enlightened ideals. But the events of the war—the Pétain regime and his own experience in a labor camp in Tunisia—fostered the realization, as he writes in the preface to *Portrait of a Jew*, that his "destiny did not necessarily coincide with that of Europe."[1] Thus began Memmi's long intellectual trajectory, explored across genres, which conceptualized the social dynamics of colonization as he himself had experienced them and as they perpetuated themselves through notions of race and power relations. As he put it in the 1965 preface to *The Colonizer and the Colonized*, "The colonial relationship . . . chained the colonizer and the colonized into an implacable dependence, molded their respective characters and dictated their conduct."[2] At the heart of Memmi's concern about colonization was the relationship between the oppressor and the oppressed. In his 1994 work *Le racisme* he sought to define and understand racism as a defensive response, a rationalization of heterophobia.

For Memmi the experience of being a North African Jew marked a particular intersection of both categories. Hence Memmi often resorts to his own experience in his writing, even in his more theoretical work. In the 1950s and 1960s Frantz Fanon and Jean-Paul Sartre were some of his closest interlocutors, sharing his interest in analyzing the Jewish Question, the race question, and the colonial question by

---

1. [Albert Memmi, *Portrait d'un Juif* (Paris: Gallimard, 1962).]
2. [Albert Memmi, *The Colonizer and the Colonized* (Boston: Beacon Press, 1965), ix.]

conceptualizing their ideal types.[3] Memmi also took part in the French debates about Jewish identity taking place at the Colloque des intellectuels juifs de langue française, though not among the most regular participants.

While many of the thinkers in part 3 struggle to conceptualize Judaism as simultaneously an ethnic particularism and a religious universalism, Memmi opts clearly for particularism. But this is not a matter of preference; it is not an ethnic nationalism chosen in pride. Rather, it is the consequence of centuries of exclusion. For Memmi, "To be a Jew is, first of all, not a choice . . . it is, first of all, a fate: to refuse that fate does not change much either, for it depends more on other men than on oneself."[4] While this position led Memmi to strongly embrace the State of Israel as a solution to the problem, it also made him resist a religious version of Zionism and a religious justification for its existence. He has spoken out vocally for the rights of Palestinians, for the necessity of a Palestinian state, but as recently as 2003 also expressed concern that the future of the State of Israel was at risk, and that Jews had lost sight of the risk this represents. He suggests further that the marginalized status of the Jew that he described in the first edition of Portrait of a Jew in 1962 remains a description germane to the twenty-first century.

ONE

I have written elsewhere that as adolescents and later as young men we refused to take seriously the persistence of nations. We lived in enthusiastic expectation of a new age, such as the world had never known before, signs of which we thought we could already detect—the death (which had certainly begun) of religions, families and nations. We had nothing but anger, scorn and irony for the die-hards of history who clung to those residues. Today I see more clearly why we expended so much energy on cultivating those hopes. Certainly the impatient and generous nature of adolescents which drives them to free themselves, and the whole world, of all shackles, is particularly suited to revolutionary ideologies. But, in addition, we were Jews: I am convinced that this had much to do with the vigor of our choice. Beyond our desire to be accepted by the families, religions and nations of non-Jews who rejected and isolated us because we were Jews, we longed to be one with all men and so, at last, become men like the others.

3. [Kwame Anthony Appiah, "Foreword," Racism, trans. Steve Martinot (Minneapolis: University of Minnesota Press, 2000), vii.]
4. [Memmi, Portrait of a Jew, 208.]

Unfortunately, whether we were deluding ourselves, whether we may have relapsed since then into a period of regression, or whether it is simply that I have grown older, I have to admit that those residues were as stubborn as weeds and persisted in remaining fundamental structures in the lives of nations, essential aspects of their collective being. War was waged in the name of nations and peace stabilized the oldest nations and brought new nations into being. The postwar period saw an indisputable religious revival which swept the orthodox parties to power throughout Europe. Because they understood that situation, the Communists, who keep their fingers on the pulse of nations, extolled the "Catholic communicants," offered their "outstretched hand" to Christians and called themselves patriots and nationalists. The Socialists did not even need to resort to trickery; their chauvinism was very real; colonial wars soon gave them an opportunity to expand. To all appearances we were doomed to religions and nations and for a long time. Once again I am not passing judgment, I am simply stating facts.

What was going to become of us, of our adolescent hopes? What we felt confusedly, what we were trying to suppress by rejecting the society of those days, I neither can, nor do I wish to make a secret of any longer. The religious state of nations being what it is, and nations being what they are, the Jew finds himself, in a certain measure, *outside* of the national community. And here again, of course, people are going to protest, and I am ready to concede, out of weariness, and to avoid a discussion in which reason alone does not speak, that this is particularly a question of, let us say, a personal situation. Because, even today, people live their collective lives as nationals, I feel more or less set apart from that life of communal nationality; I cannot live spontaneously the nationality modern law grants me (when it does grant it).

So then, is the accusation confirmed? As a Jew, you admit to being stateless and cosmopolitan? Of your own accord, you reject the nation! I do not reject anything! What is confirmed? Do I really suffer from my own refusal or from what other men refuse me? As if, on this point, I had enough strength and pride, serenity and independence to be able to refuse! I have often wished, but so far in vain, that like a former lover who has become indifferent, I could refuse dispassionately, that I could be calmly ironical about those residues, about what I liked to think were relics. But one does not really scorn till after one has been surfeited, and my non-Jewish friends manage this infinitely better than I do. The truth, on the contrary, is that I have longed with all my might for that integration, I have longed to become a citizen like other men. Yes, on this point I confess my humiliated disappointment. How heart-warming it would have been to the stranger to feel that he was an integral, definitive part of the institutions of the country, instead of finding himself constantly called to account! The Jew's enemy shouts for joy at the slightest confession of that non–co-existence, that rootlessness of the Jew. How can he call us to account for the very object of our nostalgia, for that misfortune imposed on us by fate, not to say by the enemy himself? How can he make capital of our exclusion? I have not rejected anything; unfortunately it is the nation that has rejected me, that leaves me outside. Whether I like it or not, the history of the country in which I live is, to me, a borrowed history. How could I feel that Joan of Arc is a symbol for me? Would I hear with her the patriotic and Christian voices? Yes, always religion! But show me a way to separate national tradition from religious tradition. I cannot forget that the national heroine carried a sword shaped like a cross: like most of the heroes of history, the dying Bayard, for instance, asking to kiss his sword, a double symbol. How could I have identified myself with Clovis, that good, naïve and glamorous ancestor of primary school textbooks, but who, it seems, would willingly have exterminated the wicked Jews? Or with Napoleon, so ambiguous, so annoyed by the Jews of his era? Or, with even greater reason, with the Czars and their pogroms or with Oriental sovereigns? It is impossible for me to identify myself seriously with the past of any nation.

For a great part of the citizens of the country, it is true, that history and that past are not exactly theirs, either. But they are not aware of it. Happily for them, the great collective oblivion has been going on for a long, long time. Their foreign ancestors intermingled in the vast cemetery of the past, that common grave in which all disappear together. Today the descendants reap the benefit of anonymity: Where could they come from if not from here? He who succeeds in inscribing his name on the genealogical tree, salvages enormous roots, and ends by believing that he has sprung from time immemorial, makes himself legitimate and legitimizes his descendants. There is always something mystical in all collective memory. The Jew himself, because he is a Jew, preserves his relationships integrally. Even though he be more ancient than all those successive grafts on the body of the nation, no matter how long ago he first appeared, by definition people agree that he is an outsider, because he has not always been there. Thus in Tunis, we sometimes used to boast of being authentic Berbers, or Phoenicians, settled there before anyone else, since the days of Queen Dido. That alleged nobility isolated us even more.

There is, in short, neither anything to reject nor anything to rejoice over. I live out my social and political destiny not as something marvelous and exceptional, but as something separated cruelly from the lives of my fellow-citizens. From this come my embarrassment and my apprehension the moment they speak in my presence of anything that touches on that historic past. No Gauls, please. Enough of Celts, ancient Germans, Slavs, conquering Romans and conquering Arabs! For then, I find myself naked and alone: my own ancestors were neither Gauls, Celts, Slavs, ancient Germans, Arabs, nor Turks. How can I be sure of that? Who is sure of his ancestors? But this is a question especially of the heart's confidence and of the approval of opinion. And, above all, not of a positive, but of a negative feature of Jewish existence. Difference in this case is negatively fundamental: my fellow-citizens may not have been Gauls or Arabs, but that has no importance. As for me, I may not have been an Arab or a Roman; but that is considered a certainty. I have never been able to say "We" in referring to those historical pedigrees on which my fellow-citizens pride themselves. I have never heard another Jew say "We" without wincing, without vaguely suspecting him of an inadvertent blunder, of complacency or of a slip of the tongue.

I must add that I seldom express myself this way. I detest historical grandiloquence, past or even future. I scorn the slogans "immortal France," "imperishable Tunisia," or "eternal Judaism." I believe that, sooner or later, death shows its face entirely and that all those eternities and immortalities, so auspiciously asserted, are merely the pathetic guarantees we try to give ourselves against death. "It is just that you are a Jew," someone will retort. "You scoff at countries because you haven't any!" That is only partially true. I have said too that several of my non-Jewish friends were much more violent than I, more calmly scornful of their collective myths. Unfortunately I do not have their confidence and their serenity; my mind also argues and decides, but my heart suffers and protests. I would so much rather have shared in those illusions, if they are illusions, even though with ironical dignity I rejected them afterwards. I would much rather have been part of them the better to free myself of them. A man may succeed in being casual about the collective past of his own nation, history and traditions, but it is almost unbearable to have them denied to him by other men. André Gide noted in his diary that it was almost impossible for him to think like Maurice Barrès, whom he admired, because he, Gide, was Protestant and not Catholic, and because his father and mother came from two different regions of France; in a certain measure he felt that he was too scattered, heterogeneous, as it were, and he suffered because of it. And yet no one thought of calling him to account; no one doubted him and he had not the slightest doubt himself that his destiny and the destiny of France were one. With what country, what corner of the earth, am I sure of identifying myself? With what culture, what collective experience? It is true that I can pretend to find a certain strength in that dissipation, a greater freedom: "See, I do not belong to anything, I am therefore free of hindrances!" There may be some pride in that solitude and distance I am obliged to keep. And I do not scorn those days of courage and health. But I believe that the price for them is too high. Illegitimacy sharpens the mind, to be sure, but it is a very uncomfortable condition, and one that is better to be spared. One of my friends, a somewhat scatterbrained psychologist, told me: "I come from Lyons, my father comes from Lyons, my grandfather too ... But with most of my Jewish friends, their father comes from one place, their grandfather from another, and their uncle lives in still a third place." And she added consolingly: "Compared to my Jewish friends, I feel a little cramped, a little poor."

Those, however, were a rich woman's words, the romantic regret of someone who has the wherewithal to live and enjoy life, and sighs after poetry. If she only knew how her Jewish friends would have preferred her solid poverty to their too rich dispersion, her geographical and historical uniqueness to their volatile instability.


TWO

I can do nothing to prevent that constant rupture and gnawing negativity from weighing significantly on my destiny. They are among the major signs and components of my oppression. It really seems that one of its most serious attacks is directed against the historical dimension of the oppressed person; leveling it out, flattening it, in the hope perhaps of clarifying it, of making it less awkward. The oppressed person is not credited with any historic past, and if the oppression lasts, history being stolen from him progressively, he has less and less of it and ends by forgetting it altogether. For several generations colonial troops have paid for the plans of European nations with their suffering, their blood and their death. But are theirs the profit and the glory, if there is any glory and since it is permitted to speak of glory? The battle for Cassino is therefore "inscribed forever to the immortal courage of the French Army." Do they specify that that army was composed of a large percentage of North Africans and Jews? In the very heart of the nation, women, as women, have almost no position: the history of all nations is a purely masculine history. In that masculine world, also, there are rich and poor. Historical memory seems to be dispensed according to power; only the leaders and men of importance have a right to a specified past. Who would ever think of drawing up the genealogical tree of a poor family? It is all right that they participated collectively in the genesis of the world, that they have served as the raw material, that they have been regimented masses or tremendous forces with desires that had to be deceived. The Jew does not even have the right to that vague collective participation. Historically he seems never to have fought, or conquered, or suffered; never to have invented anything, to have left nothing behind him, no monuments, no traces, no memories. If it were not for a few accidental references in the archives of the non-Jews to such and such a collective slaughter or such and such an extraordinary tax imposed on him, one might doubt that the Jew had ever lived in the land. How could it have been otherwise? History being national, and the Jew not actually part of the nation, how would he have had a historical past? Did he even have a past at all? Did he even exist? That may seem paradoxical when one looks at that splendid testimony of a splendid past, as they say to be kind to us. But that past is too splendid, too remote as a matter of fact, too far past, with no continuity with what we are today: it is a *mythical* past, the past of the Bible, of the Passage through the Red Sea and of the manna in the desert. Since then, nothing—or almost nothing. To be sure, the history of nations is also in great part mythical, but it is not lived only as a myth, it is renewed, brought up to date and revived daily. The Jew has to balance between his legendary history of which he is often ignorant and a contemporary history in which he is not recognized, in which he has no place. Carried to extremes, the truly oppressed person no longer has a past at all.

How could my removal from the universe fail to have serious and very concrete consequences? I do not suffer from my non-integration in the body and continuity of the nation because of any fetishism for nation, history or the past. I would not have made myself clear if I had not succeeded in suggesting that the negative conditions of the Jewish existence were as heavy with consequences as the more positive. Far beyond any sentimental claim, any purely emotional frustration, I am not on a truly equal footing with my fellow-citizens in the life we share, in our common history which is being made every day. Most often I am prohibited from looking forward to the same expectations even when I no longer fear them. Since the past is far from reassuring, I dare not believe completely in my national future. Many Jews, I know, act as if they did believe in it, as if they were fooled by it. But it takes very little to discover their hesitation and doubt. To make future plans in common, one has to be sure of staying together. Now, my marriage with the nation is always in danger of being questioned. How, under these conditions, can I settle down forever without a worrisome, secret fear of having to argue or even to move on? I live, I cohabit, in the hope that it may last, that I shall be left in peace. Perhaps (supreme hope) in the end they will have become so used to me that my children will finally be adopted. But any day, at any moment, an incident may remind me that the tacit contract is weak, that I do not have the right to the same considerations, the same security as my fellow-citizens. A few years ago, the French were thrown out of Egypt. Then, when relations between that country and France improved, they were again authorized to return ... all except the French Jews. That, strictly speaking, could be the point of view of Egypt, at war with Israel, which has frankly adopted an anti-Semitic attitude, but not the point of view of France which, nevertheless, forsook her nationals of the Jewish religion. "The French government," writes one of them, "in aiming to renew relations with Egypt at all costs, has accepted the principle of sacrificing the French citizen of Israelite faith ... We therefore consider that the mother country ... has sacrificed a group of her children ... by ignoring the sacred principle of racial non-discrimination guaranteed by the constitution." (*Le Monde*, August 25, 1958.)

Would the nation as a whole have consented so easily to abandoning the inhabitants of Brittany or of the Midi? Let us not forget the protests against the treaty of 1870 which ceded Alsace-Lorraine to Germany, albeit under pressure of force. The Alsatians are still bitter about it today.

That questionable integration of the Jew with the collective body denotes after all an actual insecurity, a latent historical weakness. The Jew cannot look behind him, but he cannot even look ahead except with due precaution. The past is denied him, the future challenged, and this is even more serious. Behind him, emptiness; before him uncertainty to say the least, if not threat. Do we need to look farther to find the sources of his unrest and his permanent dissatisfaction?

### THREE

As a matter of fact the Jew's whole relation to history and time is thus perverted, constantly agitated, constantly prone to upheavals. Again and again it has been said that the Jew is interested only in the present! By that is meant, undoubtedly, that he is a sensualist and a swine; that he is lacking in respect for traditions, for the most sacred foundations of national life, that he has no "sense of the past." Presented in that light, the statement is stupid and as false as usual; how can one reconcile the Jew's preoccupation with the present with his anxiety, acknowledged in other respects by a stubborn adherence to a secular tradition? Besides, it would be hard to find a pig who is as dissatisfied and disturbed as the Jew.

And yet that accusation is not entirely false. I admit that I am essentially interested in the present: it causes me enough worries! Cut off from the past, rejected by history, with no assurance for the future, I have nothing left but the present: it is not a preference, it is an obligation. The only choice permitted me is, in short, between eternity and the immediate present. To be on the safe side, I always keep eternity in the innermost depths of my being, as a last resort for my thought, an ultimate recourse in times of catastrophe. If violent death were to strike one day, perhaps my lips would instinctively move in the ancient prayer for the dying. What can one do when the present fails, when men become too cruel, history unbearable? "Our eternal God ... Abraham ... Avinu," our time-honored fathers, that is to say, beyond the ages ... Meanwhile my present as a Jew has neither the same coloring nor the same burden of anguish and hope as has the present of my fellow-citizens. I remember discussing the meaning of the last war with my non-Jewish friends. I read in the war memoirs of the German novelist Junger, all the names of the French writers who received him in the midst of war, and who had excellent relations with him. I do not even reproach them for it. We did not run the same risks, our stake was not the same, our evaluation could not be identical, I willingly admit that. A great French novelist whom I like and admire, wrote at the beginning of the war in Spain: "*Anything, rather than war! Anything, anything!* (the italics are his). Even Fascism in Spain! And do not press me, for I would also say: yes ... and even 'Fascism in France'! ... Nothing, *no test, no* servitude, can be compared to war, and all it engenders ... Does the partisan stifle the human being in you? *Anything*, Hitler rather than war!" (Roger Martin du Gard in a letter dated September 9, 1936, published in *N.N.R.F.*, December, 1958).

Are those the sentiments of a class? No, not entirely. After all, every human deed is justified by a balance sheet, profits and losses. The French could think they would lose more by going to war than by accepting the German conditions. They thought so for a while; why would they not have hesitated? What was Roger Martin du Gard risking? He could believe that the misfortune of war outweighed all else. For us, Nazism managed to surpass even war in horror: children separated from their parents, little girls turned over to the brothel, the gas chambers, the dehumanization of the camps, and torture. In truth, we were not at all equal to the present that was moving towards us. The King and the Belgians had permitted the Germans to pass through Belgium; was he wrong to do so?

Was he right? I have heard many discussions on this subject in Belgium and it is perhaps questionable; by yielding he saved his country from destruction, he could swiftly rebuild his few ruins and re-establish the nation's economy.

"When we saw the destruction in other parts of the world, the number of your dead," Belgian friends told me honestly, "we were not so harsh towards the King." Many people, I believe, would have adapted themselves to Hitlerism, to any Fascism whatsoever, at least in the beginning. Many thought, and perhaps with reason, that they personally would come out of it. In the long run, perhaps they would have discovered that they had made a bad historical calculation. For the Jew, there was no discussion, no delay, no adjustment possible. It was an immediate fact, a matter of life or death, and of utter degradation before death. One month after the Germans arrived in Tunis, we understood that everything was at stake and almost everything was already lost: our dignity as men, our children and our wives and soon even our lives. The few spasmodic efforts of the terrified community would have only served to delay and spread out the payments.

One need not even wait for such crises to verify that insufficient integration and all the weakness that flows from it. The Jew, as a Jew, can almost never have an effect on the national destiny; he is however, part of it; but he is not consulted, and the greater part of the time, he does not even ask to be consulted: he is only too pleased to be forgotten and to have others act as if he did not exist. But were he to make demands he would immediately discover his own helplessness and the hesitant attitude of others towards him. When the Jews came back from concentration camps, from prisons or from exile, they found their apartments occupied or their possessions stolen—sometimes by their immediate neighbors. Shouldn't the thieves have been forced to make restitution? The embarrassment of governments, the horrified astonishment of the public, quickly turned to annoyance and bitterness. After so much misfortune, was it good taste to make demands for so little? Should we not be glad that we were still alive? We were so accustomed to misfortune that it was not worth the trouble to defend ourselves for such small losses.

There has been much discussion, and there still is, about the fate of Europeans in colonies that are gaining their freedom. I hasten to say that it is legitimate to discuss this: whatever political mistakes a population conquered by a new fate may make, that population becomes, as a result, worthy of attention. But, are there in those colonies only ex-colonizers on the one hand and ex-colonized peoples on the other? In North Africa the Jews far outnumber the French. Who has heard anything about them? What future has been foreseen for them? It will be said that their fate is the same as the fate of the Tunisians of the Moroccans and, tomorrow, of the Algerians. But everyone in North Africa knows perfectly well that this is a pious lie, that their difficulties and their aspirations are different: most of them have chosen French culture, the French language and French schooling. I do not say they are right or wrong; I say that this is a fact, for a number of reasons connected with recent history. And everyone knows this, but no one says or does anything about it. Can it be said, on the contrary, that their fate is identical with the fate of the French people? That is equally false: in Tunisia and in Morocco it was even legally untrue. The French who left those countries were helped financially; they are still making claims, but they have received subsidies for housing and help in finding new employment. What has been done for the Jews? As far as Algeria is concerned, we shall soon see; but does anyone honestly believe that the French Army would have revolted for the sake of the Jew? In short, each side pretended to believe that the Jews belonged to the other side, so that they would not have to bother about them.

In fact, history is made without us and we are used to it, as are the majority of oppressed persons. And like the majority of oppressed persons, we reap all the bitterness of it, we are the most afflicted of victims. The moment a nation is struck by a catastrophe, we are the first to be abandoned. Vichy promptly gave up its Jews and in Tunisia we were the first to be handed over. Don't tell me they also gave up the Communists and Freemasons! A man is a Communist of his own choice: it is a free action, which he can abandon if, for example, he considers the danger too great. Dignity demands perhaps that he continue in it in the hour of danger, but it is always a question of a choice, of a free and continuing action. To be a Jew is, first of all, not a choice. We shall see that men often add a confirmation that gives it the appearance of a decision, but it is, first of all, a fate: to refuse that fate does not change much either, for it depends more on other men than on oneself. Now the others hand over their Jews, apparently with no great difficulty, almost spontaneously as one tosses overboard the thing one values least, the thing least worth protecting. When a nation is in trouble, when the world is in trouble, I know now, from the experience of my short life, there is danger for the Jew: even if the malady has no connection with Jews. Hitler did not invent German anti-Semitism: he utilized it and brewed a poison already widely secreted by the German nation.

"From 1926 on, it was almost impossible for a young Jew to be employed in one of the great banks or one of the great industries . . . Germany was crushed under the burden of unemployment, but the percentage of unemployed Jews was much higher than their percentage in the population and certainly much higher than their percentage among salaried men." (S. Adler-Rudel, in *Jewish Balance Sheet*).

We are, in short, the forsaken as far as history is concerned. We would like to go our way unnoticed: but history in doing without us, also frequently acts against us. Everything happens as though the Jew offered himself as an expiatory victim, specially marked out for the meager imagination of executioners, dictators and politicians. This is not an accident: the Jew is, sociologically and historically, the weak point in the nation, the weakest link in the chain, the one who should, therefore, be the first to give way.

## 15 | Richard Marienstras, The Jews of the Diaspora, or the Vocation of a Minority

Richard Marienstras, excerpts from "The Jews of the Diaspora, or the Vocation of a Minority," trans. Harri Webb, *European Judaism: A Journal for the New Europe* 9, 2; *Diaspora* (Summer 1975): 6–22.

Born in Warsaw, but an émigré to Paris by his early teens, Richard Marienstras (1928–2011) was only twelve when the Second World War broke out. By fifteen he had joined the Resistance in the South of France. By seventeen, in the aftermath of the war, he was working for the American Joint Distribution Committee, securing political asylum for survivors in South America and then in Palestine. By twenty he was fighting in Israel's War of Independence. During the earliest years of its independence, Marienstras lived with his wife in Tunisia teaching at a lycée. In the early 1960s he taught in the United States; in the mid-1960s he finally settled back in Paris as a scholar of Renaissance English literature at the Sorbonne. For Marienstras, this period of wandering was more than an individual life trajectory; it was an education, one by which he developed a critical stance toward the nation-state—whether Israel or France—its hegemony, and its suppression of difference. This education was also the source of a Jewish political identity that resisted the dichotomy that the State of Israel itself seemed to impose on the Jews—a choice between exile and assimilation on the one hand and national belonging in the Jewish homeland on the other.

Marienstras propounded this political vision in his 1975 book *Être un peuple en diaspora*, arguing that the response to the Nazi genocide should entail an option beyond identification with Israel, and that what should unify contemporary Jewish life in Diaspora is not religious belief or identification with a state but, instead, shared culture, history, tradition, and the will to survive and perpetuate itself. In 1967 Marienstras had founded le Cercle Gaston-Crémieux with the renowned historian of Judaism Pierre Vidal-Naquet. The socialist group, comprising 150 academics and students, affirmed a secular Jewish identity, exploring the prewar Eastern European Yiddish culture as a source of memory and inspiration. Their perspective was particularly secularist and distinctly non-Zionist, insisting both on the value of Jewish life beyond its religious manifestation and on the possibilities for Jewish political existence outside the nation-state.[1] The Circle took positions on various issues affecting the Jewish future, or for which the Jewish experience might lend insights, and helped develop the concept of minority culture over against the French Revolutionary model of "one nation, one state." The Circle—Marienstras in particular—was thus a major player in the late twentieth-century debates over various French regionalisms and the nature of French identity in its ongoing dialectic over questions of universalism and particularism, in the late 1970s and early 1980s urging the French government to recognize the cultural autonomy of minority cultures in France.[2] Marienstras also made his mark on European intellectual life as a Shakespeare scholar and was instrumental in the development of the field of Anglophone studies in France through the founding of the University of Paris VII's Charles V Institute of English Studies, where he ultimately taught.

The selection below, from the larger book *Être un peuple en diaspora* published in English in 1975 in the journal *Diaspora*, makes the case for the collective will for Jewish survival in the Diaspora as opposed to the Zionist argument that Jewish life after the Holocaust could only be lived in Israel.

. . . There has always been a formidable dispute between the Jews and the left, of which only a few fragmentary aspects can be mentioned here. To avoid confusion it must be said straight away that those Jews who assert or confess themselves as such constitute a collective in which an ethnic and national element has never ceased to exist. In this they are more like the Armenians or the Gypsies than, shall we say, the Protestants. The left, among its many deceptions, had tried to make believe that Judaism is a religion merely (and, later, "an origin"), failing to take into account the simple fact that a religion which teaches its adherents that they constitute a people gives rise to special problems. Implicit in this long-standing judgment is that with the progress of enlightenment—capitalism first, then socialism—the Jews as such will disappear, bound as they are to superstitions which are destined for the dustbin of history.

[ . . . ]

To return to our own day, it must be remembered that it is not the "pluralist" tradition of Montesquieu, Herder, Senger and Pastoret which has been retained by the "enlightened" but that of Voltaire, the Abbé Grégoire, Lamourette and later Naquet, those who, while passionately defending the emancipation of the

Please refer to the original essay in its entirety, including the notes.

1. [Friedlander, *Vilna on the Seine*, 15.]

2. [Hyman, *The Jews of Modern France*, 206.]

Jews, said to the Assembly, "Your mission is not to make use of men as they are, but to make of them what you wish them to be." They concluded that nothing should be given to the Jews as a nation, but everything to them as individuals, for as Clermont-Tonnerre said, there can be no nations in the bosom of the one nation. The same liberating, assimilating, ethnocidal impulse that destroyed the French provinces, reduced their culture to mere folklore and made their languages a sinful reproach, offered the French Jews a bargain which in their vulnerable position they felt they had to accept: emancipation but at the expense of the national dimension and collective existence. At least the terms of the bargain were clearly formulated and nobody was left in any doubt, that, although they were referred to as a "sect" the Jews were also a "nationality." In Rousseau's words, "Moses conceived and executed the astonishing plan of making a nation out of a horde of wretched fugitives." Rousseau analyses correctly the role of the Jewish religion which he interprets as a symbolic system whose constricting rules are essential to ensure communication between its members, and their resistance and endurance.

[ … ]

This choice, put before an infinitesimal proportion of Jewry in 1790 and 1791, is of capital importance, for it has served as the model for liberal and marxist thinking on the subject. The prestige of the French Revolution was so great that it was impossible to conceive, for the millions of Yiddish-speaking Jews of Eastern Europe, any other desirable fate but assimilation. Very soon the French Jews were offering themselves as an example to the rest of the world, and the value of that example was in no way diminished for them by the Dreyfus affair. The "solution" to "the Jewish question" must be integration or assimilation. So they vehemently rejected any national dimension or recognition of a Jewish nationality. On the international level they fought against the idea that Jewish communities could constitute autonomous political entities. The only form of organisation acceptable to them was that of a religious sect. No Jewish national minority in Eastern Europe, no Jewish State in Palestine. The fact is that French Jewry, almost to a man, rejected Zionism until after the creation of the State of Israel. It is only more recently that they have embraced the *ideology* of political Zionism with the zeal of converts and have transferred to it their chauvinistic French patriotism. (Remember that under the Occupation they considered themselves "different" from the more recently arrived Jewish immigrants) and to this day they revere the Nation-State, whether French or Israeli, with a remarkable continuity of devotion.

But the choice made during the Revolutionary epoch was significant not only for the fate of the Jews, but for all minorities within the framework of Nation-States. In 1791 there was a vital relationship between the Nation-State and the ideologies of emancipation. The ideologies had need of the state to become a concrete force, the state made use of the ideologies to camouflage its fundamental imperialism. The model of the state established by the French Revolution and fulfilled after Thermidor, together with a choice of all previous forms, has been reproduced on a world scale, acting on peoples with the inevitability of a law of science. It has given humanity a body of law more deadly than the oft-denounced "bourgeois legality," for its rules are established and respected by bourgeois states and self-styled revolutionary states alike. What this other legality boils down to is that license is given to the majority in the state to deal with national minorities as it thinks fit and the majority in many cases is not inhibited from using coercion and ethnocide and murder. Cultural domination is thus superimposed onto class domination. This permits the *displacement* of the will of the conquered people, who are directed according to the will of the victors. And sometimes it is class domination which follows cultural domination and ethnocide, as when a demoralised ethnic group, deprived of the guidance of its traditions, becomes the ideal lumpen proletariat of the plantations and the shanty towns, on whom the prestige of the majority culture acts more effectively than any police force.

[ ... ]

The main currents of contemporary political thought have converged in the denial of any national vocation to the Jews of the Diaspora. This is merely to state the obvious. Catholicism, liberalism, whether deist or atheist, bourgeois nationalism and proletarian internationalism have literally joined hands in this denial, infecting, as usual, many Jewish intellectuals. Many assimilated and militantly assimilationist Jewish celebrities, like Bergson and Marc Bloch will continue to "declare themselves as Jews" until the Jews are no longer persecuted. Others take upon themselves, on principle, the burden of the Jewish past, enter into its collective memory and, one way or another, do not let it become extinct within them. There is a fundamental difference. Similarly, there is a fundamental difference between the fight against anti-semitism, which the left has generally championed, and the defence of the national character of Jewish existence.

[ ... ]

Independent of ideology or regime, forced assimilation is one of the fundamental facts of Jewish life over the last few decades, whether it be through institutional and social "soft" violence, physical liquidation, ideological blackmail or police pressure. The phenomenon is constant, the means used to provoke it, even in the most unlikely circumstances, are varied, and it is justified by the most apparently irreconcilable ideologies. The murderous character of state nationalism is thus revealed. The Jewish communities themselves are reluctant to admit the truth, being influenced today by Zionist propaganda, which itself defends state nationalism and argues that only the Zionists foresaw the catastrophe that lay ahead for the European communities, that they alone had essayed realistic *political* action to avoid it, and that if they had been heeded, European Jewry would have been saved. The argument is not serious. *Before* the Holocaust, the Zionist idea was only faintly credible, either to the European powers or to the Jewish communities themselves. It was necessary for it *to have happened*, and for a special conjuncture in international affairs, before the United Nations could accept the partition of Palestine—with, incidentally, only a narrow majority, in 1948.

[ ... ]

For Zionism, in the immediate present, is the only Jewish *political* option which has even partly succeeded. Zionist propaganda exploits this situation, it seeks to discredit all the other Jewish options which have appeared over the last hundred years. It denies the Diaspora any possibility of survival, it affirms, *taking its place in the ranks of the Nation-states,* that one must have one's own State or perish.

Zionists and religious Jews alike diagnose the *fact* of the diaspora as a pathologically abnormal situation, a *galuth*. They are in unison with majoritarian thinking about the Jews, which condemns dual allegiance or double fidelity. They specify a univocal existence in the bosom of the Nation-state as "natural" and the existence of a minority as "unhealthy, unnatural, artificial." The Zionists, the religious Jews and the non-Jewish majoritarians of the right or left consider that to be exiled is to be cut off or separated from the circumstances of one's origin. They want the Jews to "come out of exile" or "come out of the ghetto," and to become one with their surroundings. They present them with mandatory alternatives: to go to Israel in order to remain Jews, or to become assimilated. The difficulty is that in the present historic situation, the original circumstances of the majority of diaspora Jews are precisely those in which they are now living. Nearly all the Western Jews could emigrate to Israel *if they wanted to*. By not emigrating they give daily proof, by an abstention which like all abstentions is a positive act, that they do not consider themselves to be in exile. Their real position is that of dispersion accepted, or better still, dispersion justified. As long as the State of Israel did not exist, they could imagine or claim that they were "in exile." Since the creation of the State, to assert that the situation of the Jews in the outside world is a *galuth* is only one ideological interpretation among many. Curiously enough it is the Zionists and the religious Jews who argue *as if* the State of Israel did not exist, and that we live in a situation anterior to its creation. The existence of the State of Israel, together with the attitude of the Jews to migration, reveal what the Zionist ideology tries to hide, that the Diaspora has become a durable and satisfactory situation, not an ephemeral and accidental one.

[ . . . ]

The will to survive in the Diaspora must be accepted as a fact, despite the absence of a common language, customs or institutions. It must also be accepted that the modern definition of the Jews, to which the majority of the Diaspora are tending despite their leaders, is essentially a national and political definition. Certainly the collective will of the Jews in the Diaspora is guaranteed neither success nor eternity. It is so situated in history as to be susceptible, both individually and collectively, to erosion and constraint, it is conditioned by the past and by all the majoritarian forces that tend to impose uniformity on ways of life, to enforce simplistic fidelities, to turn men into cogwheels obedient to the control of state bureaucracies and industrial empires. This precariousness is obvious. It is the fate in store for all stateless minorities. But it is also the fate in store for the Nation-states. The fate of any human group is not guaranteed by history or by the gods. Of course, this goes for the Jewish state, too, whose duration, like that of the Diaspora, must be measured in the long term of history, not in the short space of a few generations. The Jewish State is precarious, its character has been revealed by ancient history. All Zionist and communitarian propaganda seeks to rally Jews around Israel, arguing basically from the dangers that surround her, and thus from this very precariousness. In any case, in the age of tactical and other atomic weaponry, states far larger and more populous than Israel are no more assured of their survival. To claim that Israel alone, by some divine or historic grace, can escape from the common situation of all is the profession of a mystic faith. Finally, to imagine that Israel can be maintained without the constant support of the Diaspora, moral, political and material, is a vision in defiance of fact. Thus, a massive immigration would, by causing an outflow from the Diaspora, deprive the State of the support of the very people who help it and would weaken its capacity to survive.

Certain minorities see very well what most Jews, branded by provincialism and with a providential or catastrophic vision of their destiny, do not see clearly:

that the Jews have survived for so long in history, not *despite* dispersion but *because of* dispersion. However strong the destructive will of a nation, it has never been entirely successful because a part of the Jewish totality has always been outside its grasp. And the temptations to conversion or assimilation have been presented to the Jews in too many different forms for all the diasporas to succumb to them simultaneously. Globally, over twenty centuries, the Jewish communities have developed a prodigious defensive armoury, which has enabled them to avoid the ultimate catastrophe of complete disappearance. One cannot say so much for many "territorial" nations, assimilated or destroyed by colonisers or better organised peoples. In a catastrophic situation—and only the very greatest nations (greatest that is, in terms of numbers) can allow themselves to ignore the possibility of such a situation—the concentration of an entire people in a contiguous territory makes of it a hostage to fortune. It is no accident that the fall of Troy is at the heart of one of the foundational myths of our civilisation. Now, the Jewish Diaspora is the example which proves, by history and actuality, that non-state communities can survive and perpetuate their symbolic universe and their own means of communication despite violence which may destroy them and seductions which may weaken them. No Western community has a historic memory as long as that of the Jews, and that memory in its entirety springs from the Diaspora, independent of the language used, territory occupied, institutions adopted, or modes of production, although it makes use of all of these. It adapts itself to constraint, benefits by accidents, hazards and chances. What must be emphasised is not the boring "natural" fact that the Diasporas have adopted the ways of life, languages and customs of the lands in which they have taken root, but that, despite this diversity, they "recognise one another" among themselves. We know today that the existence of a human group outside of particular frontiers is not an historical anomaly. For centuries many such groups have lived in a minority situation, some legally, some retaining under the appearance of assimilation the characteristics on which much present-day work of "regionalist" reconstruction is based. And it may be pointed out in passing that the Jews have had long experience of this work; since the enlightenment reflexion on their identity has been their identification mark. Conversely, it is considered scandalous today that an ethnic majority having achieved its own Nation-state, should impose its political, administrative and cultural standards on all the groups it dominates. Of course this does not mean that the Nation-state is going to disappear *as such*, but it does mean that it is gradually disappearing *as a model*.

It is understandable that some Jews, dazzled by the attainment of a national existence, tend to see the Nation-state as the norm of collective existence, and that the existence of groups which do not constitute a state is, to them, pathological. But this attitude is no longer the norm. It expresses only one ideology and one option. I do not despise that option, for I affirm with Albert Memmi that "Israel is the *only* Jewish country, that is to say the only country where a Jew may go, if he wishes to, as of right, and without the permission of a power suspected of anti-semitism." But I challenge the ideology, because it makes incomprehensible the contrary evidence that five Jews out of six live outside of Israel, rooted in their respective Diasporas, with their own specific questions that political Zionism cannot answer and cannot even ask. A few of them choose or have chosen Israel, but this only throws into greater relief the fact that the majority have chosen the Diaspora. For some of them, Israel seems today to be the best refuge should danger arise. But history is uncertain. And no one can say that one day the Diaspora in its turn may not once more play the role that fell to it after the destruction of the Temple.

In short then, a Jew *may* go to Israel, but that does not mean that he *should* go, or that he should want to go. The facts speak for themselves. What political Zionism does is to convert the optative into the imperative, and that is why it has become obsolete since the creation of the State.

Undoubtedly Israel is not a Jewish community like any other. Its territorial base and its state organisation has upset the equilibrium of Jewish existence by giving it a sense of security which may be real or illusory, and a simplified identity. Since the emancipation there has been a Jewish identity crisis, in phase with the general crisis of Western civilisation, and primary nationalism as expressed in Zionist propaganda has therefore been able to exercise great influence over recent years and is still doing so. But it has done so too because majoritarian doctrine denies that the Jews, wherever they live, have the right to "a political existence among the nations." The identification of Diaspora Jews with Zionism (and which some who specifically deny this right attribute to the malevolent and misleading power of Zionism) results essentially from this negation. What pushes Jews into Zionism (a purely verbal Zionism for most of them) is not its magical or demoniacal character, it is the ensemble of ideological, political and institutional pressures which prevent them from asserting themselves as a national minority. The Zionist ideal states that Israel alone is invested with historic normality, and is a model and an example to other communities, that the history of the Jews cannot henceforth be understood except in the light of Israeli history. But when one considers the national character of Jewish existence and the totality of the Jewish condition, that idea is at once revealed as false. This ridiculous vision eclipses the existence of ten million people, it speaks the same language as those majoritarian states which want them to disappear. Once again they become *luftmenschen*, once more they are obliged to emigrate in order to affirm that they are real people.

I wish to be clearly understood: Shortly after the Six Day War I had occasion to say that "for the first time since their dispersion, the Jews had been identified with violence unjustified by any of the universalist slogans, revolution, class struggle, rights of man etc., but with violence exercised in their own name, for the defence of their own community, their historic destiny, their past and their culture." What I meant was that in today's world a group with its own culture, even if that culture is in rags, without any means of exercising violence, could find itself so gravely exposed that its members could lose confidence in their collective survival. This means that the "will to live" of the Diaspora largely depends on the existence of the State of Israel just as the "ability to live" of that State largely depends on the existence of the Diaspora. But this does not transform the dispersion into "exile," it does not make emigration obligatory, it does not make life in the Diaspora shameful or unhealthy. It does not authorise the Israeli government's policy of annexation, ignoring the Palestinian people, it does not do away with the political and moral difficulties that arise from the use of violence. It does not restore to the Nation-state her symbolic virginity. Neither does it absolve the Diaspora from analysing its own problems, recreating its own culture, modifying its institutions, or from asserting itself as a minority. Finally, it does not hide the conflicts which arise from the position of the Jews in societies themselves characterised by a serious crisis of civilisation, where class struggle, bureaucratic oppression, social injustice and tolerance impose the necessity of constant and difficult choice.

The joint existence of the Diaspora and the State of Israel shows that henceforth there are many ways of assuming and creating the Jewish destiny. National affirmation does not put an end to any problem, on the contrary it adds to those political and social problems that already exist. All that is conservative in the Jewish communities prevents them from allying themselves with other minorities, or from declaring that they themselves are a minority. The Zionists and many religious Jews have nothing but contempt for the Diaspora, in which, nevertheless, they live. So it is stated that the Jews have for nineteen centuries been content to submit to their fate and it took the Six Day War before they dared to assert themselves. If they had been merely content to submit to their fate, Albert Memmi would not be here today to perpetrate such a scandalous misjudgment on them. Scandalous because he attempts to replace them once again within the purview of those who have tried in vain to destroy them. Similarly it is a false claim that among the Soviet Jews it is only those who wish to emigrate to Israel who have "rediscovered" their Jewish identity. Some of them have never lost it, and it is premature, to say the least, that the migratory behaviour of the Soviet Jews, if they were able to move freely, would be significantly different from that of Jews living in other developed countries. The Jewish establishment itself takes the side of the centralised state and defends its activities, maintaining by so doing the old alliance between the rich Jews and the State machine.

The Jewish establishment refuses to see that the national aspirations of diverse peoples, who are today becoming aware of the irreplaceable character of their history and culture, tend to be realised, according to local conditions, on the model of the state or by territorial consolidation or by a linked dispersal. That the Nation-state shall be the exclusive model, that outside of it extant ethnic minorities are doomed, is what the Zionists want, and the Jewish establishment, and all the majority-minded thinkers whether of the right or left. They are adopting the theory and practice of the very institutions and powers who have wagered for two thousand years on the disappearance of the Jews, and who have lost their bet. They have adopted the viewpoint of the conqueror and the coloniser. They have given their backing and their active support to what Robert Jaulin has called the cultural crimes of Islam and Western Christianity. Finally, from the Jewish point of view, it is to resign oneself to the State of Israel becoming an ethnic closed shop, and all the Jews of the Diaspora lining up behind her in the drab normality of member-states of the United Nations, joining in the fundamentally iniquitous conspiracy which binds these states together whenever one of them should rediscover genocide as an elegant solution to socioethnic problems which cannot be resolved politically.

[ ... ]

Zionist militants deride Jewish life in the Diaspora. What matters above all to them is political activity which will increase the amount of the money that goes to Israel and the volume of emigration. For them, Jewish culture is only a means to these political ends. As most of the Jews in dispersal are well established in their countries the Zionisation of Jewish culture repels them. They are tempted to reject their historic tradition in its entirety. Today the Zionisation of Jewish culture in the Diaspora is itself a factor in assimilation.

Taken in the sense I mean, "culture" does not merely include the literary, philosophical, or any other sort of luggage the "cultured" individual carries around with him, but the sum total of all those distinctive characteristics that enables any human group to identify its members, and itself to be identified as a group. It can include, separately or together, means of production, institutions, a body of law, religion, language, literature, folklore, daily habits and ideology. It is not generally possible to discover a group culture in the characteristics manifested by one individual or several. This explains why certain Jews—and certain Bretons—having carried out a careful self-analysis and having discovered nothing that resembles a "culture," have decided that they are simply "French." Such individuals often become assimilated and there is nothing against them doing so. But the destiny of a community can only be truly revealed by the ideal reconstruction of the entire culture. What has prevented a generally-agreed understanding of the Jewish phenomenon has been the attempt to deduce it from such and such an individual or community, whereas the links between the communities go so deep, are so little apparent and at the same time so powerful that this method cannot but conceal the overall characteristics.

It is impossible to summarize these characteristics. One would have to describe all the different ways there are in the world of being a Jew, the various organizational frameworks of Jewish life, the historic experience of all Jews, living and dead. To simplify matters, let us say that in the Diaspora Jewish identity is seen either in a minimal activity, such as taking a Jewish periodical or reading a Jewish book, or in a deeper involvement, religious, political, "communal" or cultural. The minimal symptom of belonging may be no more than an uneasiness about one's own identity, which enables one to take a detached view of the majority culture and which, above all, enables one to see it as a *cultural* and not a *natural* creation. For what characterises Jewish existence in the Diaspora is its faithful attachment to multiple cultural entities, from which, up to a point, it is possible to become detached or liberated. For centuries, many Jews have known that to belong to their people is an act of individual will under the pressures to convert or assimilate, that their cultural entity is consciously maintained, that it is a human creation and that one can *choose* or *will* to belong to it. Whereas in the olden days one was born into one's original culture and that remained the absolute determinant, today it is only a relative determinant. And even if this consciousness is not widely shared by the greater number, we must, because of it, try to understand cultural "belonging" in new terms.

Some on the left have thought that a normal future for the Jews could only be one of assimilation, because in the age of emancipation and enlightenment, adherence to Judaism (or indeed any other religion) was seen as an individual or group act of choice, whereas adherence to the majority culture was seen as destiny. It was one's destiny to be French, it was *natural*. To be Jewish was volitional, *artificial*. But the vulnerability of national and cultural entities all over the world has radically changed that. All cultures are voluntary today, like parenthood or a planned economy. The young deculturalised Occitans, the black Americans whose "black" culture is a lot more mythical than that of the Jews, the third-generation Bretons in Paris, all these can, if they *wish*, fundamentally modify their cultural position, re-establish their links with their history, with a special group and its customs. In short they can build up their solidarity on something different from political slogans. Once again they will be able to say "we" despite the majoritarian system in which every individual is a monad before the state.

And it is no use saying that all this depends on a particular language or territory or customs handed down. Loss of memory is never total. The most dramatic recoveries are possible. Today, one may add, they are desirable. In non-state communities they occur among individuals who to all appearances have been entirely assimilated by the majority. In this the Jews are no different from the other deculturalised minorities. It is impossible to state the exact number of Jews or Basques in France. In the U.S.A. it is impossible to give an exact count of the Indians, the urbanised, detribalised ones have become assimilated and disappeared, although among these a sort of inter-tribal Indianity has appeared, which is a sign of belonging rather than of specificity. And it is belonging that matters, the possibility of being able to say "we." Besides, among many individuals, this feeling of belonging is not necessarily connected with any elaborate or complex cultural content, nor with a language or territory. The various regionalist movements, like the Jews, dream of this feeling of belonging before passing on to the stage of cultural reconstruction. In the phrase of Le Roy Ladurie, they have only to hear the echo of a "matrix-event": Montségur for the Occitans, Treblinka for the Jews. These events linger in the collective memory for a very long time. After that it is a matter of choice, perseverance, will.

[ ... ]

It must be said here that in the course of their history, the Jews have practiced various forms of confrontation with varied success, but which the outside world has as a rule belittled. These examples may be cited. There has been armed struggle, as in the Warsaw Ghetto Insurrection. Contrary to what is generally stated, this was one of the first risings in the occupied countries. There has been the stubborn assertion of particularism and otherness against the various forms of political and cultural totalitarianism. The many ruses and metamorphoses of the Diaspora are only the means of expression of this stubbornness, which in extremely difficult circumstances can be accomplished in secret as in the case of the Marranos. Then there has been participation in universalist or revolutionary movements, sometimes as communities as at the time of the German enlightenment or of the Bund. At other times certain Jews have broken with their communities or with Judaism, as was the case with many Bolsheviks or with certain leftists today. Among these forms of confrontation, some professed to be "passive" means of survival, and others active means of changing the world. But even the passive methods actively perpetuated a Jewish presence that majority groups resented as scandalous. As indeed it was, *because it signified at the very heart of the totalitarian endeavour, that the dominant system was powerless to monopolize discourse on its world.* The Jew therefore has been, and in some countries still is, a counter-type, formidable by the very fact of his existence. For in every exclusive system he is The Other, who has to be absorbed or excluded. This provocative otherness can be interpreted, according to circumstances, as a fact of civilization, religion, culture, cosmopolitanism or obstinate nationalism, political deviation, economic or moral perversity. And this otherness has manifested itself independently of the avowed purposes of the Diaspora. Under these circumstances what is subversive is the simple determination to survive in a manner deemed unacceptable by the majority.

Historical circumstances have, today, brought the diverse Jewish communities of the Diaspora willy-nilly into close contact with other minorities fighting for emancipation, autonomy or recognition of their special identity. This is obvious in the U.S.A., where the Jewish community, despite its prosperity, plays its part in the confrontation struggles of the minorities. Of course this is not so in the case of prominent Jews, who are thus in a dilemma. They can turn their back on the situation, enter into alliance with the powers that be, with some help from Zionists and Jewish capitalists, and turn away from the struggle of the minorities. This is a dangerous choice, whatever the particular issue may be. If they win, the dominant groups will apply to the Jews the means used against the other minorities. If they lose, they will drag the Jews down with them. On the other hand, if the leaders take the minority claims into account, as certain of the religious Jews now do—ethnic pluralism, economic equality, social justice, the struggle against imperialism—they will help to entrench the uniqueness of the Jews in the American mosaic, and strengthen their right to be different.

The situation is not radically dissimilar in France, where confrontation with political, administrative and cultural centralism is increasing. The Jews, *as a minority*, have an important part to play in this criticism, and this is bound up with their survival as a group. Therefore they must oppose their leaders, all of whom turn their back on this situation, and perpetuate modes of thought and organization obedient to the dominant theology: exaltation of the Nation-state as the only form of normality (so making common cause with the Zionists, the Jacobins of the right and left, the so-called liberal bourgeoisie and the communists), perpetuation of authoritarian community organization, monopolisation of community organization by the Zionists and the religious, who cling to their bogus status as "representative" which they only are by grace of the powers that be, refusal to play any part in the struggles which are of importance to the majority of French people.

For with the Jews even more than with any of the other minorities, the assertion of their nationality in France today appears as a progressive and creative act of indiscipline. If part of the struggle for a better society has got to be waged against capitalism, it has also got to be waged against the State as it exists today in fact and in people's minds, a State that transforms citizens into subjects, producers into cogwheels, public servants into agents of power, and the majority culture into an instrument of propaganda and domination. In the present situation, the assertion of culture and nationality is one of the forms of civil disobedience that the Americans do so well. Thoreau refusing to pay his taxes was an early example. It is a fundamental disobedience, ideologically and institutionally. Individuals have to come together again to practise it, and to these it offers an intellectual and subjective foundation which enables them to resist the blandishments of propaganda.

Here the historic experience of the Jews can help the other minorities as well as themselves. Dispersed and disunited, the minorities are nothing. Together they can organize and co-ordinate the struggle against the centralized Nation-state, claim a portion of sovereignty, decide what institutions they should set up, break-up the state bureaucracy, bring in new national and international legislation. It is a long-term program. But that is what they must have the will to accomplish if mankind's true qualities are to survive.

# 16

# André Neher, The Jewish Dimension of Space

## Zionism

André Neher, "La dimension juive de l'espace: Le sionisme,"
*L'identité juive* (Paris: Payot & Rivages: 1994), 121–46.

Few postwar Jewish thinkers had as much impact on the postwar renewal of French Judaism as André Neher (1914–1988). His extensive writings on the Hebrew Bible and its implications for modern Jewish identity have been influential in France and widely translated abroad. Raised in an observant family in Alsace, educated during the summers at a yeshiva, he had originally planned to be a scholar of German. However, after losing his post as a German teacher with the 1940 statute barring Jews from civil service, he spent most of the war in hiding with his family in a small town in south-central France, and he decided to turn his attention wholly to Judaism and become a rabbi. Given his observant background, this was less of a dramatic turning point for Neher than for some others of his generation; he nonetheless likened his decision to a "new birth."[1] In a prolific career spanning over forty years, Neher published nearly twenty books, including a two-volume *Biblical History of the Jewish People*, which he wrote with his spouse Renée Bernheim-Neher, also a prominent scholar of Judaism who actively participated in the Jewish resistance during the war.

Aside from his extensive publications, Neher was instrumental in postwar Jewish renewal in France on two additional fronts. First, as chair of ancient and modern Jewish literature at the University of Strasbourg from 1955 to 1974, he cultivated a generation of Jewish scholars and established the university as a center of Jewish thought. Second, along with Emmanuel Levinas and Edmond Fleg, he played a role in establishing the Colloque des intellectuels juifs de langue française. He served as president of its first preparatory committee and, in 1965, became president of the French Section of the World Jewish Congress, the organization that sponsored the meetings. Neher's biblical lessons, like Levinas's Talmudic lessons, regularly provided the core around which the meetings were organized. Finally, in his capacity as one of its leaders, he also played a key role in thematizing the

---

1. [Victor Malka and André Neher, *Le dur bonheur d'être juif* (Paris: Le Centurion: 1978), 8, cited in Szwarc, *Les intellectuels juifs*.]

colloquium's focus on contemporary issues. It is clear that for Neher, as he put it in the preface to the 1963 publication of the first volume of the proceedings, the function of these meetings was to reorient the model of the Jewish intellectual from one in which intellectual activity was the means to transcend Jewish identity toward one in which Judaism itself was a source for conceptualizing the modern world.[2]

The other major event that transformed Neher's outlook was the Six-Day War, which altered his attitude toward Zionism and ultimately toward Judaism. He began to transfer his life and teaching to Israel in 1968, and he definitively made aliyah in 1974. As the passage below, originally published in *Clefs pour le judaïsme* (1977), makes clear, Neher came to regard the relationship between Jews and the Land of Israel as central not only to the tradition but to the history of the world.[3] He fully embraced the messianic significance of Zionism, calling in 1968 even at the colloquium, a bastion of Diaspora Judaism, for the ingathering of Jews to Israel, and ended up curtailing his relationship with French Judaism, participating in the colloquium for the last time in 1969.[4] For the last eighteen years of his life Neher worked mostly at home because of heart trouble, but still managed to write and publish extensively.

It is commonly said that the supreme merit of the Jewish people consists in having given a God to the world. It should be added: a land. Because the singularity of the divine idea revealed throughout Judaism has its only equal in the idea of the land (Eretz), also elaborated within Jewish thought and history, and just as remarkable. This "monogenesis" is indeed familiar to all the "monotheists." Christians and Muslims know, along with the Jews, that neither Rome nor Mecca establishes the world. According to the biblical expression, its "navel" is, rather, in Jerusalem, and the cosmic organism grows from the embryo that makes up the "Eretz." The typically Jewish components of this "monogenesis" help us better understand that for Judaism Eretz Israel is not only an element of a sacred geography, but something much more powerful and significant, which implicates the existence of the Jewish man and the history of the Jewish people in their most key aspects.

2. [Elaine Amado-Lévy Valensi and Jean Halpern, eds., *La conscience juive, données et débats* (Paris: Presses Universitaires de France, 1963), v.]

3. [The title was changed to *L'identité juive* when the book was reissued in 1989.]

4. [Szwarc, *Les intellectuels juifs*, 185–86.]

## ERETZ ISRAEL IS THE LAND OF GOD

Solidarity first exists between Eretz and God. Eretz is the Land of God. It is not, like Egypt, a land that man can tread with his feet in all its breadth. The eyes of God encompass it; it is turned toward God, offering itself to the heavens, drinking from the sources of heavenly rains. It is not a land plunged with all its roots in the earthly depths, and nourished by them. It lives from the blessings that God sends to it from on high. Between Eretz and Heaven, the dialogue is constant. This land, unlike the others, which are all concave, lifts itself up toward the heavens in a convex movement of expectation and welcome.

## GOD OFFERED "ERETZ" TO ISRAEL

But did not God also choose a people, which is itself in this position of awaiting and welcoming the heavens? Israel, unlike the others, will be the second companion of the land. Only a people that finds itself at the border of the divine and the human could be one with the Eretz, itself at the border of the heavens and the earth.

This double solidarity of Eretz with God and Israel is not mentioned in the Bible as something merely sporadic. It is accorded conjugal symbolism, and in such a way that its true nature can be examined. The Bible compares the alliance made between God and Israel to a marriage, which allows Moses, the prophets, and the inspired cantors of the hymns and the Psalms to describe the history of this alliance as a love passing through the most varied and moving phases: awakening, first encounter, engagement, marriage, birth of children, but also jealousy, bickering, separation, divorce, widowhood and, finally, a passionate return and reconciliation. From this perspective, Israel is the feminine partner of God. But, from another perspective, more in line with reality, Israel is the virile being. What will then be the feminine partner of this Israel-man? Eretz, precisely, the earth that waits to be loved and wed. But this earth (and here again, vigorously departing from the literal, the symbolism rises to the spiritual interpretation of things), this earth was not "conquered" by Israel, contrary to what the national history might suggest, with its war stories from the era of Moses and Joshua. A longstanding "promise" was "offered" by God to Israel. God entrusts this gem to Israel, this precious pearl, protected by him, and asks Israel to be the loyal companion of this spouse without equal. The code of fidelity is carefully outlined; it is nothing other than the Torah, only scrupulous observance of which can maintain the marital connection between Israel and Eretz. Like a father over a beloved daughter, God does not stop watching over Eretz even after the wedding. He implores the husband to obey the high spiritual and moral demands of the Torah; only at this price is he worthy of Eretz. Otherwise, the land will "vomit" him out, as it had previously "vomited out" the Canaanites, to which, by a kind of hasty imprudence, God had entrusted it. God will take back his blessing by awaiting, not another people more loyal than Israel (an important nuance), but... the repentance of Israel, its return to the Torah and, by that itself, its return to its role as spouse of Eretz.

Such is the biblical theme of the land. As the elements are dispersed across the whole Bible, we will be exempted from giving references [to all the verses here]: the reader, habituated to the Bible, will find them without struggle, from Leviticus to Isaiah, from Deuteronomy to the Song of Songs. It is the highest theme in this evocation of a land in which *space* is just as indispensable as *time* for human history, up to the building of the Kingdom of the Alliance. It is in this space, and in it alone that the destiny of Israel plays out. It is in it that the success or failure of its mission is realized. Eretz is the testing ground of its election.

> The Land of Israel
> is the marriage contract
> of God and of Israel

One might have thought that the crisis of exile would have impaired the primacy of Eretz in Jewish thought and attributed some of its virtues to the lands of the Diaspora. This is not the case. On the contrary, from the first moments of the Diaspora, and in a steadily building rhythm, Jewish thought, Talmudic first and foremost, then philosophical and mystical and finally, political, seized on the biblical theme of Eretz, not to bowdlerize it but to give it even more weight, a more profound gravity. Because if, in the Bible, the debate between God, Israel, and Eretz is conducted dramatically and thereby remains open, undecided, and adventurous, in later Jewish thought this debate acquires a hieratic permanence that permits us to speak no longer of a drama, but of a situation. Eretz is still the privileged land of God, the only place the Torah can be fulfilled, and soon it will be said: the only one whose spiritual and physical atmosphere can foster the gift of prophecy. Tradition and inspiration can manifest themselves only within it. We continue to use the marital symbolism in speaking about it, but with a fine nuance: the *Zohar* wants Eretz to be the ketubah, the marriage contract of God and Israel, and one can feel how much this image aims to make the presence of the land material and unchangeable in the Jewish religious economy. But Eretz is more than a divine space and more than a guarantee of the election of Israel. It is the *center*. And founded on this *central position* of Eretz is what we could call a *geo-theology*, without which the history of the Jewish Diaspora, thousands of years old, would not be comprehensible.

In effect, Eretz is the *center of the world*. A theme already sufficiently rich in itself, and which Christians and Muslims would themselves adopt. An incomplete theme, however, because Copernicus and Galileo took care to establish its scientific nullification, and Christians and Muslims would be effectively obligated to abandon this theme or to be satisfied with it as spiritual symbolism. But for the Jews, despite the Copernican Revolution, the theorem of the centrality of Palestine remains valid because, for them, Eretz was not only the center of the world, but also the *center of exile*. And this exile was not over [*révolu*]. On the physical plane, which no science came to contest, the exile endured, scattering the Jewish people to the four corners of the world. The centrality of Eretz gave a meaning to this exile, which was not an arbitrary dispersion, a senseless scattering throughout space, but a geometric blossoming, coordinated, considered, oriented around a center. Like rays in relation to a center, the regions of exile stretch toward Eretz. As far away as they were, they kept their point of reference toward the center, in Eretz. From the center issued the nourishing sap that brought life to the most remote branches; or, better yet, this center is the source whose living water irrigated all the distant canals, and each stream, drinking from this source, knew that one day, in a grand cosmic reversal, whose creator would not be a new Copernicus or Galileo, but the eternal conjugal couple God-Israel, it would climb back up the stream and come, with the others, to "gather" in the unique source, Eretz.

## THE SERIOUSNESS OF GEO-THEOLOGY: THE JEWISH PERMANENCE IN PALESTINE FUND

The magic of this geo-theology, which takes seriously the most literal form of the prophecies of Return, is practiced without confusion in the most diverse domains during the millennia in exile. By way of it, prayers are "oriented" (for the Jews from the European regions, in the most strict sense of the word: they were directed toward the Orient, toward the Mizrah, which became like the North Star of each synagogue and each Jewish home). Also by way of it, charity is organized, the fundamental offering being that which, through the institution of the halukkah (cradle of the present Keren Kayemeth),[5] reached the pauper in Eretz: it was, despite the remoteness, him, the "neighbor" who must be loved and respected, he, who helped the exiled patron attain solidarity with the Jewish vocation by accepting his offering. Finally, by way of this geo-theology, life and death were organized in compatible, harmonious significance. Life in exile is nothing but a slow death, but burial in Eretz is a path to resurrection; the failure of Jewish existence in galuth is compensated and transmuted by the serene victory of sleep in the Holy Land. And if the difficulties of the transfers only allowed few exiled Jews to come to rest in Eretz, all the Jews in exile tried at least to have a bit of dust from Eretz in their foreign grave.

But all these efforts to elaborate and maintain the Eretz-galuth polarity return and are intensified in the greater attempt to assure Eretz of its absolute value. In intimately associating the biblical theme of the *land of covenant* and the galuth theme of *centrality*, the Jews were led to the *messianic* consciousness of Eretz. Here there were no more compensating ideologies nor transfers of rites, but an immediate decision: aliyah is the only means capable of inaugurating the instantiation of messianic redemption, through an immense and sacrificial act of faith in the mystic virtue of Eretz. And thus the *olim* [immigrants], the infinite procession of those who, in a crucial moment of their existence, decide to direct not only their prayers, their offerings, and their hopes, but also the concrete and final reality of their life to the land.

Among them, from the Middle Ages to modern times, a few—Judah Halevi, Yechiel of Paris, Nachmanides, Isaac Luria, Sabbatai Zevi, Moshe Chaim Luzzatto—gave a meaning to their experience of aliyah such that it could then nourish, guide, and illuminate the upcoming generations of the Hibbat Zion and Zionism.[6]

Sometimes the motives are cultural, meaning half political, half spiritual. For Yechiel or Nachmanides, it is about maintaining the Yishuv, reinforcing the strong community of Jews in Eretz, so that the solidarity between Eretz and Israel remains embodied in reality.[7] Sometimes the causes are clearly political, but

5. [Keren Kayemeth LeIsrael is the Hebrew name of the Jewish National Fund, which was established in 1901 to buy and develop land in Ottoman Palestine. The term "halukkah" refers to the Diaspora practice, in the days of the Old (pre-Zionist) Yishuv, of sending money to support religious pilgrims in Palestine.]

6. [Hibbat Zion was a movement that preceded Zionism in the 1880s, advocating the revival of Jewish life in Palestine.]

7. [Yechiel of Paris was a Tosafist and a defender of Judaism in the 1240 Disputation

from the Jewish perspective of a messianic politics that can have only one spiritual objective. That pertains to Sabbatai Zevi,[8] who was not the only dreamer of the messianic kingdom in Eretz. On a more realistic level, the renowned exegete of the Mishnah, Obadiah Bartenura, noted on his arrival in Eretz at the end of the fifteenth century: "Ah! A handful of men like me, and we could conquer Palestine and establish the Jewish Kingdom!" Sometimes it is a vague but irresistible urge—a calling. One leaves tranquility and shelter (Judah Halevi, the Spanish refuge; Luzzatto, Amsterdam) and faces the storms and pitfalls, even if only to die, in the prime of life, at the moment even of reaching Eretz![9] What does it matter! What would otherwise be an absurd tragedy is here, in an experience that synthesizes all the others, a mystical conquest of the Absolute.

This Absolute, this constant accompaniment, whether muted or with fanfare, from Zionism back to its biblical roots, this Absolute of a religious nature, was almost put in check by the powerful movement of desacralization that, since the end of the 18th century (the emancipation of the Jews by the French Revolution), urged Jewish thought to liberate itself from its *religious* past. The sacred was by and large replaced by a secular and universal humanism that made it possible not to recognize "Jewish thought" in the theories of a Karl Marx, a Ferdinand Lassalle, a Henri Bergson, or an Émile Durkheim, despite their Jewish existential origins. But, in the last third of the [nineteenth] century, a movement would be born that would implant secularization within the most rigorous Jewish spiritual identity and that would burst the sacred realm of the religion, without, for all that, forfeiting Jewish particularity in its "profaning" energy, rather ratcheting it up to a level rarely achieved until now. It was from this paradoxical movement of desacralization of a thought that proclaimed itself authentically Jewish, that the various currents would flow together into what came to be called toward the end of the century, Zionism. The term would be created by Nathan Birnbaum in 1890. Its advent marks a decisive turning point in the history of contemporary Jewish thought.

---

of Paris; Nachmanides, his Spanish contemporary, was a scholar, rabbi, and philosopher who helped reestablish the Jewish community in Palestine. Both are said to have died in Acre, in Palestine, though Yechiel's journey is disputed.]

8. [Sabbatai Zevi was a seventeenth-century messianic figure who eventually converted to Islam.]

9. [Judah Halevi, an eleventh-century poet, physician, and philosopher, author of *The Kuzari*, died soon after reaching Jerusalem. Moshe Chaim Luzzatto, an eighteenth-century rabbi, philosopher, and kabbalist, also traveled to the Land of Israel and died soon after.]

[ . . . ] Nevertheless, Zionism is, let us not forget, a solution brought about by events. It risks reducing the spiritual destiny of the Jewish people to a particularism as dangerously narrow as the humanist universalism is dangerously vast. Between particularism and universalism, on the crest line of their encounter, in a position that is in no way comfortable, but is consistent with the essence at once eternal and current to Judaism, will not Jewish thought try to forge a path? [ . . . ] In a monumental book titled *Babel and Jerusalem*, Simon Rawidowicz recalls the necessary insertion of Judaism in two geographic political, cultural and religious dimensions, that of Israel, but also that of Diaspora; thus, the inevitable dual destiny of Jewish thought, which cannot be understood in its authenticity except when it is accepted within a polarity, a tension, within several polarities and tensions, the tension between Hebraism and Israelism.

Alfonso Pacifici has admirably analyzed these poignant crossroads of the spirit, demystifying the primary options, drawing attention to the irreducible value of the terms religion and Torah, Israel and the State of Israel, community and nation, which cannot be mixed up without emptying them of their authentic contents. Before him, Nathan Birnbaum, the inventor of the word "Zionism," offered testimony of a grand adventure leading him from a committed materialism, through agnostic Zionism, to the most scrupulous and most demanding religious orthodoxy.

At this moment, numerous religious Jewish thinkers in Europe, in the United States, and in Israel find themselves at the center of these tensions. What defines them is their indestructible Zionism but also their religious orientation, placing their thinking halfway between theology and philosophy, in a demanding effort of transforming the concrete quotidian into a metaphysical radiance.

It is at the heart of these tensions that Judaism expresses itself today, in the entirety of a space whose dimensions encompass the State of Israel and the Diaspora simultaneously, and of a time when the pace leaps from the origins of the world, toward the messianic horizon . . . and, to start, toward a challenge posed to the year 2000.

*Translated by Beatrice Bourgogne*
*and Sarah Hammerschlag*

# 17

# Henri Atlan, Jerusalem

## The Terrestrial, the Celestial

Henri Atlan, "Jérusalem, la terrestre, la céleste,"
*Les Nouveaux Cahiers*, no. 108 (1992): 4–9.

To refer to Henri Atlan (1931– ) as a Jewish thinker is to pass over the significance of his contributions to the natural sciences. A doctor of medicine, a biophysicist, and a philosopher, Atlan in his work crosses boundaries to ask questions that few thinkers have been able to broach. He has made significant contributions to the fields of cognitive science and cellular biology, all while posing the most fundamental philosophical questions concerning the nature of complexity and systematicity, determinism and freedom. To answer these questions, Atlan has had recourse not only to the history of science and philosophy—he considers himself a Spinozist of sorts—but also to medieval Jewish thought and Kabbalah. The fundamental nature of these questions and their applicability across various fields has led him also to tackle such ethical issues as the nature of fraud, the corresponding question of bad faith, and the nature of belief. In many of his recent works he moves effortlessly back and forth between the discourses of biology, cognitive science, philosophy, and Jewish thought, often challenging our presuppositions in each realm of inquiry and practice.

At the same time, in light of his contributions to French Judaism, Atlan should by no means be omitted from a growing canon of French Jewish thinkers shaped by the postwar revival of French Judaism. A native of Algeria, he was raised in an assimilated Jewish family for which Judaism was to be observed only on the High Holidays. As a teenager during the war, he became involved with Gamzon's Éclaireurs israélites de France as a means of responding to the new reality for Jews under the Vichy race laws, which revoked the 1870 Crémieux Decree granting French citizenship to Jews. After the war Atlan was recruited to l'École Gilbert Bloch, Gamzon's school in Orsay, which was established to train leaders for the postwar Jewish community.[1] The transformative experience of this coeducational school, in which "a group of youngsters was offered the opportunity to search for

1. [See also entries on Robert Gamzon, Jacob Gordin, Léon Ashkénazi, and Stéphane Mosès.]

meaning in their lives after their various war experiences," led Atlan deep into the study of Jewish texts after his time at Orsay.[2] He went on to study Kabbalah with Zalman Schneerman, brother of the late Rebbe. In the 1950s Atlan remained active in the Orsay community, editing *Targoum*, a journal of Jewish literature and philosophy produced by the alumni of the school, and serving as its director after Léon Ashkénazi's departure in 1958. Thus, even as he became a scientist of international renown, Atlan continued to publish on Jewish themes, first in *Targoum* and then elsewhere. The essay below is from *Les Nouveaux Cahiers*, which was something of a successor to *Targoum* but was sponsored by the Alliance israélite universelle and ultimately had a larger purview. It takes the heavenly city and the earthly city as its theme, one that is familiar in Christianity since Augustine's *City of God*, but offers a Jewish perspective on it and shows that the dichotomy that sets Christian universalism against Jewish particularism is misapplied. Instead, Atlan identifies two species of universalism. Against the "abstract universal"—which, he argues, "ends with chauvinism, exclusion, and the spilling of the blood of others," Atlan identifies in Judaism the "concrete universal" as maintained by the law, which, in its very function of creating distinctions, accords with a vision of peace.

Many times destroyed and built back up in the last three thousand years, Jerusalem has come to be associated with wars, profanations, persecutions, tears, and desolation. For the last two thousand years in any case, this has been the consequence of religious fanaticism; and not just any fanaticism but the fanaticism of the one and only God,[3] of monotheist religions with a universal vocation dedicated to the search for unity, peace, and harmony extended to all of humanity. This is the paradox of this city for, unfortunately, the universal vocation of monotheism is too easily distorted into a missionary and proselytizing vocation that lies at the source of intolerance and annihilating violence toward the other, made all the more radical as these faiths claim the one and only God.

Let us recognize from the start that monotheism is not necessarily missionary and proselytizing, and inversely that monotheisms are not the privileged

2. [Henri Atlan, "From French Algeria to Jerusalem," in *Religion: Beyond a Concept* (New York: Fordham University Press, 2009), 341. See this chapter for a more detailed introduction to Atlan's thought (339–53).]

3. [See also Henri Atlan, "Un peuple qu'on dit élu," *Le Genre Humain* 3–4 (1982): 98–126. A condensed version was published as "Chosen People" and collected in Arthur A. Cohen and Paul Mendes-Flohr, eds., *20th Century Jewish Religious Thought: Original Essays on Critical Concepts, Movements, and Beliefs* (Philadelphia: Jewish Publication Society, 2009), 55–59.]

possessors of an imperialism that imposes the uniformity of morals, discourses and beliefs by force and for which all difference is subversion.

In fact, the first acts of violence against this city in antiquity were the product of paganism against Jewish monotheism, the latter having chosen Jerusalem to house its sanctuary as a place of gathering and for the dissemination of the Law. This dissemination, however, was performed by means of public readings during annual pilgrimages, by its teaching and its practice, and not by the fire and sword of holy wars and missions, as was the case much later when other monotheisms tried to expand across the entire planet.

This means that we should go back to the antiquity of Israel, to the foundation of Jerusalem as its capital by King David, and to the construction of the First Temple by his son Solomon—before the degeneration that followed—for the emergence of the vocation of this city in all its power for universal peace, founded on the Law and not on the arbitrariness and violence of empire.

As the Bible reports, this vocation manifested itself already in the very circumstances of the construction of the sanctuary of Jerusalem. It was reiterated ceaselessly and in all circumstances in the discourse of the prophets of Israel and it was ceaselessly thwarted by the violence that the Law unleashes among those who believe only in the peace of empire; that peace of uniformity—not to be confused with the universal—that peace of oppression that very quickly becomes the peace of cemeteries and genocide.

After the first destruction of Jerusalem and its Temple by the Assyrian Empire, its restoration thanks to Cyrus the Great, king of the Persians, then the new destruction by the Roman emperor Titus, it was Pax Romana, the Roman peace, that imposed its force on this city. For this new emperor, as for those who came before and after, the study and practice of the Law of Moses and the prophets was an intolerable scandal that had to be eradicated by every means, including fire, exile, or torture.

But the tragedy of the Law combating violence and succumbing to the use of this same violence in its turn reached its climax when two great monotheist religions, inspired by the Law of Moses and the prophets, claimed to crown the unique God as sovereign by taking the reins of these empires. It was in the name of monotheist religions stemming from Judaism and from which they had separated that the oppression of the city and its sanctified places became the symbol of imperial power; it was in the name of the one God that Rome continued to reign, then Byzantium, then Islam. But, unfortunately, this God, unique in principle, was multiple in fact because professed by each of these religions in an exclusive and very particular manner, indeed by each of the churches and rival currents interior to Christianity and Islam. Henceforth there followed a succession of periods in which the sovereignty of this city was synonymous with oppression or exile for all those who did not accept forced conversion to the triumphant religion, whichever one had achieved victory by way of the latest Crusade or the latest holy war.

By referring not to this historical Jerusalem but to the Jerusalem of the biblical and prophetic project retold by the tradition of Israel in its exile, it is possible to glimpse a little hope—enough to enable one to live in this city—emerging from a historical fact, but a contemporary one this time. Even though we are still so far from true peace, that of consensus, of justice, of love and of truth, since 1967 when the city was reunified and the State of Israel chose it as its capital, ensuring its Jewish administration, after nearly two thousand years of being chased out, for the first time in history a complete religious liberty exists in Jerusalem and, in particular, the holy places of Christianity, of Islam and of Israel are freely accessible without restriction for the respective faithful adherents of these traditions.

## THE VOCATION

According to the Bible, the role of Jerusalem within the Jewish tradition emerged with the construction of its sanctuary. King David, who made Jerusalem the capital of the Kingdom of Israel, was not judged appropriate to construct the Temple for even though he was the inspired author of the Psalms, his reign had not been able to avoid war either from within or without. Only his son King Solomon could do it, because he had not known the inherent impurity of bearing arms, the experience of war, nor even that which would otherwise provide the possible justification of legitimate defense—against aggression in particular. His name in Hebrew, Shlomo, in Hebrew means "his shalom," his peace, that peace and that universal radiance which, according to the Bible, characterized his reign.

He would thus construct this sanctuary, the Temple of Jerusalem, such that it also would be dedicated to peace and perfection, because in Hebrew the connotation of peace (*shalom*) is achievement and perfection (*shelema*) [sic]. Previously this sanctuary had been nomadic, since the time of the exodus in the desert when the presence of the God of Israel among his people was incarnated in a mobile sanctuary, that "tent of meeting" in which Moses received his inspiration.

With its installation in the Promised Land and the settlement of the people, this tent had to be transformed into a house, and that is in effect how we designate the Temple in Jerusalem in Hebrew, the house [the *bayt*], Beit HaMikdash, the house of sanctification. The purpose of this house, taking the place of the tent of meeting, was to assemble together the conditions that allow the God of Israel to be present, visible despite his invisibility, to reside among men. The Bible recounts how the Hebrews received the decree to construct this sanctuary during their liberation from slavery and from exodus, through which they also formed a society. By the fact of this birth in the exodus and in the desert, this society had established a relationship with its God that was neither progenitorial nor territorial, as is the case in most mythologies, but a relationship of face-to-face, founded by a treaty of alliance and redacted in a text, which was itself nothing other than that of the Law, the Law that organizes and guarantees social peace, the obligations of individuals, and their rights that—we can say without oversimplifying—are derived from two fundamental values: life and liberty.

## ISRAEL

For our purposes it is interesting to consider how this injunction to build the sanctuary is formulated and then explained by the tradition: "They will make me a home and I will reside among them," states the biblical text. The commentary points out that it does not say "among the people" but rather "among them," that is to say among individuals, indicating that the visible residence of the collective sanctuary does not have to be there in order to permit the only true, if invisible, residence within each individual.

The fact remains that the construction of the collective sanctuary creates a sacred space and when this sanctuary is implanted in its house in Jerusalem, it creates the holy place in the proper sense: the only holy place, by the way, for the Jewish tradition since we know that the synagogues do not have the same status at all, being essentially houses of study and gathering, without particular sanctity outside that which the practice of public prayer and the ritual reading of the Torah scrolls give them.

And already, owing to the existence of a sanctification of space, we see emerge the source of future perversions when the existence of sacred space will be the occasion for division and violence, when this space should only be a site of gathering and of peace.

In fact, first and foremost, sanctification and the sacred imply division, separation, distinction from the ordinary, the profane, and the vulgar. It is this, as a Talmudic text explains, that only transposes the organization of the sacred onto

Jerusalem in concentric zones that were already those of the sanctuary in the desert. Ten levels are enumerated from the sacred land or the Holy Land at the periphery, up to the Holy of Holies or the sacred of sacreds at the center of the house of sanctification. We make use in effect of these two words, "sacred" and "holy," to translate the same notion (*kodesh*) in Hebrew. For Emmanuel Levinas it is the transformation of the sacred into the holy that would bring about the purification of the slag in what is religious, of the deadly impurity, and of the shadowy and suspicious numinous material that the Bible condemns as the idolatrous world of sorcerers and spirit conjurers. From this point of view it would be the desacralization of the world that would permit its disenchantment.

Moreover, we are used to considering the religions of the Book, the monotheisms that emerged out of the Bible, as clear progress in relation to the polytheist religions in this transformation of the sacred into the holy. It is worth qualifying this judgment because of the crimes committed in history precisely in the name of these monotheisms, from which it rightly emerges that the holy no more than the sacred is safe from the perversion of the devil who only exists, in fact, in their shadow. The worm is found in the fruit of the one as much as the other when, instead of being an aspiration, an always-renewed search, the holy and the sacred become a substance, a definitive realization, an inalienable possession. There is no doubt that those religions that are spiritualized and desacralized but conquering and missionary have more to learn from the experience of the sacred that one finds in the East and Far East, in Africa and Native America, where the multiplication of spirits can also serve as a springboard for the discovery of Spirit or Brahman.

In addition, it is necessary to maintain an undifferentiated usage of these words "sacred" and "holy" to render this notion of separation that Georges Hansel proposes in translating *kodesh* as distinction, which designates different levels in the scale of a pedagogy of being. Philosophers will pardon this expression, but there is no other way to designate this permanent objective of the tradition of Israel than as the progressive transformation of human nature, judged to be bad since its childhood—"what forms the heart of man is evil from his youth" as Genesis says—but perfectible, and capable from the beginning of attaining the heights of adulthood characterized by a liberty and total responsibility that even the invocation of the God of love—that above all—cannot diminish. Then comes old age, built up wholly of memory and of wisdom, to be used by the next generations to ensure that this process of rising education in the levels of refinement and distinction has opportunities to be transmitted, so that the process does not have to be restarted from the beginning with each birth, triumphant over death in a certain measure, all while permitting the renewal of generations.

## THE LEVELS OF DISTINCTION

Thus, in this description according to the concentric levels of holiness, we are told that Jerusalem, the holy city, is more holy than the other cities in the Land of Israel surrounded by walls, they more holy than this holy land, this land more holy than other lands. And within Jerusalem, seven other levels of holiness characterize the different enclosures of the Temple, separated by as many barriers up to the Holy of Holies where the high priest goes only once a year, during the special ceremony of the Day of Atonement and the redemption of sins, a day that plays a central role in this pedagogy.

But we obviously see, right away, in the institution of these concentric barriers, the source of divisions that the sacred establishes between men: between Israel and other nations, between free men and slaves, between men and women, between the pure and impure (it being understood that impurity was something temporarily acquired through moments of contact with death, making them part of the processes of life, such as birth, evacuation of genital secretion, burying of corpses, etc. . . .). There is separation again between the Levites and the different categories of priests, and the other children of Israel, the latter not having dedicated, as had the former, their entire lives to the study of the Law and to the service of the sacred in this house where the way of life had to serve as a guiding light along the path of this ascension to which men were invited.

It is in these barriers and the divisions that they institute that the danger of idolatry, which takes the means for the ends, evidently lies. Fanatical intolerance too is such a danger when these levels of sacredness or holiness are attributed to things, places, or individuals, in a possessive and inalienable way, as properties that would define them.

Here is where it becomes imperative to read closely the Talmudic text in question, for it defines each one of these different levels through an additional obligation, additional work, and additional responsibility. As numerous authors have pointed out, along with Maimonides, and more recently Emmanuel Levinas and Yeshayahu Leibowitz, holiness does not belong to anyone, it is not an attribute but a responsibility; and the successive elections established by these different barriers of sacredness are not elections of rights but elections of duty.

This is why it is especially necessary to insist on the point that there are not holy places per se nor holy things per se. Things and places can be made sacred through opportunities of surpassing oneself, by the addition of greatness and responsibility that they offer to men and to the people who encounter them. Things and places can be charged with history and myth, permitting memory to enrich the present and to transmit the life of the spirit from one generation to another, from one era to another. But things and places cannot be for all that automatically sacred or holy: they only become so if men make them such through their actions, which testify that they are seizing on the occasion of the encounter to accept upon themselves a surplus of distinction, that is to say of responsibility, duty, and obligations.

That is why, against the danger of idolatry of the sacred place, of the holy place in itself, the tradition of Israel puts up a guardrail—another barrier if you will —but this time within the heart.

It begins with the internalized reading of the biblical decree to build the sanctuary, which we have already adduced: "And let them make me a sanctuary; that I may dwell among them," meaning in the middle of the body and the heart of each individual. This implies that the house of visible stone, the Temple with its different chambers, was there only to permit men to make this presence reside within themselves: the true residence of sanctification is found in each individual capable of building it and bringing it into existence. The house of collective sanctification, objective and visible, is the necessary condition for individuals of this kind to exist, a necessary condition *but not a sufficient one.*

## THE HOUSE OF STONE AND
## THE INTERNAL SANCTUARY

This vision of an internal, invisible sanctuary corresponding to the house of stone opens naturally onto that of a heavenly Jerusalem corresponding to the earthly Jerusalem. This celestial Jerusalem is also built by each individual insofar as he fulfills the obligations of the Law that the terrestrial Jerusalem imposes on him. In other words, the one here below is still the condition for the one beyond, but once again, the necessary condition but not the sufficient one. As Rav Chaim of Volozhin of the eighteenth century said, the earthly Jerusalem and its sanctuary would have never been destroyed if the heavenly Jerusalem had not first been destroyed by the faults of the men who lived there. It is through the body, the heart, and the conscience of each individual that the universal vocation of Jerusalem is truly achieved. For it is truly a matter of the universal, not the missionary and conforming universal, but rather the universal of the sacrality of the individual whose differences are reconciled without being abolished and whose peace is that of multiple perfections and not that of amputations.

There is in fact a remarkable dialectical reversal here: it was by barriers that create more and more circumscribed spaces that the delicacy and fragility of the internal life of each individual could finally be protected. It is by deepening the internal and cultivating one's humanity, here and now, thanks to a relative isolation, that one has the best chance of attaining humanity in its universality. This is a path headed in the opposite direction from that of the abstract universal, which ends in chauvinism, exclusion, and the spilling of the blood of others.

To start from the singular and then discover the universal, then from there to learn love and justice, and not to pose the universal in words in order to ultimately find divisions of selfishness and violence, this is what the Rav Avraham Y. H. Kook, who worked for the return of Israel to its own land as a necessary condition for its rebirth in sanctity, taught at the beginning of the century, citing the *Zohar*: "The side of evil begins with convergence and ends with division, the side of the sacred begins with separation and ends with convergence; its proper name is shalom, peace."

These words echo those of the prophet Isaiah, according to whom building a future reconstructed Jerusalem entails building a house of sanctification for all the nations: "Awake, awake, Zion, clothe yourself with strength! Put on your garments of splendor, Jerusalem, the holy city. The uncircumcised and defiled will not enter you again. Shake off your dust; rise up, sit enthroned, Jerusalem. Free yourself from the chains on your neck, Daughter Zion, now a captive!" (Isa. 52). It continues in Chapter 56: "This is what the Lord says: Maintain justice and do what is right, for my salvation is close at hand and my righteousness will soon be revealed. Blessed is the one who does this—the person who holds it fast, who keeps the Sabbath without desecrating it, and keeps their hands from doing any evil. Neither let the foreigner who has joined himself to the Lord say, The Lord will surely exclude me from his people. [ . . . ] And foreigners who bind themselves to the Lord to minister to him, to love the name of the Lord, and to be his servants, all who keep the Sabbath without desecrating it and who hold fast to my covenant—these I will bring to my holy mountain and give them joy in my house of prayer. Their burnt offerings and sacrifices will be accepted on my altar; for my house will be called a house of prayer for all nations. The Sovereign Lord declares—he who gathers the exiles of Israel: I will gather still others to them besides those already gathered."

Henri Atlan | 167

Such is this universal vocation of Jerusalem, earthly and heavenly confounded, Yerushalayim—the Hebrew name of this town is a plurality in which one can read this duality as reunited.

But, once again, it is not in inspiration and ecstasy, in the dream of the return to Zion, or, as the psalm says, "when we return, we will be as we are in a dream"; this is not where the safeguard will be found that protects this vocation against all of the internal and external obstacles found on the path.[4] This dream is necessary as a point of departure, but in order that the awakening not be a nightmare, it is necessary to make an appeal to ceaseless inquiry, to lucid knowledge, to all the resources of critical intelligence, and to the demystification of falsehood, in the pronouncement of law, right and justice. Because Jerusalem, for the prophets, is not so much a holy place, seen as a place of worship and adoration with all the dangers of idolatry inherent there, but rather, and above all, a source of knowledge, as Isaiah says (2:3): "For out of Zion shall go forth the law, and the word of the Lord from Jerusalem."

In order to try to understand what the wise men of Israel understand by Torah and the word of God, it is perhaps necessary to refer to the famous story in the Talmud about the way they had of "promulgating the Torah," and of making the word of God issue from their discussions in the form of the reasoned consensus the sages took from it, eventually even against ecstatic revelation, that of the holy and of the prophets themselves.

The story of Rabbi Eliezer ben Hurcanus is well known. A master inspired and respected by all of his colleagues and followers, he disagreed with the majority of the masters of the Sanhedrin, the legislative assembly, on a point of law. Convinced that the majority was wrong, he invoked a judgment "from on high" in order to decide between them, and succeeded in making signs appear and hearing a voice that ruled in his favor. Whereas the authenticity of this voice, heard by all, and its heavenly origin were not called into question by any of his adversaries, any more than the depth and authenticity of its inspiration, not only was his opinion not accepted, but it was ruled out by the Sanhedrin for the reason that "The Torah—the Law—is not in heaven." The Talmudic parable goes on to ask: "And what was God doing then?" and responds: "He was laughing, saying my children have defeated me, my children have defeated me" (Babylonian Talmud, Baba Metzia, 59b).

Here we see an illustrated example of the following Talmudic principle taken

4. Psalm 126.

to the extreme, according to which: "The sage wins over the prophet." The sage who analyzes the consequences of the Law ("Who is wise? He who sees the consequences") wins out against the prophet who receives inspiration from it.

Such is the Torah, the teaching "that goes out from Zion, the word of God that goes out from Jerusalem."[5] We see that it is opposed to the arbitrary, even if divine. It is the teaching of the right that compels God himself; this teaching is not in heaven because it concerns the law to be established on earth and not only the rapture of the holy.

There is another particularly striking expression of this dialectic between heaven and earth, between holiness and righteousness, in a Talmudic commentary that exactly accords with this tradition of a two-sided Jerusalem, earthly and heavenly, to which verse 3 of Psalm 122 makes allusion: "Jerusalem is built like a city that is closely compacted together."

If we understand this statement as an allusion to a Jerusalem associated and unified with another city, another Jerusalem, precisely the heavenly, the commentary nevertheless warns us that the divine presence will not come into this city, meaning the Jerusalem on high, until it comes to the Jerusalem below. The realization of righteousness and peace below, between men, is a necessary condition for the holiness and the inward purity that cannot truly exist without it.

THE PATH TO PEACE

In relation to this project, where are we today? We are witnessing a confounding of time: onto this past laden with history and myth is grafted a present, that of the Israeli democracy and its problems of integration, not only of communities but also of individuals, and the inspiration that it receives from Western models of parliamentary democracy among others.

The earthly Jerusalem currently under construction is in a process of renaissance that is only beginning, with its universities, research centers, hospitals, museums and concert halls, not to mention the Talmudic schools, multiple churches, and mosques, the abundance of international scientific and other symposiums that take place year-round. This new city, associated with the old one, has not blushed from irreparable shame before the ambition of the project and the vocation that carries the name *Yerushalaim*, "that we inherit of peace and its perfections." Even though the relative peace that currently reigns here is

5. Isaiah 2:3.

also established in the shadow of wars that preceded it and those that threaten, even though there are too many guns, too much distrust, too much potential violence in Jerusalem, it is a city of rights and liberties, not only religious liberties, which are far from negligible given its history, as we have seen, but also its opening up to the arts and sciences of our days. Because we cannot forget in this endeavor the great contribution of our century, through and thanks to atheism and secularism, what the philosopher Eugen Fink calls "the luck of modern atheism." Nothing authentically universal can come about if the grandeur and the responsibility of atheism are rejected, on the condition that it is a true atheism—atheistic with regard to all the gods comprised within it, the modern and secular gods engendered by ideology. This true atheism has the unrivaled merit of protecting against the enchantment of the holy and the murderous wrath that only it can bring about.

We continue, even though we live there, still to say "next year in Jerusalem" as has been said for two thousand years of exile because we are still exiled; because as long as peace without weapons does not reign, as long as violence threatens, we are not yet settled in this unified Jerusalem of the above and the below, of the holy and the just. This is the response to the ancient call "next year in Jerusalem," that after having kept alive over centuries an attachment to this project of the dispersed Jewish communities, now we strive to find all possible avenues capable of bringing about this peace.

*Translated by Beatrice Bourgogne*
*and Sarah Hammerschlag*

# 18

# Shmuel Trigano, Klal Israel

## The Totality minus One

Shmuel Trigano, "Klal Israel: La totalité moins un," *Pardes*, no. 49 (2011): 41–46.

One of the most active voices in French Judaism today, the sociologist and philosopher Shmuel Trigano (1948– ) is among a generation of Jewish intellectuals that has inherited the question of the nature of Jewish political identity. Unlike so many from the previous generation, Trigano has a conception of Judaism in France that is marked not, however, by a personal experience of disillusionment stemming primarily from the Second World War, but rather by his experience as a Jewish adolescent in Algeria during the Algerian War. As Trigano has written, "For me this experience was certainly that dreadful moment when my world came to an end, when the French state abandoned in 1962 what were constitutionally French departments and a population of one million French citizens under the threat of massacre by the Arab nationalists."[1]

While not all Algerian Jews understood the war in such stark terms, one cannot overestimate the impact of the colonial conflict on the character of French Judaism. First and foremost, these conflicts fundamentally changed its demographics. The independence movements in French-speaking North African countries in the 1950s and 1960s were accompanied by new waves of antisemitism leading to the mass migration of Jews from Morocco, Tunisia, and Algeria. In Algeria, where Jews once again held French citizenship after the Vichy regime, whatever their political leanings, it was widely understood by 1962 that Jews would emigrate along with the Pieds-Noirs. Those who did not go to Israel, namely, the more affluent and well-educated sectors of the population, went to France. This entailed an enormous influx of Jews to the metropole, with 220,000 arriving from the mid-1950s to the mid-1960s.[2]

Trigano finished lycée in Paris and then studied in Israel. He found, however, that Israel represented its own form of exile, an exile from the very yearning that had always characterized Judaism. "Only later was I able to name this state of

---

1. [Trigano, "In Search of Eternal Israel," in Hava Tirosh-Samuelson and Aaron W. Hughes, eds., *Jewish Philosophy for the Twenty-First Century: Personal Reflections* (Leiden: Brill, 2014), 458.]

2. [Hyman, *The Jews of Modern France*, 194.]

affairs in terms of normality," Trigano has written.[3] Settling, thus, in France, he pursued an ambitious intellectual itinerary that was one part sociology, one part social history—concerned in both cases with the political status of Jews in France, the nature of Jewish identity and identification in the post-Holocaust, postcolonial moment—and a third part philosophy and Jewish thought. In his philosophical-theological writings, Trigano plumbs the Jewish sources for alternative teachings to Western philosophy on its most fundamental topics, such as time, space, and political identity. In the essay presented here, for example, Trigano argues that Judaism offers a different way of viewing the universalism-particularism dichotomy. Even as these intellectual paths involve different methods, the strands of Trigano's project are deeply intertwined, particularly because, as he has argued, the very drama of European Judaism, the emancipatory bargain that demanded the relinquishing of corporate Jewish identity and culminated in extermination of the population as a collectivity, "indicates a structural failing of the philosophy of man and of citizen rights that leaves no room for the dimension of collective identity."[4]

Trigano has been hugely prolific and influential over the past thirty years, launching the journal *Pardès* in 1985, heading the Alliance israélite universelle's Beit Hamidrash study group in 1986, inaugurating a Popular University of Judaism in 2013, writing over twenty books, and editing many more. At the same time, he has not been uncontroversial, particularly as he has not only been publicly critical of France's historical treatment of its Jewish community going back to the emancipation, but also has been an outspoken critic for the past fifteen years of a "new antisemitism" driven by Islam. Trigano has often charged that France has shown preferential treatment to its Muslim minority community and swept Muslim-driven antisemitism under the rug.[5]

*We are twelve brothers, the son of one man in the land of Canaan and behold, the youngest is this day with our father and one is not. (Gen. 42:13)*

The difficulty of conceiving and formulating the Latin notion of the "universal" in Hebrew is well known. If one follows the etymology, that which is

3. [Trigano, "In Search," 458.]

4. [Ibid., 461.]

5. [See, e.g., the exchange in the *Jewish Review of Books* between Trigano, Maud Mandel, and Ethan Katz. Shmuel Trigano, "The Journey through French Anti-Semitism," *Jewish Review of Books*, Spring 2015; Maud Mandel and Ethan Katz, "Strange Journey," *Jewish Review of Books*, Summer 2015; Trigano, "The View from Paris," *Jewish Review of Books*, Summer 2015.]

universal is that which is "versed in the one." That which is thus in play in the universal is the one, unity, the unification of all men. Coming from an entirely other root (*kol/*all), *klal* seems to be the most adequate term to translate this notion into Hebrew and Jewish terminology. When Klal Israel is habitually invoked, it is to encompass all Jews, of every denomination, beyond differences and conflicts.

### THE TEST OF THE ALL

Are all one? The Hebrew perspective overturns the centrality of the one in the notion of the universal to put the focus on the all, the totality. Its test, if you will, is not the one but the all. Totalization is the danger that effectively threatens every group, every collectivity. In the debate proper to Jewish thought this challenge is viewed in terms of the opposition of Babel and Jerusalem. Babel produced a totalizing unification of all men. They spoke "one language, unified words" (Gen. 11:1) to the point that their lips could no longer stop their voices at the end of formulating, pronouncing and communicating words. The divine judgment underscores the extent to which this totality is monolithic: "Nothing will keep them from doing *all* that they propose to do" (Gen. 11:6). In Babel everything is in everything [*tout est dans tout*], "unified [*ahadim*] [*sic*] words," a monolithic, corporal, massive unity.

The other side of this totality is equally defined by the men who make up Babel: they construct a tower "for fear that we will be dispersed over the surface of the earth" (Gen. 11:4). Here the *kol*, the possible whole [*tout*] is set up as parallel to and in opposition to "the dispersion" (*tefutsa*), the separation. The same text of Genesis previously asserted that all of the earth had been "peopled" by the three sons of Noah using the same verb that suggests "dispersing" (*nfts*), as if to tell us that the ensemble of humanity is only possible on the model of dispersion and by a multiplicity of peoples. The plurality of languages and the separation of peoples will come to reinstate it. The totality of Babel is thus fractured in order to bring humanity into life and into history. It is necessary in effect to leave a vacant place for the assemblage of humanity to pass into the world.

We have an articulation of this paradigm in the story of the Garden of Eden. "You will eat from *every* tree in the garden and from the tree of the knowledge of good and evil you will not eat" (Gen. 2:17). There is a significant paradox here. Why does it say "from *every* tree you will eat" when one tree is forbidden for consumption? What is this totality if a part is removed? It is a totality minus one. The only form of totality thinkable and viable: *klal*.

This totality minus one emerges again with the doctrine of election, by virtue of which humanity is rendered possible in the removal—the election—of Israel. In this sense, the election of Israel serves the function of the tree of knowledge, the prohibition of which governs all of the Garden of Eden. The existence of Israel revitalizes the Garden of Eden within humanity. "Has any God tried to take for himself a nation from the midst of another nation?" (Deut. 4:34). Israel was removed from the tally of the peoples.

## THE ONE OUTSIDE THE ALL

But the removal of the one from the all, its isolation, does not only apply to the relation of Israel to humanity. It serves as an injunction for itself. Thus from within its midst, a tribe, the Levites, are removed from the assembly of tribes to manage the Ark of the Covenant, and they do not receive territory. By this removal the totality is understood to be circumvented even within Israel, without, however, the generality, the collective being abandoned. The paradigm equally concerns the Levitical condition by which the priest is himself separated from the Levitical collective. At a lower level, it applies also to individuals of the assembly of Israel, called to separate themselves by the rituals of sanctification (*kedushah* = separation), by the tithe, and so on.

## A SUBLIME STRUCTURE

What is the meaning of the impressive structure of the *klal*? Confronted with totality, it helps to preserve separation in Being—the condition of every alliance between two beings. It helps to avoid fusion, the confusion that is creation's opposing principle. On the plane of the individual and the collective, this procedure aims to avoid the subject or the *klal* identifying completely with itself. For the hiatus between self and self is the condition for safeguarding the *nefesh*/ identity of individuals and for the self's articulation to the *klal*, to the whole of the city.

Accordingly, this was the role of the Tabernacle (Ohel Moed) in the camp of the desert, at the center of the tribes, surrounded by four Levitical families, bearing within it the Holy of Holies, where no one but the high priest could enter, a void at the center of the city. Thus there should equally be such a space within the individual to avoid his being fused with himself.

The Ohel Moed is the opposite of a re-public, insofar as the foundation of the public is not a thing (re[s]) but concealment, a void, a hiatus, an absence.[6] Its principle is the prohibition against representation, the principle of hidden presence, outwardly absent. It is that which is hidden, meant to be prohibited, which keeps the totality from constituting itself. This hidden part is not, however, a nothingness. It is a void but it is the seat of divine presence, the place where the Torah, His word, lies. It is a place with a name. In reference to the people Israel in its election, this place in humanity, which is Israel, is defined as "the Lord's portion" (Deut. 32:9).

## PARTICULARISM IS NOT AT STAKE

From this perspective, the identity of Israel, as a part removed from the totality of humanity, is an obstacle to the Babelian fusion of all of humanity, and guards against the danger, the snare of totality. In this sense the existence of Israel is a major obstacle to all imperialist totalization, to every "universal." But this is not, as it is sometimes understood, a consequence of its particularism. Such an interpretation is a complete misunderstanding. In fact, the Hebraic *klal*, thus conceived, is fundamentally different from the Latin universal. The *klal* is not in any way one "versed" in the one, in monolithic unification: rather it is a separation. The one is separated from its other elements, which it gathers potentially but never realizes. It is by way of the separation and the concealment of the one that the multiple are gathered, assembled (Knesset [Israel] has this sense of assembly) without being made uniform, neither annulled nor suspended. It is the one, rather, that is put on hold.

One arrives, in Hebrew, at the universal by bypassing totality, which always constitutes a danger, because it [totality] exposes being to exteriority in a world that remains unfinished, because the One, the Divine, contracted himself in the act of creation that made all of reality. In this sense the verse about the Garden of Eden, "every tree except for one tree" states the principle of creation, the key to the vault of the whole edifice of the universe. The project of the imperialist universal is always to realize the one in its withdrawal, to re-verse the world into the one. This is a perversion of the Divine. In other words an idolatrous approach whose consequence entails only the grasping of power and the divinization of the human: a repetition of the eternal temptation of Babel.

6. [*Res* is Latin for "thing" or "object."]

This is the principal reason—on the metaphysical plane—for the universal hostility toward Jewish existence, specifically as the Jewish *people*, as a nation. We find here the contemporary aspect of the question that concerns us, a situation defined by a considerable augmentation of the hatred toward Israel in the epoch of globalization.

Let us try to understand this [hatred] from the perspective we have been considering. The new antisemitism is in fact quite strange: it essentially manifests itself through the currents of postmodernism and multiculturalism, and no longer through nationalism. It is even the enemy of the latter. The phenomenon that has been defined as globalization implies the end of borders, the multiplication of interactions, the diasporization of populations and identities, the effacement of nations and the weakening of states. It is a paradoxical conceptualization: defending the affirmation of identities and at the same time calling for their effacement, through mixing, hybridization and miscegenation. But this is not the only paradox. The apology for identitarian affirmations meshes with a radical hostility toward one (supposed) identity: Jewish identity. Certainly it is indexed to Israel and thus to a state, a nation, all the more identified as such so that it has a resolute enemy to confront, but it extends to diasporic Judaism as well, unless it dissociates itself from the State of Israel.

Furthermore, the situation is even more complicated. In the affirmation of brotherhood [*fraternité*] and universality on which multiculturalism is founded, there is an illusion, or rather a falsehood: it is not the other who is celebrated in the neighbor, but the similar [*semblable*], that is to say, the one who is the same. Multiculturalism has the illusion of a recognition as the neighbor as other. But in fact he is recognized only as *similar*. A new Babel is on the way. It is under construction. The "unified words" of this new Babel, of our time, take the form of political correctness. And its new proponents have understood that Israel's difference entails the project and the horizon of a much greater alterity, a transcendent alterity. What they hate is not the national difference of Israel, but divine alterity, the transcendence of the Ohel Moed (the Levitical withdrawal), even against its will [*à son corps défendant*]. They perceive it, but cannot see it, like the prophet Balaam (and they perceive it better than a good number of Israelis and Diaspora Jews who do everything to be similar [*des semblables*] to the world's nations rather than to be their neighbors [*des prochains*]. They ask Israel to give up its status as nation and state, to be part of a hypothetical "international community." But would Israel even be admitted to such a community? It is not the singular identity of the Jewish people that is at stake but the election of Israel, the one withdrawn from the All, the non-Babelian architecture of humanity. Paradoxically, thus, in the perverse arena of current debate, it is the affirmation of this singular identity of nation that makes reference to the universal and is opposed to the illusions of globalization.

## THE PEOPLE OF THE *KLAL* TODAY

It is an assumption of popular opinion that the Jewish people incarnate the quintessence of particularism and ethnicity, that is to say ethnic supremacy, with its doctrine of election. This vision is inherited from the Pauline tradition, which carnalized and racialized the Jewish people in order to better exalt, in a hierarchical order, the (Christian) Israel reputed to be universal and spiritual: the people of Israel became "Jews according to the flesh," circumcision was defined as ethnic marking. . . . Today in the new version of this discourse, notably taken up by Alain Badiou and Giorgio Agamben, the Israeli nation-state, necessarily defined as "racist" and "colonialist," appears always as an obstacle, this time to the unification of humanity in its globalized version.

But does the real Israel correspond in truth to this mythification, to this mystification? Let us consider the Jewish people across the board. It is a global people, present in all the nations of the world, in all their cultures, languages, and political regimes. They are present across the globe not only as marginalized pariahs or parasites, but—in the modern centuries—as true members and creators. Today this people is present in every country of the world, except for those from which they have been chased out or excluded.

If we consider the Israeli people, we are far from the received idea of a narrow and blunt ethnic identity, closed off to the external world. Instead what we find is the vibrant image of a truly global people, assembling more than 120 origins and every race (from the Ethiopian to the Asian). Every language is spoken there, every culture represented. Arabic is the second language of the country, and the Arabs have their own education system. And despite this extraordinary diversity, Israel constitutes more than a nation of immigrants; it constitutes a people. A (hidden) principle of unity gathers together all these origins: it is the *Jewish people* that plays this role for these natives of the universe; it is the *Israeli nation* that plays this role for the Arabs through citizenship. Hebrew is this universal language shared by all of these populations, with the symbol of Israel uniting Jewish natives from every origin without fail, even if this does not unify all of the Arabs.

In this diversity, the horizon of unity is never lost. It is the inherent message of the notion of the Jewish people. The Israeli people thus witness simultaneously to the unity of humanity, to their ingathering in a unique place, and to its infinite and irreducible plurality.

*Translated by Beatrice Bourgogne*
*and Sarah Hammerschlag*

# IV | Identification, Disidentification

Already in 1935 Emmanuel Levinas described the impact of Hitler on Jewish identity as "without precedent" for "the Jewish conscience. . . . One can no longer flee it. The Jew is ineluctably riveted to his Judaism."[1] Despite a sharp increase in Jewish name changes in France in the first few years after the Second World War—which might seem to indicate precisely the desire to escape one's Jewish background—it is clear that after the war, in France and elsewhere, the nature of what it meant to be Jewish had changed.[2] It was no longer a matter of religious confession but a fact of being. One of the catalysts for the ensuing discussion was Jean-Paul Sartre's 1946 *Réflexions sur la question juive*, published in English as *Anti-Semite and Jew*. On the one hand, Sartre treated Jewishness as a category without content, a state of being determined by the gaze of the other, one that he predicted would eventually disappear. On the other hand, his description both of antisemitism and the experience of being the object of this hatred struck a chord with a generation of young Jews after the war, many of whom felt as if they were being seen for the first time. Claude Lanzmann said his whole way of walking was transformed by reading the book. Pierre Vidal-Naquet reported feeling "avenged."[3] Even for those who disagreed with Sartre's description, particularly its lack of attention to the content of the tradition, it raised the possibility for new nonreligious ways of thinking about Judaism, such as Albert Memmi's and Robert Misrahi's.[4] That, in turn, raised questions about what such a nonreligious Judaism would entail and how it could be expressed. It provoked as well the counterclaim that the only way to be Jewish is in fact to rid oneself of the cultural baggage

1. Emmanuel Levinas, "L'inspiration religieuse de l'Alliance," *Paix et Droit*, no. 8 (1935), 4.

2. Mandel, *In the Aftermath of Genocide*, 161.

3. Cited in Pierre Vidal-Naquet, "Remembrances of a 1946 Reader," *October*, no. 87 (Winter 1999): 7, and "Sartre and the Jews: A Felicitous Misunderstanding," *October*, no. 87 (Winter 1999): 64.

4. See Misrahi, *Un Juif laïque en France*.

that has defined the Jew from the outside and thus go back to the tradition for the answer to the question of what a Jew is.

In this part we encounter Léon Ashkénazi, who aims to retrieve the authentically Hebraic origins of Jewish identity as opposed to what has been imposed on it and to determine how to harness the Jewish past to Jewish renewal. For Stéphane Moses, there are forms of continuity that assert their relationship to the past by emptying its traditional forms and regarding it critically. In the view of Alain Finkielkraut, born after the war, the very claim to possess the identity of the Jew is improper in light of the disparities between traditional Jewish life and the postwar context. For Jacqueline Mesnil-Amar and also for Hélène Cixous, to be a "lost child of Judaism" is a way of being Jewish. For Jacques Derrida it is the endeavor of coming to terms with the inherent contradictions of identity claims that is the most fruitful, and perhaps the key to the inevitable ethical and political implications of such endeavors. For all these thinkers there is a dialectic between inside and outside, between tradition and modernity that has come to light in and through the French Jewish experience of persecution, exclusion, and the shifting ground of what constitutes religious and racial identity. It makes the very question of what it means to be a Jew inextricably complicated, but its exploration politically and religiously fruitful.

# 19

# Jacqueline Mesnil-Amar, The Lost Children of Judaism

Jacqueline Mesnil-Amar, excerpt from "Les enfants perdus,"
*Aspects du génie d'Israel* (Paris: Les Cahiers du Sud, 1950), 293–312.

Born into an assimilated bourgeois family, Jacqueline Mesnil-Amar (1909–1987) might have easily described herself as one of the "lost children" of Judaism. In a later essay, published in 1977, she described the Jews of her milieu as "the Jews of forgetting." She grew up in the wealthy Paris suburb of Passy with every comfort and privilege and little awareness of the entailments of Judaism beyond synagogue attendance during the High Holidays. Until the outbreak of the Second World War, she was the perfect exemplar of the *Israélite*, French by national identity and Jewish only by confession. Her life during the war was characterized by upheaval and the realization that she was an outsider in a culture she had theretofore considered her own. She is perhaps best known for the book *Ceux qui ne dormaient pas* (Those Who Did Not Sleep), composed of excerpts from her wartime journal and published in 1957. It received little notice at the time but was published in a second edition in 2009, and she now plays a prominent role in accounts of French Jewish women during and after the war. The journal describes her participation in the Resistance, in particular her experiences after her husband André was arrested and deported. Miraculously, he escaped a train to Auschwitz a few days before the liberation of Paris, and the two were reunited. Both became noteworthy figures in the postwar French Jewish community. Although Mesnil-Amar did not publish extensively, she participated actively in the Jewish literary community and befriended important figures, such as Edmond Fleg and André Spire. In journals such as *Les Nouveaux Cahiers*, she articulated a unique perspective on the nature of French Jewishness as transcending the categories of religion and nationality and described the sense of the liminality that arose for those who had believed in the unattainable promise of Frenchness, even as it insistently eluded them. This feature, she suggests, magnifies the most fundamental human drama. Marcel Proust was for her the exemplar of these "lost children of Judaism." Shaped far more by the experience of being alienated than by Judaism, and by the failure of assimilation than by the tradition itself, she maintains that these "lost children" nonetheless carry within a remnant of the thousands of years of Jewish diasporic consciousness.

In his essay "From Shylock to Swann," Levinas described her as exploring the representations of Jews in literature so as to reveal, "behind the conventional ignominy or estrangement of these figures, their wild and sovereign energy . . . an authentically human nobility."

In writing these pages I am thinking of those vagabonds, lost from Judaism, who, voluntarily or by circumstance have abandoned Israel, turned away: the rebels against the law, those ignorant of the tradition. I think of those among them who were great by virtue of their genius, and of those lost children who were in a certain sense true Jews, irreproachable and pious, whom we can nonetheless also call abandoned children! They were lost to their community that they forgot or disowned, which in its turn rejected them; lost to that dispersed people who so struggled and who so long wrought iron on all the forges of the universe so as to conserve the purity of its blade. They are lost also for the Christians to whom they went and for whom they remain Jews for eternity. What are we to do with these absent ones? Where do they reside? Must they be completely lost? Have not their works contributed much to the human heritage? In studying their case, I believe I have discovered that they have truly betrayed neither their inner nature nor even sometimes the highest inspiration of Judaism.

There are many types of lost children. There are those Jews indifferent to "religious questions," raised in rationalism and the cult of the universal and abstract man, so dear to the preceding generation. There are all those assimilated Jews of the West of infinite variety: from those who maintained their religious traditions and transmitted the faith of their ancestors to their children through their civic pursuits to those on the other side of the spectrum, those ashamed Jews of the "imitative" type, so concerned to camouflage their origins and to copy others, to change their milieu, change their country, change their name, change their nose, forgetting only to change their outlook and their souls, remaining thus the only dupes of their enterprise and the only ones confident in the disguise, reaping nonetheless the recompense so desired in a world that mocks cowards, but accepts them tacitly. Finally there are those refined Jews, but also long-suffering, those Jews who have been *split* for so long, whose exquisite and difficult duality has given way to weariness, ravaged by an intolerable suffering, by an irresistible love of their country that remains a lasting part of their being; these Jews, half alive, half dead are like the two-headed eagle: where one head is going to die, the other will fall sick too, because they have been so enamored of assimilation, with a culture so perfect, so classic, of infinite seductions, so enamored of its realities and also its lures.... Perhaps they are like those eternal Marranos, before the eternal tribunals of the Inquisition, eternally choosing Spain. Didn't they understand the true demands of the adherence that was asked of them? Didn't they understand that they were not being asked for resemblances so much, or ardent submission, sacrifice, or even naive confidence in these attachments, no more than they were asked to fade out... to forget their drama sometimes to the point of denial. Rather, they were asked for something somewhat paradoxical in the world into which they were thrown. It was a demand that they fight themselves, without conviction or aggressivity, but openly, at the crossroads peopled by their enemies.

Of course, there are also half Jews by birth, who are not responsible for the darkness in which a watchful entourage interrogates this obscure part of their being, until the hour of reckoning that rings always only once, when the price of conscience and knowledge of the self imposes itself like a fatality. There is finally the infinitely delicate, often painful case of the authentically converted who awaken with both sides full of passion, the case of those who have voluntarily embraced the Christian faith, found truth and love, and cowardice, often without knowing it, without ever having examined the faith of their ancestors.

Can one conclude that all these Jews, distant by different degrees from the tradition—de-Judaized, seemingly lost to the Jews, but not won over to Christians, isolated at times in this strange solitude—have held onto nothing, transmitted nothing, given nothing that testifies to this long past of suffering? Do they bear nothing of the tradition's sensibility, so rich with resonances, a tradition of such particular ancestral customs, which at the end of all this heritage is freighted with death and the stone face of the same destiny? The opposite would seem to be true. Having voyaged so much across the vast world, wandered so, searched across spaces and societies, over the varieties of the human spirit, the lost children of Judaism have in their diverse works added to the vision that offered them a field so vast. They have added an extremely subtle and mixed message, one in which Israel in a return of flames, blown by a contrary wind, has brought to each flower of the gardens of the world a mysterious pollen full of millennial seeds with the far-off perfume of a perennial Orient.

It is sometimes easy to quit Judaism, but it is less easy to be acquitted by it. [...] It is necessary to conclude that there is another sort of Judaism that envelops and surpasses the strict Law of Moses, the words of the prophets, the teaching of the Talmud, a strange Judaism, emanating certain of God's commandments, but transposed, bathed in all sorts of climates, filled with and resonant with familial customs, the mysterious residues of anxiety and feeling.

Jacqueline Mesnil-Amar | 183

Lost children of Judaism, in France and elsewhere, at the heart of the twentieth century, caught up in the intensification of forces that have entangled us all, each one of you turns toward an integration that reassures and exceeds you. If you have not chosen a return to your ancestors—like those who have returned to the ancient religion of their fathers in a great effort of truth, or those of Palestine, land of fire and love, who have refounded a nation and a fatherland out of the same desire for integration, but also one of marvelous authenticity—if you have chosen other means is the fault solely yours? Lost children, this is the drama of extreme assimilation, from intoxication to failure in this modern and fatal search for the roots of being, in this thirst for *rootedness* or *engagement*, in this anxiety about the void. . . . Separated from the others for so long by the particular life of our communities and since the emancipation, through our mixing, separated again sometimes by a face, by a word or by a great event, alas, isolated by so many obstacles and sometimes by our internal difficulties, it is natural that the intoxication of assimilation and that the nostalgia for rootedness haunts the hearts of Jews.

The drama is already entirely in force with the child: the irresistible intoxication of assimilation, the nascent power of adherence that develops with it. The most perfectly assimilated of the Jews is the child. All the Jewish children of our country are the hyperassimilated who suffer the charm and enchantment of the world, obscurely presenting the pain with which the world will one day bless them.

Who will describe the passionate momentum that carries the Jewish child toward the milieu that surrounds him outside his family, toward those comrades of his class, toward those blue eyes, of another hue, toward their manual mode of address, their force, their games, their cousins, their parties, toward this gaiety, which is more natural and easier, which seduces them and makes them happy? What impression does this exchange make, of what love do they so often bear the brunt? What impression does it make on these young careless beings when the presence that reproaches them one instance in the same universe gives them the next a mysterious happiness? Which writer, which poet will make himself known to the ancient and receptive soul of the Jewish child? They already exist perhaps, perhaps they are called Marcel Proust or Max Jacob or there are others?

But we all know, if we are sincere, that this period of harmony, this marriage of love does not last forever. Much later the development of a diverse and particularistic intelligence and the attitude of society will bring about the youth's first injury, will foster the slow development of his difference that he we will forever work to hide. And the passionate child of yesterday, the young, starry-eyed Jewish child changes as he is able; failing to make himself loved, he becomes an aggressive young man avid to affirm his talents and to be assured of his position, or perhaps he becomes a rebel who returns to his [Jewish] origins, or one of the docilely assimilated, who takes a beating. Whichever he becomes, it is within a destiny so complex, one that brings our singular battle into the context of all man's battles. All of us continue under the masks and charades, carrying with us our dreams, the child's yearning, our obscure desire for unconditional integration, our thirst to enter into a human group, to share its fate, its suffering, and its ideals and to penetrate, together with other men, into the heart of a truth that transcends us.

The nostalgia for society, for reality, so as to enter into the world of men and of things, that supreme yearning for an emotive and redemptive mysticism, all these temptations and all these remainders call to and recommence the voyage of these lost children who are hardly ever found.

But it is a strange voyage, in truth, whose aim seems less to arrive than to depart again, passionately to belong, but then all of a sudden to refuse integration and belonging that has been obtained and merited, but along with the thousands of difficulties that the limits of this paradise of rootedness impose on us. Who will heal these lost children of Judaism of their soul's wandering, of the mobility of their faith?

*Translated by Sarah Hammerschlag*

# 20

**Léon Ashkénazi, Tradition and Modernity**

Léon Ashkénazi, "Tradition et modernité," *La Parole et l'écrit*, vol. 1
(Paris: Albin Michel, 1999), 127–37.

Born in Oran, Algeria, Léon Ashkénazi (1922–1996) came from a long line of influential rabbis on both sides of his family. His father was chief rabbi of the city and the last chief rabbi of Algeria; his mother's family was a font of kabbalistic learning, tracing its lineage back to the earliest generation of students and to the great masters of sixteenth-century Safed. As he describes in the following essay, during the 1930s Ashkénazi simultaneously attended yeshiva and the city's lycée and thus acutely felt the bifurcation of his two worlds. At the age of seventeen he joined the Éclaireurs israélites, the Jewish Boy Scouts, becoming one of its most influential leaders, and taking on the scout name Manitou for his charisma and dynamism, the name by which he was best known among his students and disciples first in France and then in Israel.

Ashkénazi's life, like those of many of the thinkers in this volume, was affected by the Second World War, an event that for him and many others precipitated a quest to differentiate the Jewish heritage from its Christian-Greek counterpart. Before the war he had begun studying philosophy at the University of Algiers, but in 1942 he lost not only his place in the university but also his citizenship when Vichy repealed the 1870 Crémieux Decree, which had granted Jews (but not Muslims) automatic French naturalization. Nonetheless, in the final years of the war, he fought in a battalion reserved for Jews and served as its chaplain. In 1944 he participated in the liberation of France and was wounded in Strasbourg. It was during his period of recovery that he learned from Robert Gamzon about the École d'Orsay and eventually met Jacob Gordin, whom he would refer to as his greatest master. He began as a student at Orsay in its first year, became a teacher after Gordin's death, and then the school's director in 1950 for the next eight years.

Ashkénazi was most influential as a teacher, and most of the essays that make up the two volumes of his work began as oral presentations. Along with Emmanuel Levinas and André Neher, he was an important contributor to the Colloque des intellectuels juifs de langue française. Whereas Neher offered biblical readings and Levinas gave Talmudic ones, Ashkénazi's contributions drew mostly from the kabbalistic tradition. As is evident in the following essay, he was partial to a method of reading the tradition that centered on the claim that the Genesis stories of the lineage and generations (*toledot* in Hebrew) of the patriarchs held, in fact, the secret of human history and could be used to understand the particular task of the Jewish people as well as human history's unfolding. In this endeavor, he draws on a line in Jewish thought from Judah Halevi through the Maharal of Prague to Rav Kook. It is a lineage that has received far more attention in modern French Jewish thought since the 1950s than it did in the heyday of German-Jewish thinking.

The most profound shift in Ashkénazi's thinking, perhaps less evident in this essay, arose with his trip to Israel in 1956 and his attendance at the seminar of Rav Zvi Yehuda Kook, the son of Abraham Isaac Kook, the first Ashkenazi chief rabbi of Palestine. Until this time, following Gordin, Léon Ashkénazi had recognized a spiritual and messianic function of the Diaspora and, in an essay from 1954, described the Diaspora as the source of Judaism's saving power. The Israelis would reap the joys of nationhood, while those in exile toiled for world salvation. After his meeting with Kook, however, he came to the conclusion that the time of deliverance, of *geulah*, had arrived, and that Kook's thinking was the logical continuation of that of Gordin, who, he claimed, would have himself become a Zionist had he met Kook. The essay's emphasis on the Hebrews reflects Ashkénazi's conviction that a new historical era had arrived, and the crucial task was once again to become a Hebrew in the Land of Israel. It was a time, he contended, comparable to that of Moses, when the Israelites did not have the confidence to leave the exile. Like the slaves in Egypt, Jews who remained in the Diaspora were unwilling to believe that the stage of exile had passed. This was not a sign of a crisis of faith; it was resistance to recognizing the new age. Ashkénazi's interpretation stemmed from a desire to harmonize a vision of Judaism's messianic mission with the reality of the State of Israel. But the only form this could take was grafting the diasporic messianism of Gordin onto the Jewish state.

In 1969 Ashkénazi finally made aliyah, eventually founding Mayanot, his own Institute of Jewish Studies in Jerusalem, which became an intellectual center for Francophone Jews.

The terms used here have a history. We are expressing ourselves in French, but the concepts to which we make allusions concern Hebraic categories. Now Hebraic culture is different from Greco-Latin culture and more specifically from French culture, which also has a very long history, not only in its classification but also in its implications. The words that designate the realities have changed meaning in the course of the great cultural epochs, but they also seem to take on a life of their own; even when one is a contemporary of such and such cultural implication, the intellectual resonances and connotations, and above all the emotional connotations, are different. When we use, for example, a term like "tradition," there are at least two possible responses: the positive response from the traditionalists, who find in their tradition the axis of reference to their values, and for whom the term "modernity" will accordingly appear to have negative implications; or the contrary: if one falls on the side of the cultural choices of modernity, the term "tradition" carries negative implications.

To grasp the European Jewish sociological context, let us consider the generation that had access to cultural lucidity immediately after the Second World War and the events that followed, who encountered this problem in a specific sense: the inheritors of the tradition had to confront modernity. But it seems that, these days, we have the reverse problem, or at least the meaning of this problem is reversed. This is more for sociological than ideological reasons, but the two planes intersect. A great number of Jews are participating in a movement—one that transcends, moreover, the limits of Jewish society—a call to return to the source.

The problem of "tradition and modernity" is in the process of assuming a meaning that it did not have for the previous generation. The "men of modernity" tried to invoke a tradition of identity to which, for purely sociological reasons, they had to address themselves in order to respond to the great question of self-knowledge, which is not merely an intellectual formula but also concerns the profound existential identity of each of us.

That being the case, as a precise historical point of reference, the example of the identity of Israel has existed over the course of universal history for a considerable time; it began in the times of the Hebrew patriarchs, some 3,600 years ago, and inevitably, it has known—even if the term is a bit contradictory —transformations, it has confronted the problem of "tradition and modernity," and the precise question of revitalization. Do not mistakenly view archaism with reference to what came before, as the source of an identity that has a history. In the contemporary moment in which we live, this is perhaps the most serious pitfall that we need to avoid: in the demand for revitalization, [in the desire for rejuvenation,] in wanting to go toward "the ancestral," toward that which is the source of identity, toward that which we confront when we confront ourselves, we encounter the temptation to move toward archaism.

In the identity "Israel" there was first the Hebrew period: Israel is the Hebraic nation to which the Bible refers, which knows itself as such and is known as such in the cultural environment of the era. A Hebrew is known as a certain manner of being a man, whose awareness had a specific history and a considerable impact on humanity in its entirety; this way of being a man has its own religion, the Mosaic law, its own spirituality, prophetic events, its own language, and its own conception of the world.

The Hebraic history lasted until around the beginning of the Christian era; it was destroyed in two stages: first by the Babylonian civilization, 2,600 years ago, then by the Roman civilization. The Jewish period, properly speaking, succeeded it. Two thousand years ago there was a change in identity that transformed the original Hebrew way of being into the Jewish one. There are real differences between these two modes of Israel, the same Israel but with two radically different historical indexes.

The Jew is always known in reference to the Hebraic identity and, as a consequence, his problem of revitalization was a problem of returning to the roots of Hebraism. Today, at the same time that great upheavals are occurring for humanity on the universal level, we are once again grappling with historical events that are both sociological and political, events that lead us to believe that the Jewish community finds itself confronted anew with a shift in identity. On at least one level, this identity tends toward becoming once again Hebraic. Here are posed the problems of revitalization and here appear the risks of adopting archaic contents in their undifferentiated form, deposited by the past over the course of our history, for their revitalization.

Those who are familiar with it know that when the Bible tells the story of our ancestors, it is not to recount what existed in a past characterized and desired as bygone, but rather to speak to us about the problems of our deepest identity, as it appears from the first unfolding of the story—of that way of being man that the Bible calls Israel. Whatever the attributes of the cultural era in which we find ourselves, it is always this existence, this way of being, that is at stake in our history.

One of the clearest examples is the marriage of Jacob's son Judah, to which the Book of Genesis devotes all of Chapter 38. The identity of Israel resulted entirely from an effort of selection within the Hebraic identity. Starting with Abraham the Hebrew, there are three levels of selection that lead to Jacob who becomes Israel. In the meantime, other Abrahamic lines appeared that established themselves in history as the rivals of Israel, disputing its profound identity as the descendant of Abraham, which is a whole other problem.

But at the end of the day, the identity "Israel" was born to this world; it is conceived, it emerges, such as the story is told, at the level of the third patriarch, Jacob. Not all of Abraham becomes Israel; one lineage was separated from him, the one that would become Islam, with Ishmael. Not all of Isaac becomes Israel—and the story continues; that is, the tradition of the Hebraic identity, confronted with the endurance of time, finds itself to be identical through all the changes that time brings and throughout all of the different clans that the children of Jacob-Israel created.

In order to continue the story of the identity of Israel, the children of Jacob must find wives; in order to conceive children, there must be a mother. Judah, settled in the countryside, among the righteous, says the Midrash, thus marries a Canaanite, Bat Shua [the daughter of Shua]. This attempt to procreate, to continue conceiving according to the Canaanite way, is destined for infertility: Judah has his first son, Er, who marries a woman named Tamar, but he dies before having a child. Then he has a second son, Onan, who pursues the same woman, but refuses to make a son with her; a third son is finally born who, according to the midrashic context, is incapable of having a son with any woman. It is an impasse. So Judah takes the traditional Hebraic identity upon himself through the fertility of Tamar, so that she can get out of the impasse and traverse time.

This is where the Midrash explains the difference between revitalization in the archaic mode, which was headed toward sterility and a dead end, and rejuvenation in the undifferentiated past that can become fertile. Indeed, Tamar is not a woman like all the other ones in Canaan. She is, according to the Midrash, the daughter of Shem himself—Shem, the founder of the lineage of Semites of which the Hebrews were a branch, essential, but one among other branches. There is a guiding thread in this story that seems simply to tell the story of ancestors, but in reality analyzes conditions of identity, this identity that is put into play in the history of Israel from the beginning: over the course of time, each time it appears, there is a risk of seeking out and encountering only the archaic, which is taken to be the ancestral, while in reality, it is necessary in fact to go much further for fecundity to reappear, much deeper into the most undifferentiated past.

The current generation of Jewish society encounters these same problems, with nuances all their own. It is certainly the case that a great number of Jews are today confronted with this problem of revitalization, because they have been disappointed by modernity and are searching to rediscover their traditions; they risk going down the wrong path and falling into the archaic. But what is the archaic? The archaic is what was once living and has become obsolete. When it existed, it was the apex of the tradition's modernity; but time having passed, what has been truly living has become what we call in Hebrew a *klipah*, meaning a shell, about which we can never know in advance if it encloses a spark of life or a deadly poison. The waste of prior history, when it is nothing more than waste, risks, in fact, becoming a deadly poison. To revitalize oneself in archaism is to attempt to revive the past. Life happens elsewhere.

The story of Judah's marriage, as the Midrash suggests, provides an indication about the search for the most undifferentiated. It is not in order to have a chance of unanimity. A tradition is first the tradition of a collectivity and consequently must search out the unanimity of the nation and not any identification too particular to the tribe, or family in the tribe, or at the extreme, to the individual. In the time within which we live there are beautiful flowers, but time will pass and only the flowers that carry fruit will bring forth in their turn trees that will have flowers and fruit. The contemporary generation of Jews is, it seems to me, confronted with the grave danger of seeking out its revitalization in the obsolescence of history, when it must search for it in the undifferentiated past of Hebrew history.

When the source of Hebraic history is revived—it is never dead—the various cultural heritages of Jewish time become a resource. As an illustration, let us consider an example on the level of language. Our generations must take note —sometimes with great sadness—that the "Jewish languages" risk no longer being spoken. They will certainly be studied, will serve as material for many more works, theses, memoirs, but ultimately, we are quite possibly the last to have known a time when Jews spoke "Jewish languages." It is certainly good that there have been efforts made, in the Diaspora and in Israel, to preserve the heritage of the languages. Two thousand years of culture elaborated the considerable wealth of what was alive in its time. But when these Jewish languages live on a Hebrew canvas (because they come from a Hebrew source), they represent wealth, enrichment; by contrast when they are disconnected from their Hebraic origin, they instantiate an archaic obsolescence.

The first time "Israel" was conscious of being confronted with the risk of disappearing in the clash between its own tradition and modernity, in the course of one of the great shifts in its history, was when the Judean identity encountered Greek identity. From the perspective of our own Hebraic identity, modernity began at the time of the philosophical method that finally gave Western culture its identity as we know it today. For a Hebrew, modernity in the non-Jewish cultures begins there.

It is important to make a remark here: we, Jews, are accustomed to using the categories of Western culture to analyze the problems that concern our own identity; the lens that the Western culture places on the fact of being Jewish, that is to say Hebrew, has produced a series of misunderstandings. This is without taking into account the fact that this conflict doubles as a theological conflict, because, ultimately, the religion of Western culture is the Christian religion, which, with respect to our problem, is a radical transformation of the Hebraic tradition establishing itself in competition with the Jewish tradition. There are a multitude of complicated and difficult misunderstandings to clear up, particularly in the ambivalent nature of the idea that the Jew has of himself when he makes use of Greek categories. And inevitably, since we have had access to the universities, we have adopted more or less unconsciously the categories of Greek thought, that is to say Greco-Latin, Christian even when they are de-Christianized. There is an obstacle to returning to our roots in a language other than Hebrew.

From the point of view of the Hebraic tradition, the first appearance of philosophy, in its method of reflection for understanding the world and above all the relationship between man and the world, the destiny of mankind, can be dated. Man had not yet begun to think in the way philosophers do about the problem of the meaning of existence. There is a "secondarization" of thought that appears at a certain time in the Western tradition: the first philosophers began to think at the moment that the last Hebrew prophets fell silent. The Hebraic period was the period of prophecy. And then the Bible announces that prophecy is going to fall silent. It does not go quiet completely or all at once: there is an important phenomenon of persistence, the *ruach hakodesh*, the "holy spirit," which continues up till now. But prophecy as an objective experience of revelation—a tradition of speaking and carrying forth a message about the meaning of existence from outside human consciousness—ceases to be experienced, but it leaves a trace, our books. Books to which we are faithful, insofar as we are capable of doing a traditional reading.

The Jewish tradition, inasmuch as it is the inheritor of the Hebraic tradition, teaches that this phenomenon of the prophetic experience was first universal and did not concern only the Hebrews. We refer to a very ancient time that needs to be retrieved from memory. An important phenomenon: if the Hebrew prophet speaks of One God, he speaks of a universal revelation. If there is a one and only God, he reveals himself to all of his creatures. And actually, not only in our own tradition, in the Midrash in particular, but in our memory, even if it has faded over time, and in all the human traditions, there is memory of a time when prophecy was a universal phenomenon. Its cessation had extremely important implications for our subject: if it was a universal phenomenon, its cessation also had an implication on the level of the universal. In the West, this cessation explains the appearance of the philosophical mentality. Before the time of philosophers, to take the unique case of Greece, there was a time of the sages. According to the assertion of even the Greek tradition, in the time of the sages, the sages understood their own message. This message is not ours; it may be impure wisdom, but it is wisdom nonetheless.

When I was in sixth grade, we studied the history of antiquity. I was about ten years old, I was in a state-run school and I was also going to Talmud Torah where I studied my own tradition, the tradition of the Hebrews. Imagine the reaction of this little Jewish boy that I was, in history class, reading his textbook and listening to the teacher say that he had read the Hebrews, this professor who did not even know what Talmud Torah was. For an essay, he gave the subject "The Hebrews": inevitably, I went first, and the professor discovered what Talmud Torah was. I said to myself then: "If one is capable of saying such nonsense about the Hebrews, maybe the case is similar regarding the other chapters of the same textbook, on the Egyptians or Greeks from antiquity." Maybe the "moderns" are incapable of understanding what there was in the wisdom of the ancients; the Greeks, for example, are described as heroes of all forms of culture, but as soon as it comes to spirituality, we look at them as childish. It is as if something had not happened. As for the past of the Hebrews: in my Talmud Torah, it was alive. For the university, the history of the Greeks is dead, and so one projects a type of mentality derived from contemporary modernity onto the wisdom of antiquity, one that we are incapable of understanding. As Paul Ricœur says, "the myth gives itself to be thought." It took two thousand years to rediscover that behind myth, there was wisdom.

In the time of the prophets, in the time of the Hebrews, this experience was accessible to all people, says the Midrash. When the one and only God revealed himself, He revealed himself on the universal level; but when this revelation stops, the impact of this cessation is also at the universal level. Each culture sensed the prophetic message through the prism of its own psyche. There is a cultural personality in each way of being man; each nation perceived this same revelation through its own language, its own way of thinking, and through its own way of being human.

The premise of the Jewish tradition is that there was neither mediation nor screen between the transmission of revelation and the human identity of Israel.

Where does this arrogant ambition "Israel" come from to claim that since the beginning, there was no mediation between God and Israel, when one knows there was mediation between God and all men?

The etymology of the word "philosophy" at the time of its emergence demonstrates the point well: the philosopher is he who loves wisdom in a time that follows the time of the sages. The wise man is he who receives wisdom; the philosopher is he who searches for it—therefore he does not possess it. For a philosopher who is honest with himself, there are only questions and no answers. The dignity of the philosopher tends toward the question of wisdom: he knows, and it is because of the transformation of modernity that emerges in this time that he questions a wisdom that does not respond. He does not believe in it anymore, because he was deceived by the contents of ancient wisdom, which, as it was passed down by the mythologists in modern language, has become incomprehensible. When one moves on from the time of the sages, the pre-Socratics, to the time of the philosophers, one reads this wisdom and these myths as childish writings because one is no longer capable of recognizing them.

The wisdom of the Hebrews was allowed to thrive among the Jews, for the essential reason that there was no prism. The revelation was made *face to face*, without intermediary, and the Jew continued to understand the revelation given in Hebrew. Everywhere else, it was obscured over a variable amount of time and according to different modalities. In the East, where there is still a sense that these things have meaning, people continued to believe but in a mystical way; the response was the emergence of mysticism. Whereas in the West, and that is where our problem lies, the premise of the philosophical method comes from an absolute immanence. Man questions a silent wisdom, and when he receives an answer, he knows that he is the one answering the question. Hence the tragic tone of modernity, its positive and negative aspect. There is, in the autonomy of the human being, an assumption by reason of the value of the human being —but at the same time, an entry into the tragic world, a foreign world to the Jewish soul.

This explains why the Jew has a difficult relationship with theater. I am opening a parenthesis here. A Jewish conscience that occupies itself with theater grapples with difficult impossibilities, because the tragic dimension is foreign to him. Tragedy is at the boundary of blasphemy for the Jewish soul: we get that from the Hebrews. Tragedy is truly the experience par excellence of the Greek soul. Not only would the Jew, as an individual, in other words as a human, not be capable of being tragic; as the carrier of the Hebraic tradition he would not even know how to be. The Bible recounts dramas, certainly, but be mindful of the vocabulary, especially the adjectives; intense dramas, paroxysmal dramas—but there is always a solution. The Hebraic consciousness is optimistic, messianic, while the Greek consciousness is essentially tragic, not that it was incapable of optimism, but it rejected it as an implausible hypothesis. From whichever side one approaches the problem, it is evident that by the fourth century BC, almost everything had been thought; ever since then, there is commentary. We would say that modernity is *immanentism*, and thus the experience of solitude. A serious philosopher cannot be anything other than tragic. During adolescence, we are seized by the enthusiasm of this excitement; when maturity comes, we discover derision: if it is indeed me who answers my question when the question concerns the meaning of my existence, that is derision. This is how the Jewish tradition has understood it.

Over the centuries, we have more or less known these same confrontations between a modernity and a tradition that takes root through memory in the experience of a prophecy. With each contemporaneity, this experience of the independence of "immanentist" thought, proceeding by way of a disillusionment from a lack of understanding of earlier traditions, reoccurs. In a slightly different register, we find the same disillusionment, the same uprooting. One finds only the same obsolescence of the archaic, even when one looks for the undifferentiated anterior. The conflict between the sage of the Talmud and the philosopher is the most illuminating illustration of the problem.

How is it in Jewish society today? How can a man of tradition react when he encounters the philosophical phenomenon of modernity and the principled rejection of the authority of all prior wisdom, once again a result of the experience of a radical disillusionment issuing from a phenomenon of occultation?

Imagine a child to whom we say: When you grow up, you will be given wisdom—and who grows into adulthood and receives nothing but childishness. It is from this disillusionment in relation to its own ancient tradition that philosophy is born and it is from this disillusionment where it enters the tragic that modernity is born. For Jewish society, grappling with its risks and its difficulties of transmission, passing from one cultural era to another, it is essentially a phenomenon of translation, in the broader sense of the term. Modern men, under the sociological pressure that pushes them to ask themselves about their own identity and seek out their own tradition, find themselves bifurcated.

Moving from the individual to the collective, to the social, to the community, in order to understand what is happening in our time and the impasses where people of good faith so often get stuck, we can turn only to the time of the Judeans, to their encounter with philosophical culture. There were two perspectives: the one from the Pharisean school and the other from the Sadducean school. For the Pharisee, the source of faith is in the meaning of the ancient tradition to which he is tied: the content of the prophecy of the Hebrews is a true wisdom. This faith can, sometimes, arise in a subjective fashion. Some people receive "proof" through knowledge or experience on a particular point. If it is true on one point, maybe it is true in general. For others, this faith arises through values other than knowledge, strictly speaking; more than a sentiment, there is first an experience of certainty: this book, the Bible as the identity card of Hebrews, has a meaning. We study it to know what we believe in. This is the Pharisaic tradition. It is a certainty of the nature of the prophetic faith; afterward, one studies the books that speak about it. This is the Jewish tradition as it has been for centuries.

The Sadducean attitude, by contrast, a sort of mixture with the philosophical attitude, is starkly in opposition: we duly note that there is a prestigious cultural phenomenon, books, great books, old books; we know there is something important there: one studies them to try to understand, and believes what one understands. The method is reversed. The result is the failure of the tradition, because modernity encounters only archaism, and again at the level of each individual who reads. [ ... ]

There is no space, it seems to me, for the Jewish people, to add a philosophy to other philosophies. Such a philosophy could only be of the Sadducean type. It would be of Jewish origin, certainly, but in reality it would be of the Greek method. This is the obstacle to overcome.

All this can be seen as a form of battle between the human person and time. To speak of change, Hebrew has two very different terms. The first, *shinui*, means the change when one becomes something else; time has conquered the identity of man. To be able to survive time, he had to change, but in changing, one became something else, one is changed, one changes oneself or becomes obsolete. Modernity, essentially, is what is going to go out of fashion very fast. There is a line of degradation that leads to death. *Shinui* leads to death. It is the change through which one becomes something else in order to survive, to persevere in being, finally leading to disappearance, to denaturation.

But there is another Hebrew word to say change, *hiddush*. *Hiddush* is renewal: to change while staying the same. If there is no adaptation through *hiddush*, through the rejuvenation of the identity while remaining the same, there is a disappearance. If there is *shinui*, changing to something different, there is disappearance. Contemporary Jewish society is confronted with two pitfalls: the choice of *shinui*, to traverse time while changing according to the criteria of time, at the risk of disappearing; the refusal of the *hiddush* at the risk of ending up obsolete and so, again, of disappearing. Are there criteria that allow one to distinguish between *shinui* and *hiddush*, between the change that kills and the change that revitalizes? It is an open question; it is the problem of revitalization of the tradition. *What we have to avoid is going back to the archaic, as prestigious as it may be, in order to go back to the earliest undifferentiated past.* Such is the task of our time.

*Translated by Sarah Hammerschlag*

# 21

**Alain Finkielkraut, From the Novelesque
to Memory**

Alain Finkielkraut, *The Imaginary Jew*, trans. Kevin O'Neill and David Suchoff
(Lincoln: University of Nebraska Press, 1994), 35–54. Originally published as
*Le Juif imaginaire* (Paris: Éditions du Seuil, 1980).

The child of Jewish Holocaust survivors from Poland who settled in France, Alain
Finkielkraut (1949– ) was raised in a secular home where his parents encouraged
his French assimilation. Nonetheless, as he was growing up, Finkielkraut's Jewish
heritage and the suffering that he associated with it provided an unquestioned site
of identification. His subsequent critical journey, described in *The Imaginary Jew*,
was not so much a matter of disidentification as one of self-realization. By means
of his French education and postwar upbringing, Finkielkraut came to the realization that he could claim the inheritance of Jewish suffering no more than any other
child of his generation. At first attracted by the Cercle Gaston-Crémieux's secularist approach to reclaiming prewar Eastern European culture, he eventually also
grew distrustful of the possibility of reviving Yiddish culture. That world had gone
up in flames, he concluded. The question then was how to show reverence to the
dead. The approach to Judaism that he develops in *The Imaginary Jew* involves
both a commitment to preserving the memory of the past and the concomitant
possibility that Judaism could be "no longer a kind of identity as much as a transcendence. Not something that defines me but a culture that can't be embraced,
a grace."[1]

In later works, Finkielkraut's suspicion of his own Jewishness as driven by a desire to identify with the victim developed into a criticism of multiculturalism and
what he understood to be its dangerous valorization of cultural particularism, a
politics he traced back to early German nationalism. He is known thus as a staunch
defender of Enlightenment universalism and the ideals of Republican France in
which his own secular education was steeped. In the more than twenty books he
has written since *The Imaginary Jew*, he develops a philosophical position and a
theory of culture influenced by Hannah Arendt and Emmanuel Levinas, drawing
from their respective works confidence in the superiority of deliberative democ-

1. [Finkielkraut, *The Imaginary Jew*, 176.]

racy and respect for the alterity of the other, a position he contrasts with the mere lauding of difference. Since first publishing *The Imaginary Jew* in 1980, Finkielkraut has become a well-known public intellectual, but not an uncontroversial one. He has been widely criticized for his staunch insistence on Western values, his defense of the French tradition of laïcité, his critiques of multiculturalism, and occasional controversial comments in the press.[2] He has also been much celebrated: in 2014 he was elected to the Académie française, one of France's oldest and most revered institutions of culture.

*I must acquire everything, not just the present and the future, but also the past,*
*that thing of which every man receives a share free of charge; I must acquire that too,*
*and this perhaps my most difficult task; if the earth turns to the right—I don't know*
*if it does—I must turn to the left to catch the past.*

FRANZ KAFKA

To claim as my own: for many long years, this was my unique and glorious mandate.

I was never one of the feckless who took the easier path, chose a French-sounding name and fled the burden of identity in silence or apostasy. "So what are you?" I never would have exploited the confusion that reduced Judaism to a religious category by replying to this question with: "Me? I'm an atheist, I don't believe in God." For me, atheism was no hideout, no pretext for an irreligios-ity that would allow me to abandon my people for the free-thinker's cozy and peaceful confines. I was a Jew without God, but a Jew before all else. No conduct seemed more odious or degrading to me than that of the *turncoat.* My own frank-ness was the very opposite of such cowardice. By reclaiming my tradition I could beat my eventual aggressor to the punch, assert I was a Jew before another's malice could label me such. I was thus proud of my origins, and my Jewishness had no content beyond this wariness and pride.

The Holocaust I never forgot. On the contrary, I couldn't stop thinking about it. Deep ignorance, curiously enough, went along with this obsession. Why did I need to know every detail of how the Holocaust took place? A few family stories, indelible images from *Nights and Fog*, a number repeated interminably

2. [See, e.g., the controversy surrounding his comments about the 2005 Parisian riots in an interview to *Haaretz*: "M. Finkielkraut s'excuse pour ses propos dans le quotidien israélien," *Le Monde*, November 25, 2005.]

—six million Jews exterminated during the last war—were enough for me. The rest mattered little. Leave scholarship to the experts, my instincts were proof enough. Jewishness coursed through my veins, was my inner truth, my flesh and blood. The culture of the ghettos and scars of deportation still dwelled in the depths of my soul. My character had been molded by twenty centuries of suffering: I was one of the earth's living repositories of the *Jewish spirit*. I never would have thought of using the much maligned term *race*, and yet, imbued with the sensibility of my people, an authentic part of a larger process, a link in an uninterrupted chain of being, I pledged implicit allegiance to the determinism of racialist thought. Unwittingly, I followed Barrès. I could therefore do without memory, for Jewishness thought and spoke through me.

What I didn't see then was that by appropriating the Holocaust as my own, I mystified and softened its horror. Five years had been enough to destroy an entire civilization. It had disappeared. And while it wasn't courage or vigilance that brought me to face that fact, I acted as if I were one of the victims. Eager to assume responsibility for Jewish destiny, and wishing to stand by my people, I forgot this: they no longer existed. A disaster without precedent cut me off from Jewish culture, and I, a simmering rebel, reforged an artificial and reassuring continuity between present and past. I filled in the gap that held me distant from generations gone before. Because I was Jewish, I felt I had been born to a tradition of exile, but the Holocaust had exiled me from the experience of Jewish collectivity itself. Experiencing the travails of my people in dream, I denied this rupture; orphaned from Judaism, I wrote myself back into its genealogy and the trick was done: I had domesticated Auschwitz, turned the massacre into a strictly numerical and therefore reparable state of affairs. Only sufficient effort would be needed to move beyond it: with fecundity, and a little time ... At heart, my piety evinced a casual attitude toward the disaster, as if it were merely a painful parentheses in a story which, for all that, hadn't lost its thread.

Today, I would no longer rely on my Jewish spontaneity. I am nothing instinctively, unable to claim any specific kind of cultural difference. My gestures, language, habits, appearance and way of life have been washed clean of every particularity. In public as in private, I am identical to non-Jews, an impeccable likeness. Nor has such typicality been mine to choose or reject. It is the result of neither a fading culture in decline, the homogenizing power of capitalism, nor of progress and its ineluctable course. Could the West, that vast, elusive entity signified with a capital letter, be behind this leveling effect? Will we once again condemn, in absentia, the society in which equivalence rules? No. Jewish life was suddenly reduced to folklore by a specific, singular, and quite recent event: the Holocaust. Hitler's achievement cannot be diminished on the grounds that his task remained unfinished, and that he lost the war. The success of the extermination is measurable not just by the number of dead, but also by the poverty of contemporary Judaism. Chaïm Kaplan erred on the side of optimism when he wrote in his account of the Warsaw Ghetto: "Our existence as a people will not be destroyed. Individuals will be destroyed but the Jewish community will live on."

Certain communities, to be sure, remain practically intact, those whom the Nazis' lethal violence was unable to reach. The rest belie Kaplan's prediction, and show that the opposite has come to pass. Only in numbers did the Nazis fall short, despite their monstrous toll of victims. While defeat prevented them from completing the final solution, they achieved a qualitative success: Yiddishkeit was erased as one of the world's unique cultures. That's why I, an Ashkenazi am a Jew without substance, a *Luftmensch*, but not a beggar or wanderer in the traditional sense. Today's *Luftmensch* is the Jew in a state of zero gravity, relieved of what could have been his symbolic universe, his personal place or at least of one of his homes. To console myself, I always rehash the same subject: my profundity. I avenge myself in psychological complexity for the diaphanous slice of Jewishness I actually possess. If I can't be a member of a living Jewish community, I can devote myself at a moment's notice to the pleasures of self-interrogation: he who is deprived of Jewish ethnicity finds in the Jewish question endless food for thought.

The force of things has made me an introspective Jew, leaving me but a single faculty for escaping the monotony of the inward gaze: memory. Willed, laborious, faulty, untiring memory, a far cry from two thousand years of History at the tip of my tongue. Jewishness doesn't come naturally: an uncrossable distance separates me from the Jewish past. With the Jewish community carried off in catastrophe, my homeland is gone. Memory's imperative springs from the painful awareness of this divide. Unquenchable nostalgia for the Jewish life of Central Europe is the entire legacy I have been left. Jewishness is what I miss, not what defines me, the base burning of an absence, not any triumphant, plentiful instinct. I call that part of myself Jewish that remains at odds with life in its time, and which cultivates the powerful supremacy of what *has been* over what is. "It happens that peoples lose their connectedness: it's a great loss, of course, and consolation is hard to find; but here comes Doctor Soïfer with his own loss to bear. . . . For he is one of those who are in the process of losing their people. . . . What? . . . What's that he's losing? . . . We've never heard of such a loss!"[3]

A young bourgeois, spared by History, feels a growing fascination for the times in which his people lived. Must such curiosity be seen as a return to roots? The image is tempting but inexact: it conjures up hordes of former progressives, now scouring bygone eras, waiting for the past to divulge the foundational truth of the self. If only tomorrow could be like yesterday—those were the days! Genealogies have become the rage, as everyone looks for the meaning that contemporary life so cruelly lacks. Deep disillusionment has seized old devotees of the meaning of History; today, relish for one's origins has replaced the taste for revolt. The sickness specific to this last quarter-century is the need for roots. But how the devil would I go about tracing my roots in Galicia or prewar Warsaw, knowing only a few curses and terms of endearment. and two or three Yiddish and Polish turns of phrase? This murdered world moves me, haunts me, precisely because I am completely excluded from it. Instead of examining the past for images of myself, I search for what I am not, what it is now impossible for me to be. Far from ending my exile, memory makes it deeper by making it more concretely felt. No feeling of recognition ties me to Poland's lost Jewish community. To know it, to visit it repeatedly through books (the only locales where it still exists), is only to measure my own estrangement from what has been lost. These prewar Polish Jews brought back to life by certain scholarly and literary works, these are my people. Yet to sound, search and excavate my inner depths would be in vain, no trace of them remains, except perhaps my taste for poppy seed bread, scorching hot tea, and the way I hold sugar in my teeth rather than let it dissolve. Tenuous and fragile roots, to be sure.

What I have here called memory is thus the useless passion a vanished civilization stirs in me. Not just useless, you might say, morbid as well. What's dead is dead. Why spend time energetically sifting through the ashes, when the effort would be better spent fighting for Jewish renewal or social justice? If only for this reason—and I offer it here in the name of a Jewish way of life, surrounded by its absence: that today, everything conspires to make us believe that such a civilization never existed. Everything: the uncommitted and their indifference, the pressures and everyday worries of contemporary life, and even the way our era remembers the Holocaust, however reverential it might seem. We spare no

---

3. [From David Bergelson, "A Candle for the Dead." The quotation appears as an epigraph in André Schwarz-Bart's *The Last of the Just* (New York: Overlook Press, 2000), 199.]

expense and produce an irreproachable commentary on these occasions, superlative heaped on superlative, choked voices and torrential sobs abound. The process of erasing the history of these people, so recently robbed of life, is apparent in two recent tearjerkers: *Holocaust*, the TV series judged to be worthless, and *Guichets du Louvre*, a film praised for its lucid intelligence.

Only two types of European Jew existed at the war's start: white, Western, normal ones, with the average man's clean-shaven look—and Jews from the olden days, picturesque throwbacks and medieval remnants, recognizable by their black caftans and sidecurls. The former spoke the majority's language with exemplary correctness; the costumed silhouettes, on the other hand, expressed themselves in Yiddish, and found nothing better to do as their hour of doom approached than to don their ceremonial shawls and sway rhythmically in prayer. Television will tell children what a Jew used to be: a figure constantly swaying back and forth. The image, of course, is hardly malicious: our era drips with compassion for these rockers-in-prayer, with no words harsh enough for the barbarians who put them to death. In guilty pity and its zeal, we're almost moved to think the world inhabited by those pallid scholars of the synagogue was Eden. Their swaying in prayer, we imagine, was a spiritual ideal whose like will not be seen again. More than bewail these psalmists in beard, we're meant to envy the wisdom we have lost, to grant them our compassion as a kind of homage. What can be said after such an orgy of goodwill? Simply this: that the opposition on which it rests is false. Between the wars, the Jews of Europe were anything but a homogeneous community, and certainly not a community divided in two, split between a group of doctors-lawyers-bankers and those who wore traditional garb. Yiddish was no exotic dialect, spoken by a few fossil throwbacks as the world left them behind. Three million Jews lived in Poland; their culture was a varied space in which the observant and the secular, Zionists and Bundists, Orthodox and Reform Jews, cosmopolitan citizens and inhabitants of the shtetls rubbed shoulders and confronted one another. You could keep the sabbath without looking like a bearded prophet, enjoy the Yiddish theater as well as Bizet's *Carmen*, study the Torah and play Ping-Pong or volleyball, be fully Jewish and reject the Talmud's rules. Modernity and Judaism were not the two mutually exclusive options, one set against the other, that we have retrospectively made them to be.

Even in our beloved France, Eastern European immigrants were so visibly Jewish that their coreligionists became uneasy. Assimilated Jews for the most part rejected these aliens who "vulgarly" betrayed their origins, while the assimilated, by contrast, outdid themselves trying to make their own Jewishness disappear. Everything about the newcomers spoke against Israel: accents, gestures, physical appearance—everything except religious ways. Local craftsmen from Belleville, La République and the Marais truly enlarged the scope of synagogue architecture: classifiable as neither assimilated nor traditional, they remain absent from our reconstructions of the past. In *Guichets du Louvre*, a film devoted to their portrayal, they appear dressed in Levite coats, which they in fact never wore; while waiting for the police to raid, they sway in prayer, the perfect image of the Jew. In our desire to see clearly, we no longer see at all. We commemorate, in amnesia, the destruction of a nation. And so the Jewish people have been made to suffer a double death: death by murder, and death by oblivion. Collective memory reserves space only for those who look like we do, or for museum artifacts or circus freaks.

They're even better than the Mona Lisa, these Jews from another age: in portraying the actions and gestures of the ancient Hassidim, pathos is de rigueur. It all seems inevitable. By reducing Jewish life to something archaic, the Holocaust is implicitly defined as a rapid historical advance. Haste may be cruel and inhuman, but weren't they victims—those anemic scholars who studied, interpreted and chanted nothing but the sacred word—of progress itself? A death by natural causes for Jewish culture would of course be preferable. Hitler disagreed. The elegiacally inclined can still visit Mea Shearim in Jerusalem, or certain neighborhoods in Brooklyn and Anvers. There they will see those freaks in flesh and blood: our era's last representatives of the Jewish civilization of Central Europe.

This is our official cult of the dead, a debasing distortion. With an outpouring of tears we're offered the image of a senile community being put to death, when it was a vibrant, multifaceted and creative culture the Nazis killed. Blatant indifference would surely do less harm than commiseration of this sort. For when all is said and done, and the public mind has been presented with the image of these helpless dotards—swaying, wasted bodies bemoaning their worldly woes —what else is there to think? Only that they were led to the slaughter in resignation, like docile sheep, and that they met their destruction with the calm and absolute passivity of those who firmly believe the Messiah will come. Religious hope doesn't foster the military calling, and you can't forge a resistance from people who sway over the prayerbook from dawn to dusk. By now, of course, the Warsaw Ghetto uprising has attained universal recognition and even receives fervent celebration, as if to better emphasize its exceptional status. Good thing they were there, the rebel few, to salvage, in extremis, the honor of an anesthetized people! Such unique prowess, moreover, is imputed spontaneously to those least Hebraic of Jews, the aberrants, those already-Israelis, our alter-egos, counterparts and brethren, who possessed the anticipatory courage to shed superstition and its ancestral yoke.

It's tenacious, this legend of Jewish passivity, a vile myth worse than oblivion. Victims of the Holocaust are treated as if they *collaborated* in their own destruction. The ss were filthy murderers, of course, but it must be said, must it not, that the Jews—bewildered, taciturn and afraid—did their part. A suicidal propensity? Masochism? Scapegoat complex from time immemorial? Did they render themselves unto God in a kind of mystical fervor? Was accepting their fate their way of obeying God's command, or did they refuse to face it in outright denial of reality? While religion and psychology endlessly dispute the key to the riddle, Auschwitz is gradually transformed into evidence of man's dizzying capacity for passivity. No longer the mystery of Nazi horror that piques the popular imagination, but the far more exciting mystery of Jews who failed to act. "There was no way to escape these kinds of stories. Why didn't the Jews revolt? Why didn't they fight? Why didn't they form an Underground? Why were the Germans able to say: *Die Juden sind die billingsten und willingsten Arbeiter?* The type of question you are asked by those with hearts of stone and eyes of ice."[4]

It's unbearable, this arrogant summoning of ghetto dwellers and camp prisoners to answer before an abstract tribunal, a scandal. Yet for all our disgust, the indictment still requires a response. Jews who forty years ago suffered through Hitler now need lawyers for defense. Today and for the foreseeable future, we are reduced to justifying the victims for a massacre carried out against them. The task of rehabilitation rests with us, there's no escape: for Jewish memory is nothing but an incessant struggle we must wage against majoritarian memory, to reclaim the Holocaust's dead from the creeping conformism disguising them for posterity as confused and consenting prisoners put to death. [ ... ]

The world has seen other genocides since the war. Only vanity would claim moral privilege or a monopoly on extermination for the Jews, for in this domain the Nazis were precursors rather than exceptions to the rule. Something unique, nonetheless, remains specific to these four years of dereliction, and it is not, as the familiar cliché would have it, the victims' resignation. "Unique in 1940–1945 was the abandonment," as Emmanuel Levinas writes. No petitions then, no

4. Adolf Rudnicki, *Le Marchand de Lodz*, trans. Gilberte Crépy (Paris: Gallimard, 1969), 62.

press campaigns; no media to "cover" the Holocaust, no march, no swaying of public opinion. Not a sign from the world outside. An impenetrable wall, made of hostility, detachment, skepticism or ignorance stood between the suffering and those beyond. It is useless to cover up this silence with impenitent blather about Jewish passivity: it remains as dizzying, as incomprehensible today as it was forty years ago.

It's natural these days to look ahead. "Onward" is the word on practically everyone's lips. Eccentrics who look back must explain themselves. Nostalgia must give meaning to contemporary life, must be of use here and now; preoccupation with the past must be part of a triumphant vision of the time in which each of us pays homage to a future that rules supreme. Consider the arguments that those who refuse to forget the Holocaust, wanting to retain a link with their vanished culture, are compelled to use. Memory, they claim, is nothing but a form of vigilance: "Of course we return to the past, good people, it's this very obsession that keeps us modern: it's our way of assuring that such a past will never return." Some zealots of modernity reject the excuse; the Jews, they say, open old wounds out of complacency, create a distraction. They say: Jews who harp on the Holocaust by continually bringing it up draw our attention away from crying injustice and more pressing instances of genocide. Such modernists blithely compare Jews of today with yesterday's anti-Semites: the former are said to dwell on yesterday's disaster when their efforts would be better spent facing up to contemporary history, just as the latter used racial hatred to divert social unrest that might have shaken the very foundations of capitalism itself. If one were to believe these censors of memory, today's honoring of Auschwitz is carried out for the same reason that hooked-nose parasites were hated before: to exorcize collective violence, using fictional unanimity directed against a helpless enemy to mask real social conflicts beneath. The Elders of Zion gave shelter to those responsible for human misery: of course, every memorial of the Holocaust serves to mask the torture chambers of Uruguay, Chile, or Argentina, if not refugees from Indochina, the Soviet gulags or unemployment in France. Thus, during the broadcast of *Holocaust*, few were the critics who brought out the film's deficiencies (and notably the total absence of Jewish life): innumerable, on the contrary, were the editorials that denounced it as a dangerous distraction. The time is past, they cried, to bewail the plight of the Jews. Make way for the Young! Make way for a new class of the damned!

The partisans of Jewish memory declare: The dead teach the living, warn them and open their eyes. The enemies of Jewish memory declare: These dead serve no purpose, weigh us down, enfeeble our vision, mystify what's at stake today: Both sides can conceive of the dead only in terms of their *usefulness*.

As for myself, I too spent all of my long adolescence making use of the dead. Shamelessly annexing them to myself. Voraciously appropriating their destiny as my own. Gorging myself on their agony. Now I know that memory does not consist in subordinating the past to the needs of the present, nor in painting modernity in dramatic hues. If the future is for all things the measure of value, memory has no ground: for he who looks to gather the materials of memory places himself at the service of the dead, and not the other way around. He knows that they have only him in the world, and that if he turns his back to the manner in which they lived and died, then these dead Jews who were at his mercy will truly perish, and modernity, in love with itself, absorbed by daily intrigues, will not even notice they have disappeared.

# 22

# Hélène Cixous, Albums and Legends; The Dawn of Phallocentrism

Hélène Cixous, excerpt from "Albums and Legends," *Hélène Cixous,*
*Rootprints: Memory and Life Writing*, ed. Susan Sellers, trans. Eric Prenowitz
(London: Routledge, 1997). Originally published as Hélène Cixous and Mireille
Calle-Gruber *Photos de racines* (Paris: Des femmes–Antoinette Fouque, 1994).

Hélène Cixous, excerpt from *The Newly Born Woman* (with Catherine
Clément), trans. Betsy Wing (Minneapolis: University of Minnesota Press,
1986), 100–104.

The author of scores of books — critical essays, novels, plays, and theoretical works
that often mix genres — Hélène Cixous (1937– ) is an icon of the French feminist
movement. She is best known for her notion of "feminine writing," her call for new
writing practices as modes of resistance against the suppression of women, "writing that can serve as a springboard for subversive thought," the first means for
social transformation.[1] According to Cixous, it is by reclaiming the domain prohibited by the law — the material, the overflowing, the dangerous — that women resist
patriarchy. As she suggests in the essays below, her Jewish identity is closely tied
to her experience as a woman. She initially experienced both of these categories
as a site of exclusion and marginalization, and her work became a means to recast
that exclusion into forms of literary affirmation. "When I write I escape myself, I
uproot myself, I am a virgin; I leave from within my own house and I don't return."[2]

Born in Oran, Algeria, to two Jewish parents, one European and the other
North African, Cixous's familial Jewish history is a microcosm of Jewish experience in the late nineteenth and twentieth centuries. At the same time, Jewishness
appears in her work mostly as a site of cultural negation, as an experience of being
determined by the gaze of the other. Cixous embraces the association between
Jewishness and uprootedness, but also the alignment between Judaism and prohibition. The excerpts from her work included here explore both sides of the coin.

1. [Cixous, "Laugh of Medusa," trans. Keith Cohen and Paula Cohen, *Signs* 1, 4 (Summer
1976): 879. It was this essay that brought her to the attention of American readers in 1976.]

2. [Cixous, *Three Steps on the Ladder of Writing* (New York: Columbia University Press,
1993), 21.]

She connects with a Jewish literary history, not that of biblical or rabbinic literature but its modern literary figures, such writers as Franz Kafka, Sigmund Freud, Paul Celan, Nelly Sachs, and Clarice Lispector. Growing up as an Algerian Jew through the events of the Second World War and the Algerian War—the revocation of French citizenship, the antisemitism accompanying Algerian nationalism, and the concomitant migrations across continents—produced a particular nexus of exclusion that, in turn, allowed for the possibility of an identity divorced from structures of belonging, or as she describes below, "a literary nationality." For Cixous, consequently, expressions of communal or national disidentification are simultaneously expressions of her Jewishness.

## ALBUMS AND LEGENDS

What I am recounting here (including what is forgotten and omitted) is what for me is indissociable from writing. There is a continuity between my childhoods, my children, and the world of writing—or of narrative.

Then I arrive in France in 1955. It is the first time. My first European city was London where my mother sent me (1950) alone to learn English.

In 1955 in *Khâgne* at the Lycée Lakanal—that is where I felt the true torments of exile.[3] Not before. Neither with the Germanys nor with the Englands, nor with the Africas, I did not have such an absolute feeling of exclusion, of interdiction, of deportation. I was deported right inside the class.

In Algeria I never thought I was at home, or that Algeria was my country, or that I was French. That was part of the exercise of my life: I had to play with the question of French nationality which was aberrant, extravagant. I had French nationality when I was born. But no one ever took themselves for French in my family. Perhaps on my father's side, they refrained from not being French. We were deprived of French nationality during the war: I don't know how they gave it back to us.

Image: I am three years old. I have followed in the streets of Oran the Pétain Youth parade. Dazzled, I go home singing "Maréchal here we are." My father takes my brother (two years old) and me solemnly on his knees. He solemnly tears the photo of Maréchal Pétain that I brought back, and he explains it to us.

That logic of nationality was accompanied by behaviors that have always

3. [Cixous here refers to the two-year program following lycée that prepares students to take the entrance exam for the écoles normales supérieures.]

been unbearable for me. The French nation was colonial. How could I be from a France that colonized an Algerian country when I knew that we ourselves, German Czechoslovak Hungarian Jews, were other Arabs. I could do nothing in this country. But neither did I know where I had something to do. It was the French language that brought me to Paris.

In France, what fell from me first was the obligation of the Jewish identity. On one hand, the anti-Semitism was incomparably weaker in Paris than in Algiers. On the other hand, I abruptly learned that my unacceptable truth in this world was my being a woman. Right away it was war. I felt the explosion, the odor of misogyny. Up until then, living in a world of women, I had not felt it, I was Jewess, I was Jew.

From 1955 on, I adopted an imaginary nationality which is literary nationality.

### THE DAWN OF PHALLOCENTRISM

What is a father? "Fatherhood is a legal fiction," said Joyce. Paternity, which is a fiction, is fiction passing itself off as truth. Paternity is the lack of being which is called God. Men's cleverness was in passing themselves off as fathers and "repatriating" women's fruits as their own. A naming trick. Magic of absence. God is men's secret.

> Among the precepts of Mosaic religion is one that has more significance than is at first obvious. It is the prohibition against making the image of God, which means the compulsion to worship an invisible God. I surmise that in this point Moses surpasses the Aton religion in strictness. Perhaps he meant to be consistent: his God was to have neither a name nor a countenance. The prohibition was, perhaps, a fresh precaution against magic malpractices. If this prohibition was accepted, however, it was bound to exercise a profound influence. For it signified subordinating sense perception to an abstract idea; it was a triumph of spirituality over the senses; more precisely an instinctual renunciation accompanied by its psychologically necessary consequences. (*Moses and Monotheism*)[4]

*Jewoman*:
And in the same story, as Kafka told it, the man from the county, the one who-doesn't-know-but believes, comes before the law. A doorkeeper stands before

---

4. Sigmund Freud, *Moses and Monotheism* (New York: Knopf, 1939), 152.

the law. And the gullible man asks to go into the law. But even though the door opens, one doesn't go in. Maybe later. Nothing keeps the poor fellow from entering. Except everything: the doorkeeper, the way he looks, his black beard, the door, the fact of its being open; the fact that nothing keeps him from entering the law, except what the law is; except that it is what it is. And waiting.

In the first years he curses his evil fate aloud; later, as he grows old, he only mutters to himself. He grows childish, and since in his prolonged watch he has learned to know even the fleas in the door-keeper's fur collar, he begs the very fleas to help him and to persuade the doorkeeper to change his mind. Finally his eyes grow dim and he does not know whether the world is really darkening around him or whether his eyes are only deceiving him. But in the darkness he can now perceive a radiance that streams immortally from the door of the Law. Now his life is drawing to a close. Before he dies, all that he has experienced during the whole time . . . condenses into one question, which he has never yet put to the doorkeeper. He beckons the doorkeeper, since he can no longer raise his stiffening body. The doorkeeper has to bend down to hear him, for the difference in size between them has increased very much to the man's disadvantage. "What do you want to know about now?" asks the doorkeeper, "you are insatiable." "Everyone strives to attain the Law," answers the man, "how does it come about, then, that in all these years no one has come seeking admittance but me?" The doorkeeper perceives . . . that his hearing is failing, so he bellows in his ear: "No one but you could gain admittance through this door, since the door was intended only for you. Now I am going to shut it."

And no one is there now to learn what the man devoted his whole life to think, to reap the discovery that could come about only at the price of a whole life, at the moment of death. There is never anyone there when what has been not-open or open closes, the door, the threshold of the law. What is the law? The law where? who? whose?

But the Real has very clearly crystallized in the relationship of forces between the petitioner "outside the law" and the doorkeeper, the first in a series of representatives of the L—, the cop, the first level of power with a thousand laws. "Outside" the law? Is there an "inside" to the law? A place? A country maybe? A city, a kingdom? As long as he lived, that is what he believed.

Was he ever outside in relation to the desired inside that is reserved for every man—that place, that L—, which he believed was his good, his right, his "accessible" object. *Into* which he would enter and which he was going to enjoy.

So it is the L— that will have served as "life" for him, will have assigned him his place before the L—, permanently. Immobilized, shriveled. And no one will have been there to learn from the dying man, from the dead man, what he began to think maybe at the last second: that the law isn't within, it has no place other than the gullible man's body that comes to rot in front of the door, which has always been in the L—, and the L— has only existed to the extent that it appears before what he doesn't see it is behind, around, before, *inside him* that it is nothing without him, that its apparently absolute power is inexhaustible, because like Moses's God, it doesn't exist; it is invisible; it doesn't have a place to take place; it doesn't have anything. It "is" hence it is only if he makes it; it is nothing more than the tremendous power of the invisible.

Exploited by thousands of its representatives—supposed-to-represent-it, who draw their dissuasive, repressive power, their calm and absolute violence from this nothing that is out of sight.

You will not pass. You will not see me. A woman is before the door of the law. And the bearded watchman—his beard so pointed, so threatening—warns her not to go through. Not to go, not to enjoy. And by looking toward, and looking in, and feeling herself looked at without knowing where the L—'s look is coming from, she gets it to come, she believes she sees a glimmer radiating, which is the little flame that the constant flow of her gaze keeps burning in emptiness, in nothing. But from always being looked at without seeing, she pales, she shrinks, she grows old, she is diminished, sees no more, lives no more. That is called "internalizing," she is full of this nothing that she imagines and that she pines for. Sublimation? Yes, but negative, turning the power—whose source she is without knowing it—back against herself. Her powerlessness, her paralysis, her feebleness? They are the measure of her power, her desire, her resistance, her blind confidence in their L—. Suppose she "entered?" Why not have taken this step? Not even this first step? Does she fear the other doors? Or does she have forebodings? Or is the choice between two mockeries of life inscribing themselves in the nothingness that she embodies and that rivets her in the visible, on the lowest level, in relation to her nearest interlocutor: fleas in the doorkeeper's coat, a flea herself.

Or maybe there is an L— and it is the petrifying result of not-knowing reinforced by the power that produces it.

And they told her there was a place she had better not go. And this place is guarded by men. And a law emanates from this place with her body for its locus. They told her that inside her law was black, growing darker and darker. And the doorkeeper preached prudence to her, because beyond it was even worse.

And she doesn't enter her body; she is not going to confirm the worst, it is not even properly hers. She puts it in the hands of the doorkeeper.

So the resounding blow of this same trick echoes between Jew and woman. In the tabernacle it is metamorphosed as a box full of nothing that no one would miss. The trick of the "omnipotent." The voice saying, "I-am-who-I-say-I-am." My name is "the-one-who-is-where-you-aren't." What is a father? The one taken for father. The one recognized as the true one. "Truth," the essence of father-hood, its force as law. The "chosen" father.

And one day—as Freud sees it still inscribing itself in the Oresteia—the matriarch is done for, the sons stop being sons of mothers and become sons of fathers. The question of filiation swings, changes tack: What is a mother? And they no longer ask themselves, which is more certain, but which is stronger?

On one side there is mother, belly, milk. The bond passing through flesh, blood and milk, through the life debt. What is owed to her? A debate begins over sperm and milk, does she provide food only? Or does she also provide a germ? Who begins?

How hard it all is for Orestes who is at a turning point in time and whose action, a matricide—until now the crime of crimes—marks the end of mothers and inaugurates the sublime era! How do you estimate the value of the mother's murder? What value does blood have? What is the value of words? In the struggle between blood and words, the marriage pact—a commitment made with word and will—is stronger, Apollo claims, than the blood-tie. The link to mother loosens. The link to word tightens. We are still in the age of the organic. From now on legality is to come to the assistance of the father's order. A new relationship between body and justice will have to be instituted.

# 23

# Jacques Derrida, Avowing — the Impossible

## "Returns," Repentance, and Reconciliation, a Lesson

Jacques Derrida, "Avowing," *Living Together: Jacques Derrida's Communities of Violence and Peace*, trans. Gil Andijar, ed. Elisabeth Weber (New York: Fordham University Press, 2013), 18–44. Published in French as "Avouer l'impossible: 'Retours,' repentir et réconciliation," in Jacques Derrida, *Le dernier des Juifs* (Paris: Éditions Galilée, 2014).

His inclusion in an anthology of French Jewish thought would not have been uncomplicated for Jacques Derrida (1930–2004), the philosopher who famously introduced the world to deconstruction. While he did not shy away from examining themes and thinkers associated with Judaism, Derrida never addressed these topics from a position within the tradition, and in *Archive Fever* he reflected on the fraught dynamics of attributing a thinker's ideas to his Judaism.[1] He wrote essays on figures at the margins of the Jewish tradition, such as Edmond Jabès, Paul Celan, Franz Kafka, Walter Benjamin, and Sigmund Freud, but also on thinkers who took part in pioneering the field of modern Jewish thought, such as Hermann Cohen, Gershom Scholem, and Emmanuel Levinas. While Derrida's books and essays on these philosophers, poets, and critics address a wide range of themes often explored within Jewish thought, such as exile, law, sacrifice, covenant, the sacred, messianism, circumcision, and revelation, they also reveal an abiding interest in the issue of Jewish election and exemplarity — that is to say, in Judaism's claim to be a particularism that instantiates the universal — and an unease with the dynamics of community inscription, its mechanisms and paradoxes.[2] In numerous essays and interviews he traced both this fixation on exemplarity and his discomfort with community inscription back to his own childhood experience of growing up in El Bair, a suburb of Algiers, during the Vichy era.

Derrida, raised in a culturally Jewish but largely irreligious family, had a relatively unproblematic relationship with his heritage before the war. But in line with the

1. [See *Archive Fever*, in which Derrida discusses Yosef Yerushalmi's Jewish reading of Freud.]

2. [See Dana Hollander, *Exemplarity and Chosenness: Rosenzweig and Derrida on the Nation of Philosophy* (Stanford: Stanford University Press, 2008).]

1940 repeal of the Crémieux Decree under Vichy rule, in November 1942 Derrida was expelled from the state-run lycée, owing to restrictions on the number of Jewish children allowed in state institutions. It was not, however, the revocation of Frenchness that seems to have preoccupied him, but rather his consequent enrollment at the Jewish Lycée Maïmonide, which he found to be a kind of unbearable constraint, a forced inscription, that "mirrored too symmetrically, that *corresponded* in truth to an *expulsion*."[3] Whereas for many Jewish thinkers of his generation, Judaism provided a space to be at home when the comfortable rug of Frenchness was pulled out from under them, for Derrida it was the very dynamics of community that troubled him, the fact that determining its members entails a necessary exclusion. Philosophy thus became both the avenue of escape — to the metropole — but also a method of inquiry by which he could return to some of the structural dynamics underlying his discomfort. Much later, after he had come back explicitly to the issue of Jewish identity in his own work and begun to play with the forms of its articulation, by calling himself a Marrano and "the least and the last of the Jews," he wrote that "being Jewish would be more than and other than the simple strategic or methodological lever of a general deconstruction, it would be the experience of deconstruction itself, its chance, its menace, its destiny, its earthquake."[4] In suggesting as much, Derrida was himself asserting the very dynamic that he often criticized in the work of other Jewish thinkers, namely, the claim that Judaism represented the privileged exemplar of a universal structure. While one could easily take this for a kind of hypocrisy, for Derrida that was indeed often the point. Whereas most philosophers blame their predecessors for an error from which they claim to be free, Derrida instead would often commit the very error for which he was criticizing his predecessors, thus differentiating himself by that distinction.

"Avowing," the selection that appears here, was first presented at the Colloque des intellectuels juifs de langue française. However, unlike Neher, Levinas, Ashkénazi, and others included in this volume, Derrida was not a regular participant in the conference. It was not, however, his first time there. As he points out in the essay, he had attended once before, in 1965, at the invitation of Levinas, with whom he shared a lifelong friendship and conversation across texts, in which the

3. [Jacques Derrida and Élisabeth Roudinesco, *For What Tomorrow . . . a Dialogue*, trans. Jeff Fort (Stanford: Stanford University Press, 2004), 111.]

4. [Jacques Derrida, "Abraham, The Other," in Bettina Bergo, Joseph Cohen, and Raphael Zagury-Orly, eds., *Judeities: Questions for Jacques Derrida* (New York: Fordham University Press, 2007), 29 (translation slightly altered).]

dynamics of what it meant and could mean to be Jewish were often at stake.[5] Here this conversation continues, two years after Levinas's death, and with the explicit theme of "living together," around which the colloquium was organized in 1998. For Derrida the stakes of such a theme are best invoked in the acknowledgment of its contradictions. As he writes here, crystallizing one of the central tenets of his project, whether with regard to Jewish identity or the nature of law: "to avow this aporia does not suffice, but it is the first condition of a responsible lucidity."

*Grâce, oui, grâce.*

Yes, before even starting, I will risk these two words—of *grâce*. First word, *grâce*, second word, *grâce*. In order to attest to my gratitude, indeed, but also in order to avow while asking for *grâce*.

I would like to render thanks [*grâce*], therefore, and also to ask for your forgiveness [*grâce*].

*Rendering* thanks [*grâce*] to those who have granted me the redoubtable honor of speaking, assigning me, as if by the privilege of an election, a task to which I will always feel unequal, I would also *ask* for their forgiveness, and for yours as well. Asking that one forgive what I will soon avow, I will dare use my avowal as a pretext in order to put forth a general proposition, the formal hypothesis I submit to your discussion.

Which one?

Well, today—I do say *today*—for those one calls contemporaries, for those who one thinks, in a supposed synchrony, *live together* [*pour ceux qui* vivent ensemble], the historical now of a given time; today, therefore, in the same world, facing responsibilities (be they ethical, juridical, religious, and beyond) named by what we call, in so obscure a fashion, in *our* language, "living together [*vivre ensemble*]," well then, a *certain* avowal would announce itself as the first *commandment.*

This is not just any avowal but a singular, unheard of and improbable avowal, an avowal that, prior to and beyond any determined fault, declares before the other the un-avowable. For to avow what seems easy to avow, to avow the avowable, let us recognize, would not be to avow. Let us avow that. The avowal, if there is one, must avow the un-avowable, and must, therefore, *declare* it. The avowal would have to declare, were it possible, the un-avowable, that is to say,

---

5. [See Sarah Hammerschlag, *Broken Tablets: Levinas, Derrida, and the Literary Afterlife of Religion* (New York: Columbia University Press, 2016).]

the unjust, the unjustifiable, the unforgivable, and even the impossibility of avowing. In the same manner, to forgive only that which is forgivable, venial, would not be to forgive. An avowal, if there is such, must avow the unavowable, and forgiveness, if there is such, must forgive the unforgivable—and must, therefore, do the impossible. If such were the condition of the "living together," it would command doing the impossible.

I do not yet know whether declaring, manifesting, confessing, or avowing the un-avowable already supposes the repentance or the return of some *teshuva*: immense enigma, against whose background a globalization of the scene of avowal presents itself. Everywhere, there is the theatrical process of a *return* to the most proximate or to the most distant past, often with repentance and forgiveness asked for, a process of reparation, indemnification or reconciliation. However one interprets it, this globalization of avowal and of repentance perhaps affects or already signifies, like an announcement or like a symptom, a certain mutation of the "living together." Thus would resonate the first *commandment*—be it impracticable—dictated by all "living together."

I will not use this word, *commandment*, lightly.

But here is a first avowal before beginning to justify this word of "commandment" with regard to a "living together"—and I will do nothing here but prepare myself, until the very end, to begin again, for there can be no "living together" that is not devoted to this return, this going back upon oneself or back over one's steps, this repetition of inaugurality. I know that there has been here, in the past, a great conference on forgiveness.[6] What would have changed in the world concerning the scene of forgiveness, since that time, thirty years ago, in the time, that is, of one generation? What is new concerning forgiveness and concerning what the scene of forgiveness implies and engages of a "living together"? Since Jean Halpérin has honored me with this invitation by sharing with me the theme chosen for this encounter, namely, "how to live together [*comment vivre ensemble*]?" I avow that I now live differently with these close and familiar words, words which say something about close ones, about the neighbor and the proximate [*qui disent quelque chose des proches, du prochain*], and about *familiarity* itself, even about family. What is a neighbor [*prochain*] when one knows that no known proximity, above all not that of space and time, suffices to define my close ones [*mes proches*] and even less so my neighbor? My neighbor can be a

6. See Eliane Amado Levy-Valensi and Jean Halpérin, eds., *La conscience juive face à l'histoire: Le pardon* (Paris: Presses Universitaires de France, 1965).

stranger or a foreigner, any other or wholly other [*tout autre*], living very far from me in space and time. This truth has not had to wait for television or the cell telephone. These words, "to live together" and "how" have thus not ceased to accompany me, but they have also and at once failed or escaped my company, becoming for me, in their very familiarity, more and more strange, foreign, enigmatic. "Living together"—yes, but what does that mean? Even before knowing "how"? Is it not both a simple evidence (how could one live otherwise?) and, on the contrary, the promise always of the inaccessible? Suspended in a title and out of context, the tone of this formula remains very unstable. Following the virtual phrases that incline it toward one side or the other, it oscillates between a tone of practical serenity and an accent of tragic pathos, between philosophical wisdom and desperate anguish. Wisdom teaches us: Given that living is always "living together," and that it must be so, let us only learn "how to live together," let us determine rules, norms, maxims, precepts, even an ethical, juridical, and political jurisprudence. But despair protests and replies: "But *how*? How to live together? I will not, you will not, he/she will not, we will not, you will not, they will not, achieve it, ever"—and the variation of these persons also speaks of a deeper paradox as to the same concern: Who addresses whom in asking: "how to live together?" or still: Does not "living together" take place from the instant the concern over this question makes us tremble in our solitude and *avow*, yes, declare our despair and share it?

In a kind of discreet and discontinuous meditation, these two words, "living together," this couple of words that go together, that go well together while letting us think of an impossible marriage (one often says of unwed couples: these two "live together"), these two words, therefore, have both harassed and abandoned me, like two words that go together *without* closing themselves in a togetherness, an ensemble or a gathering—and already there announces itself, between the adverb "together [*ensemble*]" and the noun "ensemble [*ensemble*]," a divorce of which I will make much [*grand cas*]. An intense obsession, if often distracted by the memory I keep of the only time I have attended, without participating, a colloquium such as this one. To attend without participating—is that "living together"? How to "live together" with or for intellectuals said to be French-speaking Jews [*des intellectuals dits juifs de langue française*]? This is not only *my* question, and it is pregnant with so many others. I was attending this colloquium, then, without participating, quite a long time ago, in the 1960s no doubt, probably in 1965. Close to Emmanuel Levinas, near him, perhaps together with him. In truth, I was here thanks [*grâce*] to him, turned toward him. That is still the case today, differently. Another way of recalling, at the moment when I want to salute the name of the admired friend, that one can "live together" with the dead. This will be my conclusion in a moment when I will return, finally, to Jerusalem and tell you about my first visit to the cemetery of this city of which the whole [*l'ensemble*], the being-together [*l'être-ensemble*] remain to be thought. "Living together," with the dead, is not an accident, a miracle or an extraordinary story [*histoire*]. It is rather an essential possibility of existence. It reminds us that in "living together" the idea of life is neither simple nor dominant even if it remains irreducible. "Living together" with the past of those who are no longer and will not be present or living, or with the unpredictable future to come [*avenir*] of those who are not yet living in the present: if this constitutes an irrecusable possibility of the being-with-oneself [*être-avec-soi*], of a "living together" —with-oneself, in a self thus shared or divided, enclosed, multiplied or torn, open too, in any case anachronistic in its very present, at once increased and dislocated by the mourning or the promise of the other in oneself, a larger, older or younger other than oneself, an other outside of oneself in oneself, then "living together" no longer has the simplicity of the "living" in the present pure and simple, no more than the cohesiveness, the coincidence with self of a present whole [*ensemble présent*], living present, present to itself, synchronous with itself, conjoined with itself in a kind of totality. The alterity of irreducible pasts and futures withdraws [*soustrait*] "living together" from the plenitude of a presence to self or from an identity. In order to attempt to think what "living together" might mean [*ce que peut vouloir dire "vivre ensemble"*], one must therefore take into account what occurs [*ce qui arrive*] to what is called the proximity of the other in the present, and not only by way of technology, from television to Internet and cell phones, wireless communication or satellites. The alterity of past and future, the irreducible experience of memory and of the promise, of mourning and of hope, all suppose some *rupture*, the interruption of this identity or of this totality, this accomplishment of a presence to self—a fracturing openness in what one calls *un ensemble* [whole, gathering, ensemble], with the name of *ensemble* which I will distinguish here from the adverb *ensemble* in the expression "*vivre ensemble*." This cannot be without consequences of all kind, and not only ethical, juridical or political, as to what we must meditate on *together* [*ensemble*]. The adverb, in the expression "living together," appears to find its sense and dignity only there where it exceeds, dislocates, contests the authority of the name "ensemble," to wit, the cloture of an ensemble, be it the whole of a "living" [*d'un "vivant"*], of a system, a totality, a cohesiveness without fault and identical with itself, of an indivisible element containing itself in its immanence and simply larger, like the whole [*tout*], than its parts. The authority of the *ensemble* will always be the first threat for all "living together." And inversely, all "living together" will be the first protestation or contestation, the first testimony against the whole [*ensemble*].

Before beginning still, I recall therefore what Emmanuel Levinas told me in an aside on that day, and which I had evoked on the day of his death. I narrate in the present tense as is done sometimes in the rhetoric of historians in order to make things more palpable [*sensible*] to representation. On that day, Levinas speaks words that resonate otherwise as to what "living together" might mean *for Jews*, living or not. André Neher is lecturing, and Levinas whispers in my ear: "You see, he is the Protestant—me, I'm the Catholic." This *mot d'esprit* would call for an infinite commentary. I will raise only one question: What must a Jewish thinker be in order to use this language, with the depth of seriousness and the lightness of irony that we hear in it? How can a so-called Catholic Jew (outside of any conversion, any canonization, and outside of any great ecclesial scene of repentance of which we will speak again) "live together" with a supposed Protestant Jew, while remaining a Jew together with himself, and while opening himself to another Jew, probable or improbable, in this case me, who has never felt very Catholic, and above all not Protestant? A Jew who, coming from another shore of Judaism than Neher and Levinas, a Mediterranean shore, immediately remarks in the abyss of these doubles or of this Abrahamic, Judeo-Catholico-Protestant, triangle, the absence of the Islamo-Abrahamic? And how does a Jew of whom I know only too well, and from so close, that he will never have been sure of being together with himself in general, a Jew who dares not stop at the hypothesis that this dissociation from self renders him *at once* as less Jewish and as most Jewish; how could such a split or divided Jew [*un Juif aussi partagé ou divisé*] have received this remark? How could he welcome its letter according to the spirit that was undeniably breathing in it, to wit, that nothing of all these differences, dissociations or indecisions could damage [*entamer*] the complicity of a certain "living together" that had decided for *us* well before *us*—I name thus the supposed friendship, the affinity, the complicity, if not the shareable solidarity of Jews so different within themselves, so different from themselves within themselves and at their core, be they assured or not of a stable and decidable belonging to Judaism? I would not have let my memory speak, at the risk of appearing complacent, if, after lengthy debates, I had not judged irresponsible to efface, in simple politeness, my signature, that of a Jewish intellectual for whom "living together" with a non-Jewish world was no more serious or more urgent problem than that of "living together" with all the forms of what one calls the Jewish communities of the world—and first of all, for my generation, the Algerian community, the Algerian communities—the Arab, Berber, French of Algeria, French of France, communities, Israeli community, Israeli communities, and beyond. If I trust what remains for me irrecusable or undeniable, to wit, an "I am Jewish," not "I am *first of all* Jewish," but "I am *already and since forever* Jewish and I will it at all cost," this experience of the irrevocable has always tolerated, even demanded, an infinite uncertainty regarding what might be meant by or involved in a "living together" in a Jewish community—and first of all with oneself as Jewish and with oneself in general. It is in this torment that I recall the words of Levinas. In a biography dedicated to him, there is a chapter on the history of the Colloques des intellectuels juifs de langue française which recalls the impressive list of speakers who have participated in its proceedings. One can then read, and I underscore the future tense: "But, among the French philosophers of Jewish origin, one *will* never see Jacques Derrida there." As if I were dead. Or as if the colloquium had already concluded its work and ended the travels of this Booth [*Cabane*] of which Pierre Bouretz spoke so beautifully.[7] This fictitious future, articulating a future anterior, will have belonged, of course, much like the present tense I was invoking earlier, to an unequivocal grammar of the historian of the past; but through its lack of prudence, it announces something else, like my present tense earlier. The thoughtlessness [*légèreté*] of the prediction gives rise to a reflection on time and on what can "occur [*arriver*]" as to the "living together," and on a certain relation of the arrival, the coming or the event to the "living together." It is of this relation between the event and the "living together" that I would like to speak. In this respect, the unstable agreement [*accord*] or belonging, the unresolved, divided modality for such a Jew of *his* "living together" in the Jewish and French communities, without speaking for now of the Israeli community, or simply of "living together" with oneself—such is one of the indecisions, even impossibilities whose avowals I would like to unfold in order to draw a few consequences.

I do not, therefore, as I was saying, use the word "commandment," lightly nor to agree with the spirit of what should be, according to some, a meeting of Jewish intellectuals. No, in its French idiom, "how to live together," in the infinitive

---

7. [An allusion to *Sukkot*, the Feast of Booths (or Tabernacles), and to a remark by Levinas recalled by the philosopher Pierre Bouretz, which referred to the colloquium itself as a traveling booth.]

and without determined subject, a verb plus an adverb, we hear, in the brevity of its sententious ellipsis, the imperious reminder [*rappel*] to what remains an ineluctable necessity, even a *vital* necessity. One *must* [il faut] "live together." Together with the adverb "together," the infinitive "to live" enjoins, it gives at least an implicit assertion: "live together," one must, one must "live together" well and has no choice but to "live together" [*il faut bien "vivre ensemble"*]. In any case [*de toute façon*], in any fashion [*de toutes les façons*], "live together" one must, and one must do so well, one must as well do so [*et il le faut bien*].

This "must [*il faut*]," like the *well* of the one must well, can be modulated in any and all keys. Were we to do scales on an instrument in order to test the tuning of its strings, in order to adjust the ear toward the right note, or at least toward a not too discordant note (unless the false note, the right false note [*la juste fausse note*] were not rigorously required when it is a matter of discording [*détonner*] or going a little out of tune in order to think how difficult the accord and agreement are, the harmony of the "living together," a rare and always improbable thing), we would hear the harmonics of this strange expression ("living together") which has some fairly strict equivalents, it is true, in other languages. Following the French idiom which constitutes, de facto and de jure, and even more than Judaism, even more than the same feeling of supposed belonging to Jewishness, the element of our "being-together," the connotations of the "living together" are distributed from the best to the worst, by way of the last resort, here an inaccessible ideal, there a fatality that itself can be experienced as good, neutral or infernal. The best of the "living together" is often associated with peace, enigmatic concept if there ever was one, and I would have liked to have time for a patient meditation on peace, from Kant to Levinas, a perpetual peace or a messianic peace, whose promise belongs to the very concept of peace and suffices to distinguish it from armistice, from cease-fire or even from any "peace process." Palestinians and Israelis will truly live together only on the day when peace (not only armistice, cease-fire, or the peace process) comes into the bodies and souls, when what is necessary will have been done by those who have the power for it or who, quite simply, have the most power, state power, economic, military, national or international power, to take the initiative for peace in a manner that is first of all wisely unilateral. At bottom, the question of which I will speak tonight could be summarized as the question of initiative, in avowal: Who takes or must take the initiative? And to whom falls the charge of the unilateral decision before all exchange and all reciprocity to come, in the approach of peace or of reconciliation?

But another connotation of the *"bien vivre ensemble,"* that of the last resort, does not wait for peace. It is that of the "one must live together well [*il faut bien vivre ensemble*]," one has no choice. It is, indeed, always a matter of a necessity, and therefore of a law: One cannot not "live together" even if one does not know how or with whom, with God, with gods, men, animals, one's own close ones, neighbors, family or friends, with one's fellow citizens or countrymen, but also with the most distant strangers, with one's enemies, with oneself, with one's contemporaries and with those who are no longer so or will never be so, so many names that I draw from daily language and of which I do not yet presume that we know what they designate. But we sense that the regimes of this law, of the "must [*il faut*]" and therefore of the "well [*bien*]" of "one must as *well* live together," can be different. We know (the example will not surprise you but I could substitute it with so many others) that Israelis and Palestinians, Israelis and Arabs of the Middle East, already must, they must as *well* "live together" whether they are or not for "peace now," whether they are or not orthodox, as one says strangely; and the same goes for the Israelis and for all the Jews of the Diaspora (this name which arbitrarily places them in one ensemble, whether or not they want to, be it under the category of dispersion), whether they are believers or not, favoring or not what one calls the "peace process," agreeing or not with those who, here or there, concur in good conscience or cynically to sabotage the said process; well then, all of these, they must well "live together."

In the inflexions of what we declare here as our language, these "one must as well" of the "one must as well live together," can therefore have heterogeneous values to the point of incompatibility. At least two.

*On the one hand*, the "one must as well" can announce that one will have to live *badly* [*mal*] together (in hatred or in war—which are also manners of living, even of dying together, in the same space and the same time) in lack of trust, indifference or resignation to fatality—as when one suggests sometimes that, short of authentic peace, Israel and the countries of the Middle East must as well *co*-exist, *co*-habitate, *co*-operate, *col*-laborate. War, cold or not, even apartheid, but also peaceful coexistence, the cohabitation of adversaries, including in the sense of the Fifth Republic, are all forms of the "one must as well live together," be it at the price of *not well* agreeing to "live together." And under cohabitation, in the sense of the Fifth Republic, there present themselves at this time, in a nonfortuitous manner, major and conflictual stakes that divide the French community as to the "living together": Beyond the thousand problems of Europe and of social justice, in a sharper fashion yet, three fundamental questions of the "living together" put this cohabitation to the test today, questions that are no longer only French but to which Jews are particularly sensitive: the question of hospitality to foreigners, immigrants with or without permits, the questions of civil unions and of marriage, the question of national memory, in particular (since one could multiply examples) that of World War I, even before the 1930s and 40s, there where another imagery of the trenches of 1914–1918 and thus of so many other structuring phantasms come to unsettle [*inquiéter*] the most re-assuring and the most consensual foundations, foundations that are, however, non-natural, constructed and fragile, of the national "living together."

It is true that even in these negative hypotheses of the "one must as well live together," the common value of a higher interest is accepted by the partners, even the enemies, that it is better to live than to die (living, surviving, would then be, in this hypothesis, the unconditional imperative, as problematic as it remains). Even if this cohabitation is resigned, armed, organized, at times guaranteed by a contract, a constitution and some institutional jurisprudence, it answers to a common, and therefore higher, interest. This calculation supposes at least three axioms at once powerful and fragile:

1. One cannot not suppose that this reasoned cohabitation represents a temporary situation destined to save the promise of an *avenir*, a to-come, and that the *avenir* of this *avenir* should keep the figure of a "living together" free of these negative limits, of this statutory surveillance. An authentic peace to come, a peace without end or infinite remains the quasi-messianic horizon of this armed peace or of this armistice. What goes here for communities, nations or states can also be valid for families or individuals.

2. One cannot not suppose some consensus as to what "living" means, and that it is worth more and better than dying—which is far from self-evident, no more than it is self-evident that some forms of "dying" do not figure a certain manner of "living together." Dying together, in the *same* place and at the *same* moment, for those whom Montaigne calls the "co-dying [*commourans*]," some can see here the supreme ordeal of the "living together." What does "same" mean in these expressions? Here is an enigma I do not yet touch on.

3. One cannot not suppose that each partner of this coexistence or of this co-habitation is identical to himself, should be one and together with him—which is far from self-evident, whether it be a matter of humanity, the nation or the nation-state, and therefore the citizen, whether it be a question of no matter what community or class of so-called civil society, or simply a family, each individual and of what one strangely calls close ones or one's own, of "me," or whoever

says "me" and claims in all conscience—I mean, without taking account of some unconscious—to decide and to take responsibility. But, *on the other hand*, the syntagma "il faut *bien* vivre ensemble" can let itself be otherwise accented in *our* language, and signal toward a "well [*bien*]," a "living *well* together [bien *vivre ensemble*]," that no longer incidentally qualifies a fundamental or previous "living together." "Living together" then means living together "well [*bien*], according to the good [*le bien*]: not only some euphoria of a living, of the good-life, of the *savoir-vivre* or an art of living, but also according to a good of trust, of accord or of concord." This "good [*bien*]" intrinsic to the "living together," no one will *reasonably* think (but it is this reasonable that we interrogate here) of dissociating it from peace, from harmony, from accord and concord. If "living together" then means "living *well* together," this signifies understanding one another in trust, in good faith, in faith, comprehending one another, in a word, being in *accord* with one another. Why then speak of accord? Why this language of the heart [*cœur*], of the accord and concord, even of "mercy [*miséricorde*]" and of the compassion which must bring us closer and a bit more quickly, to the question of "forgiveness," with or without *teshuva*? The language of the heart reminds us that this peace of the "living together," even if it is a peace of justice and equity, is not necessarily under the law of the law, at least in the sense of legality, of law [*droit*] (national or international) or of the political contract; and here, as I often do, I will distinguish, but without opposing them, justice and law [*la justice et le droit*]. Let us turn our ear toward the French idiom: One says for example of the partners of a couple (man and woman, man and man, woman and woman) that they "live together" when, outside of the law or the instituted obligations of marriage, even of a civil union, they decide, freely and of a common accord, to share their life, their time, the places of life (the land on earth) and sometimes, with the time and the land of their history, with their memory and their mourning, the *avenir* of a generation, children by them (men and women) engendered or adopted, etc. (Hence my allusion to the PACS and to the mutineers of World War I, announcement of two earthquakes, the rumbling of which remains still discreet.)[8] Not that the "living together" demands a rupture with the normality of law or with marriage (spouses can well "live together," and legality does not exclude the "living *well* together"). But even in the cases of the most reassuring juridical normality

---

8. [PACS refers to the *pacte civil de solidarité*, the official term for civil unions, instituted in October 1999 by the French legislature to legalize domestic partnerships outside marriage.]

(with or without civil union), there is a "living *well* together" only to the extent that something which I will elliptically call here the heart, the love or the peace of the heart, the *fiance* [of *confiance*], the accord or concord, exceeds the contract guaranteed by law or state legislation. Henceforth, if some ethics of the "living together" thus appears to be implied by the idiomatic usage that I content myself for now with analyzing, it supposes accord beyond any statutory condition, not necessarily in contradiction with it, but beyond and across the normality of a legal, political, and state-controlled bond between two or more than one (male or female) who are not only spouses, co-citizens, co-countrymen, congeners or coreligionist individuals, but remain strangers, (from) others and radically other. The peace of "living together," therefore, exceeds the juridical, even the political, at any rate, the political as determined by the state, by the sovereignty of the state. This "living together," even where it is irreducible to the statutory or institutional (juridical, political, state-controlled) bond, opens another dimension to the same necessity—and that is why I have spoken of the other, of the stranger, of a hospitality to the wholly other who exceeds the statutory convention. The "good" of the "living well together" supposes the interruption of the *natural* as well as *conventional* relation; it supposes even this *interruption tout court* that one calls absolute solitude, separation, inviolable secret. This separation (which was also one of the great themes of Levinas), is precisely that which opens without contradicting, all the "must" of "one must live together well." Through paradoxes and aporias about which I will even claim shortly that one must avow, one will not say that the parts of one and the same natural, organic and living ensemble *live together*. The adverb "together" in the expression "living together" does not refer to the totality of a natural, biological or genetic ensemble, to the cohesiveness of an organism or of some social body (family, ethnic group, nation) that would be measured with this organic metaphor. "Living together" supposes therefore, an interrupting excess *both* with regard to statutory convention, to law *and* with regard to *symbiosis*, to a symbiotic, gregarious or fusional living together. I would go so far as to say—this appeared to me serious enough not to be accepted too easily—that all "living together" that would limit itself to the symbiotic or that would be regulated according to a figure of the symbiotic or the organic is a first lapse of the sense [*un manquement au sens*] and of the "must" of the "living together." Here is, therefore, a double and paradoxical prescription. It is inscribed in the idiom, that is to say, already in a mode of the "living together." "Living together" is reducible neither to organic symbiosis nor to the juridico-political contract. Neither to "life" according to nature or birth, blood or soil, nor to life according to convention, contract or institution. "Living together," if it were possible, would mean putting to the test the insufficiency of this old couple of concepts that conditions, in the West, more or less any metaphysics, any interpretation of the social bond, any political philosophy or any sociology of the being-together, the old couple *physis/nomos, physis/thesis*, nature/convention, biological life/law [*droit*]—law which I distinguish here, more than ever, from justice and from the justice of "living together." One will never think the "living together" and the "living" of the "living together" and the "how together" unless one transports oneself *beyond everything* that is founded upon this opposition of nature/culture. That is to say, beyond everything, more or less everything. This excess with regard to the laws of nature, as well as to the laws of culture, is always an excess with regard to the whole [*ensemble*], and I do not take the difficulty lightly. It is almost unthinkable, very close to impossibility, precisely. This excess does not signify that law, a non-legal law or a non-juridical justice, does not continue to command the sense and the "must" of the "one must live together well." Which law? And can a "declaring oneself Jewish," in whatever mode (and there are so many) grant a privileged access to this justice, to this law beyond laws [*cette loi au-dessus des lois*]?

We lack time to deploy this argument in the code of a philosophical analysis that would refer itself to universal and impersonal structures and would appeal to numerous texts. Under the heading of "declaring oneself Jewish," I would rather confide in you, and perhaps avow that these philosophical necessities have imposed themselves upon me through the modest experience of someone who, prior to becoming what you call a "French-speaking Jewish intellectual [*intellectuel juif de langue française*]," was first a young Jew in French Algeria between three wars (before, during, and after World War II; before, during, and after the so-called war of Algeria). In a country where the number and the diversity of historical communities was as rich as in Jerusalem, West to East, this Jewish child could dream of a peaceful, cultural, linguistic, and even national plural belonging only through the experience of nonbelonging: separations, rejections, ruptures, exclusions. If I did not forbid myself any lengthy first-person discourse (but is there "living together" otherwise than among "first persons"?), I would describe the contradictory movement that, at the time of the anti-Semitic zeal of the French authorities in Algeria during the war, pushed a little boy who was expelled from school and understood none of it to rebel, forever, against two ways of "living together": at once against racist gregariousness, and therefore against anti-Semitic segregation, but also, more obscurely, and more unavowable, no doubt, against the conservative and self-protective confinement, of a Jewish community that seeking *naturally, legitimately* to defend itself, to constitute or reconstitute its whole [*ensemble*] under the ordeal of these traumas, was folding upon itself, overbidding in the direction that I already then felt as a kind of exclusive, even fusional, communitarism. Believing that he was beginning to understand what "living together" could mean, the child of which I speak had to break then, in a manner that was as unreflective as reflective, with both sides, with both exclusive —and thus excluding—belongings. The only belonging, the only "living together," that he judged then bearable and worthy of that name already supposed a rupture with an identitarian and totalizing belonging, assured of itself in a homogeneous whole [*ensemble*]. In a manner as unreflective as reflective, the child felt at his core two contradictory things as to what this "living together" could signify: on the one hand, that he could betray his own, his close ones, and Judaism, and that he had to avow this within himself, even before others, even before God, but also, on the other hand, that by this separation, this rupture, this passage toward a kind of universality beyond symbiotic communitarism and gregarious fusion, beyond even citizenship, in this very separation, it could be that he was more faithful to a certain Jewish vocation, at the risk of remaining the only, the last and the least of the Jews [*le seul et le dernier des Juifs*], in the most ambiguous sense of this expression with which he played without playing— elsewhere and fifty years later, presenting himself or sometimes also hiding himself like a kind of paradoxical Marrano who ran the risk of losing even the culture of his secret or the secret of his culture. For, at the core of this solitude, this child had to begin believing, and he no doubt never finished thinking, that any "living together" supposes and guards, as its very condition, the possibility of this singular, secret, inviolable separation, from which, and from which alone a stranger accords himself to a stranger, in hospitality. To recognize that one lives together, well then, only with and as a stranger, a stranger "at home [*chez soi*]," in all the figures of the "at home," that there is "living together" only there where the whole [*ensemble*] is neither formed nor closed [*ne se forme pas et ne se ferme pas*], there where the living *together* [*ensemble*] (the adverb) contests the completion, the closure and the cohesiveness of an "ensemble" (the noun, the substantive), of a substantial, closed ensemble identical to itself; to recognize that there is "living together" only there where, in the name of promise and of memory, of the messianic and of mourning without work and without healing, it welcomes dissymmetry, anachrony, nonreciprocity with an other who is greater, at once older and younger than it, an other who comes or will come *perhaps*, who has *perhaps already* come—here is the justice of a law above laws, here is a paradox which I believe coherent with what we were saying a moment ago of a "living together" that does not allow itself to be contained, exhausted or governed, either in a natural or organic (genetic or biologic) whole, or in a juridico-institutional one. And this, whatever the name one gives to these natural or institutional wholes (organism, family, neighborhood, nation, nation-state, with their territorial space or the time of their history). Levinas recalled the bond between Jewish universalism and the respect of the stranger, in his lesson, "Toward the Other" with the commentary of a text from Tractate *Yoma* around *teshuva* (a lesson I will not have time to interrogate in my turn with the attentiveness I would have liked). "The respect for the stranger," he says, "and the sanctification of the name of the Eternal are strangely equivalent. And all the rest is a dead letter. All the rest is literature. . . . The image of God is better honored in the right given to the stranger than in symbols. Universalism . . . bursts the letter apart, for it lay, explosive, within the letter."[9] The faithful child of whom I speak, faithful to this solitude and obligated toward a singular interruption, believed he did not have, in growing up to salve these first wounds. If the memory of anti-Semitic persecutions, well beyond those he could have suffered himself, remained as unerasable, as present in everything he thought, said or wrote, or taught, in return, the same vigilance was warning him, warns him today, against all the risks of the "living together" of the Jews, be they of a symbiotic type (naturalized, birth, blood, soil, nation) or conventional (state juridical, in the modern sense): a certain communitarism, a certain Zionism, a certain nationalism and all that can follow as to the motifs of filiation through blood, appropriation of the place, and the motif of election, all run the risk of remaining caught—I am saying "risk" because this is not a fatality, and there is where the moment of responsibility is found—in the grip of nature or of convention. I do not have time here to develop all the philosophical and political analyses that, for the child turned adult, have sharpened this concern, but I must declare, or, if you prefer, avow that this concern was and remains with me without complacency and sometimes without pity. It pushes the said child not only to oppose, sometimes publicly, the politics of the current Israeli government and of a great number of those who preceded it, but to continue to interrogate himself in the most insomniac fashion regarding the conditions in which

9. [Emmanuel Levinas, *Nine Talmudic Readings*, trans. A. Aronowicz (Bloomington: Indiana University Press, 1990), 27-28; Emmanuel Levinas, *Quatre lectures talmudiques* (Paris: Minuit, 1968), 60-61. Aronowicz's translation is slightly altered.]

the modern state of Israel established itself. If there is a place where I do not have the right to hide this, it is here. I hasten to immediately add at least two things: (1) that one can remain radically critical in this regard without implying thereby any threatening or disrespectful consequences for the present, the future, and the existence of Israel, on the contrary; (2) that I have been able to perceive, and to rejoice at this during my last visit to Israel and to Palestine, that these questions, these "returns" (reflections, repentances, conscious realizations) upon certain founding violences are today more frequent and declared by certain Israelis, citizens and authentic patriots, and by new historians of the state of Israel, the ones and the others having decided to draw political consequences from this return to the past, as some Palestinians do as well. The child of whom I speak and that makes me speak understood in growing up that any juridico-political founding of a "living together" is, by essence, violent, since it inaugurates there where a law [*droit*] did not yet exist. The founding of a state or of a constitution, therefore, of a "living together" according to a state of law [*un état de droit*], is always first of all a nonlegal violence: not illegal but non-legal, otherwise put, *unjustifiable* with regard to an existing law, since the law is inexistent there where it is a matter of creating it. No state has ever been founded without this violence, whatever form and whatever time it might have taken. But the child of whom I speak asked himself whether the founding of the modern state of Israel—with all the politics and policies that have followed and confirmed it—could be no more than an example among others of this originary violence from which no state can escape, or whether, because this modern state intended not to be a state like others, it had to appear before another law and appeal to another justice. I recall here this classical question because I intend to take into consideration in a moment a certain globalization of law and of scenes of repentance or of forgiveness asked for when the instance in front of which this appearance is instituted is no longer national, nor does it belong to the state.

If I let a Jewish child speak, it is neither to move you cheaply, nor to shelter provocations behind an alibi. Rather it is to convince you that my questions, my reticences, my impatiences, my indignation sometimes (for example, when faced with the politics of almost all the Israeli governments and the forces that support them, from within and from without) are not inspired by hostility or by the indifference of distance. On the contrary, shared with so many Israelis who are exposed and concerned otherwise than I am, and together with so many Jews in the world, this innocent concern for compassion (a fundamental mode, in my view, of "living together"), of this compassion of justice and equity (*raha-*

*mim*, perhaps), I will claim it, if not as the essence of Judaism, at least as what remains in me inseparable from the suffering and disarmed memory of the Jewish child, there where he has learned to name justice and what in justice at once exceeds and demands law [*le droit*]. Everything comes to me, no doubt, from this source, in what I am about to say, under the title "avowing—the impossible."

"Avowing—the impossible." This can signify at once "one must avow and, therefore, avow the un-avowable," and this avowing of the unavowable remains perhaps impossible but of an impossibility that must be rendered manifest— even and precisely if it appears impossible. Put otherwise, the truth is that one must do the impossible, and the impossible would perhaps be the only measure of any "must [*il faut*]."

How and why grant *today* such privilege to the avowing of the unavowable? Since I have *chosen* to place this modest address under the sign of the avowal, you have the right to ask me why I am about to do so in such paradoxical and suspicious fashion, to the point of declaring the command to avow to be as necessary as impossible.

The choice of this theme was an election, and therefore a selection, therefore an exclusion that I could not justify in a rational fashion, but for which I would account in a solely economic and conditional mode—and this too I must avow. Economical and conditional, because I have committed myself to treating an infinite enigma ("living together") for an hour and a few minutes (on such a topic, this is the time of one of those telegrams that one no longer sends), and to do so in a language shared by all of us who are here together (first response to any injunction of the "living together"), and so a language that resists my temptations, and first of all the temptation that would consist in wagering on the double and abyssal memory that opens upon the immense question of the "living together" by multiplying allusions on the side of a philosophical memory, from Aristotle, Rousseau, Kant, Heidegger or Husserl, to Marx, Nietzsche or Levinas, to the metaphysics or to the ontology of the being-with (*Mitsein*), to the socius, intersubjectivity, the phenomenological constitution of the transcendental *alter ego*, to the social bond and to dissociation, to the relation without relation to the other, to Blanchot's "unavowable community" or Nancy's "inoperative community," and so on. And how to faithfully treat, at this rhythm, a tradition of Jewish thought on the topic of "living together" but also on the return, repentance, pardon, reconciliation and reparation (on *teshuva* or *tikkun* in the treasure of canonical texts or their repetition [*reprise*] by Leo Baeck, for example, Hermann Cohen or Emmanuel Levinas)? If I have chosen the theme of avowal, that is first of all because of what is occurring [*ce qui se passe*] *today* in the world, a kind of general rehearsal [*répétition*], a scene, even a theatrical rendering [*théâtralisation*] of avowal, of return and repentance which seems to me to signify a mutation in process, a fragile one, to be sure, fleeting and difficult to interpret, but, like the moment of an undeniable rupture in the history of the political, of the juridical, of the relations between community, civil society and the State, between sovereign states, international law and NGOs, among the ethical, the juridical and the political, between the public and the private, between national citizenship and an international citizenship, even a metacitizenship, in a word, concerning a social bond that crosses [*passe*] the borders of these ensembles called family, nation or state. Sometimes accompanied by what one names rightly or wrongly repentance, sometimes preceded or accompanied by what one believes, rightly or wrongly, must condition them, namely confession, repentance, forgiveness asked for—scenes of avowal are multiplied and have been accelerating for a few years, months, weeks, every day in truth, in a public space transformed by tele-technologies and by media capital, by the speed and the reach of communication, but also by the multiple effects of a technology, a techno-politics and a techno-genetics that unsettle [*bouleverse*] at once all conditions: conditions of being-together (the supposed proximity, in the same instant, in the same place and the same territory, as if the unicity of a place on earth, of a soil, were becoming more and more—as one says of a telephone and with the measure of said telephone—*portable*) *and* the conditions of the living in its technological relation to the nonliving, to the hetero- or homo-grafting, to prosthesis, artificial insemination, cloning, and so on. Largely exceeding the territory of the state or of the nation, all these scenes of avowal and of reexamination of past crimes call upon the testimony, even the judgment of a community, and so of a modality of the living-together, virtually universal but also virtually instituted as an infinite court or a world confessional.

I could recall a great number of different but analogous examples, and intentionally juxtapose the most heterogeneous cases, from the memorable gesture of Willy Brandt in front of the monument of the Warsaw Ghetto, the famous declaration of the bishops of Poland and Germany at the Fiftieth anniversary of the liberation of Auschwitz, that of the French Church, of the corporations of physicians and the police, to the speeches of heads of state such as Jacques Chirac who declared that France had committed the "irreparable." In all these cases, it is a matter of crime against humanity from which Jews were not the only ones suffering but of which they were massively the designated victims and always named in these declarations of guilt. As problematic as it remains, and whatever the elaborations it still calls for, the concept of crime against humanity (created, as you know, by the international court at Nuremberg in 1945) is the juridical mechanism of this globalization of avowal. This unprecedented event affects at its root a condition of "living together"; but it also marks the aftereffect of a moment in the history of humanity that keeps the wound of the Shoah, even if it is not, of course, reducible to that. This advent of a new juridical concept is the very memory of the Shoah. I would go so far as to say, since I cannot cite so many analogous examples, that the recent promises of the Vatican regarding the examination of conscience as to the Inquisition are inseparable from the same presuppositions, I mean, from the bottomless trauma of the Shoah, of its memory, whether assumed or denied. This globalization of avowal is therefore not thinkable in its inaugural emergence without what happened to the Jews of Europe in the twentieth century, nor is it any more separable from the international recognition of the state of Israel, a legitimation I would also interpret as one of the first moments of this avowal and of this world's bad conscience.

These acts of public repentance address themselves to crimes against the Jews, but one could just as well recall analogous declarations by Vaclav Havel toward the Sudetenland; by Prime Minister Murayama in his own name a few years ago and, more recently, in the name of the Japanese government as such toward the Koreans, as well as what is happening at this very moment between the Chinese and the Japanese; by President Clinton, not only regarding the sinister and significant matter of the impeachment, but first of all regarding the recognition in 1998 in Africa—without, however, any act of official contrition —of an American responsibility in the history of the African slave trade and the infinite violence of slavery—which, like the violence done to Native Americans, is inseparable from the foundation of the United States. One thinks above all of that extraordinary "Truth and Reconciliation" Commission in South Africa, which was itself preceded by analogous, if not identical, institutions in Chile and Argentina (these, however, did not address violences and traumas affecting communities as different among themselves as in South Africa). These events have, to my knowledge, no antecedents in the history of humanity, in the history of states or of nation-states which thus find themselves appearing in court, as it were, in front of an instance above the state. Yet, all these scenes have in common a feature that is at once double and indivisible. On the one hand, their common presupposition will have been the possibility opened after World War II of recognizing and judging in front of an international instance Nazi violence and, in it, the extermination project called "holocaust" which aimed explicitly and in the first place at the Jews, the Romani and homosexuals. On the other hand, and with the aim of making this extermination appear before a universal jurisdiction, the creation of the Nuremberg court and the institution in international law of the new concept of "crime against humanity"—which France in 1964 declared henceforth "imprescriptible." As problematic and insufficient as it remains in my view, as I have said, this concept announces an irreversible progress. It is implied in all the scenes of repentance, of avowal, and of forgiveness asked for. For example, the global and local fight for the abolition of apartheid, followed by the institution of the Truth and Reconciliation Commission, was possible only because of the official recognition of apartheid as a crime against humanity—by the UN among others. This international juridical act provides a reference upon which the Commission grants itself its authority. It articulates a logic signifying that any state racism (which the "living together" that called itself apartheid was), any racism, and any segregation based on birth, where it is encouraged or permitted in the laws of a state, is a crime against humanity. As imperfect as it remains, this concept is on the horizon of all the progresses to come of international law, of the difficult but irresistible institution of international courts as well as the practical setting to work of any declaration of human rights (something which still remains largely to come if one considers the incommensurable inequalities in the living conditions of human beings); not to speak of what, in the life of what are called animals and in the living together with the living ones that are called, in undifferentiated fashion, animals—for there is also a "living together" with animals—calls up tasks that exceed even the concepts of law and of duty and would have to obligate us to rethink the great question of sacrifice.

I hasten to conclude with the consequences that follow, and I will draw in general lines a series of contradictions that not only do not forbid "living together" but, were they to be declared or avowed, would, on the contrary, provide the condition of "living together" and the chance of a responsibility.

1. *First aporia. On the one hand*, we know that the globalization of avowal, of repentance and of return upon past crimes, with or without forgiveness asked for, can indeed dissimulate facilities, alibis, perverse strategies, instrumentalization, a comedy or a calculation. It calls, then, for an endless vigilance. Yet, it nonetheless resembles those events in which a thinker of the Enlightenment (Kant, in this case) thought he recognized *at least* the sign, *at least* the possibility, of an irreversible progress of humankind. It marks a beyond of national law,

even the beyond of a politics measured only by the sovereignty of the nation-state. Nation-states, institutions (corporations, armies, churches) must appear before a court; sometimes former heads of state or military leaders must give account—whether willingly or not—in front of instances that are in principle universal, in front of an international law that does not cease to be refined and to consolidate new nongovernmental powers, to force belligerent parties to recognize their past crimes and negotiate over the peace of a new "living together," to judge in exemplary fashion governing individuals (dictators or not) while being careful not to forget the states, sometimes foreign states, that have sustained or manipulated them (the important signal constituted by the removal of Pinochet's immunity would have to go far beyond his own person, and even beyond his own country). More generally, with all the questions that these developments leave open, what one calls humanitarian intervention is not the only space of such new interventions.

But *on the other hand*, if one must salute this progress which sketches a beyond of state-national sovereignty and even of the political inasmuch as it remains since the beginning, in fact co-extensive with the state and with the exercise of citizenship, one can also see emerging possible perversions of this progress: not only a legalism that replaces politics [*politisme*], a reduction of justice to law, a surreptitious appropriation of the universal juridical powers (there is no enforcing law without a force of application, as the same Kant reminded us with good sense), a logic of the alibi or of the scapegoat in the determination of the accused subjects, a hijacking of international law by different forces and camps, by economic or state-national powers which would submit this exercising of law, and even so-called humanitarian action, to unjust strategies and to a disguised politics before which the recourse to the sovereignty of the nation-state would sometimes have to remain an irreducible site of resistance. All the more so since this new legalism, sustained by technological resources of investigation, communication, ubiquity, and unprecedented speed, runs the risk of reconstituting, under the pretext of transparency, a new inquisitorial obsession that transforms anybody into a subject or a defendant summoned to "live together" according to the ensemble, while renouncing not only what one names with the old name of "private life," the invisible practice of faith, and so on but also, and quite simply, while renouncing this possibility of the secret, of separation, of solitude, of silence and of singularity, of this interruption that remains, we have seen, the inalienable condition of "living together," of responsibility and of decision. Were the time given to me, I would have offered, in order to sharpen the blade of this aporia, a reading, for today, of what happened [*ce qui se passa*] in the silence and the secret of a certain Abraham on Mount Moriah from this perspective.

If these two exigencies and these two antinomic risks are indisputable and so grave, there are no knowable and prior norms to regulate or finalize our response. The responsibility for the most just decision must be invented each time in a unique fashion, by each one, in a singular time and place. To hold myself to the letter of our theme, well then, for the "living together" that I am proposing we think beyond any "ensemble," there is no "how," there is, in any case, no "how" that could take the form of precepts, of rules, of norms or previous criteria available to a knowledge. The "how" must be invented by each at each moment. There would be no singular responsibility if a "how" were available in advance to the knowledge of a rule to be applied. What I am saying here is anything but empirical or relativistic; it responds to what I hold as the most demanding in ethical experience [*l'expérience morale*]. One must then at least begin to declare this antinomy, to recognize and acknowledge it, to avow it to oneself, to avow it before the other, every other, before the stranger, and even before the enemy. There where it seems unavowable and because it is unavowable. One must recognize and acknowledge this division, this tearing, this rift, this dissociation from oneself, this difficulty of living together with oneself, to gather in an ensemble, in a totality of cohesiveness and coherence: the first step of a "living together" will always remain rebellious to totalization.

2. *Another aporia* runs the risk of paralyzing this movement. The ethics of "forgiveness" is, I believe, profoundly divided by two heterogeneous motifs of the Abrahamic tradition, Jewish, Christian or Islamic, which has bequeathed it to us. Without wanting to reduce these three legacies to the same, far from it, and without being able here to involve myself in the treatment that this immense question would deserve without stopping either at the profound—actually Hegelian—Christianization that marks the language of this globalization of avowal (there is here an effect of what I have called globalization in process [*la mondialisation en cours*], and not only in law), I will mention only one paradox. The heirs that we are, feel that the movement of forgiveness is found between two logics, at once heterogeneous to each other and yet undissociable. *On the one hand*, there should be forgiveness only under the form of a gracious, unconditional, free, infinite and unilateral gift, without an economic circle of reciprocity—that is to say, even there where the other does not expiate, does not repent, and therefore even if the "living together" does not inscribe itself in a horizon of reconciliation, of reparation, of healing, of indemnification, and of

redemption. An unconditional forgiveness is an absolute initiative that no calculation, whether sublime or spiritual, should motivate. But, *on the other hand*, the same tradition reminds us, in a prevalent, dominant, and hegemonic fashion, this time, that forgiveness cannot be granted but in a conditional fashion, there where there is acknowledgment of a fault, avowal, repentance, return upon the past, present or future transformation, forgiveness asked. Although in his book on *Forgiveness* [*Le pardon*], Vladimir Jankélévitch had spoken of a *hyperbolical* ethics of forgiveness, he nonetheless firmly declared—especially during the time when, in France, one was debating the imprescriptibility of crimes against humanity—that forgiveness could not be granted to those who never asked for it by pleading guilty. "Forgiveness died in the death camps," he had already said, in a less polemical mode, in his philosophical book on forgiveness. What sense, indeed, would forgiveness have, there where the guilty one does not await it, and first of all does not know nor acknowledge the crime? This strong logic, this economy, precisely where it seems to me hardly compatible with this other postulation of unconditional forgiveness—we know that it dominates, even if it does not exhaust them, both the Abrahamic traditions and the actual politics of forgiveness. At the very moment in which he recalls that "the principle of Jewish forgiveness" becomes a "pure rule, unanimously acknowledged by man, and by him uniquely, before the Lord," Hermann Cohen does not dissociate forgiveness from repentance. With this "forgiveness," which is, he says, explicitly designed as the objective of the Torah, he then associates, as if it were one and the same thing, *teshuva* which, he recalls, designates repentance and means "return," "change," return to the good, return unto oneself. The instigator of sacrificial worship is also herald of repentance that figures as a major act in any "ethics and at the core of any divine worship." "Even God cannot redeem me," Cohen dares to say, "without my own moral effort and repentance."[10] As legitimate as it may seem (and I do not want to denounce it), this placing under condition of the unconditional governs the practices of a forgiveness there where the latter remains nonetheless heterogeneous, in its unconditionality, to all these orders (ethical, political, juridical) and to the goals of reconciliation, reparation amnesty or prescription. One recognizes the figure of cure, of self-healing, and

10. [See Hermann Cohen, "Die Versöhnungsidee" and "Der Tag der Versöhnung," in *Jüdische Schriften*, vol. 1 (Berlin: C. A. Schwetschke, 1924), 132, 143; Hermann Cohen, *Reason and Hope*, trans. E. Jospe (Cincinnati: Hebrew Union College Press, 1993), 206, 212. Jospe's translation is slightly altered.]

"living together," in the South African discourse of the Truth and Reconciliation Commission (above all where it is moderated and interpreted in a Christian
sense by Desmond Tutu—something that forces us to ask ourselves whether
the globalization of avowal is a planetarization of the Abrahamic concept, or
more specifically Christian concept, of forgiveness, or, on the contrary, a new
mutation that brings about [*qui fait arriver*] something unexpected, something
even threatening to this tradition—I cannot engage here this necessary but
immense question). What the South African example brings into evidence, is
a process of repentance, of amnesty or of prescription—which one confuses
too quickly with forgiveness—a work of mourning that one interprets as *healing away*,[11] an act of memory as healing that overcomes the trauma and enables
wounded communities to "live together." One dreams, of course, that other
wounded countries, each in its own way, might be inspired in the foreword to
the South African, in spite of all the ambiguities [*équivoques*] of which I speak.
But as equivocal and as conditional as it is, as threatening as it is to the purity of
forgiveness, this motif of healing is not only at the heart of all the dominant in-
terpretations of forgiveness. One finds it operating at the heart of the great Jewish reflections on *teshuva* in this century. One could cite not only Baeck, Cohen
and Buber, but also, as Dominique Bourel recalled in a recent article, Scheler
—another Catholic of Jewish origins who spoke of repentance as "*Selbstheilung*
of the soul," self-healing of the soul.[12]

Under the sign of *teshuva*, of what he translates as "return, relation with God,"
and "absolutely internal event," Levinas appeals to "unconditional justice" in his
"Text on Tractate *Yoma*," but he nonetheless submits forgiveness to condition
and asks that it be asked for: "There can be no forgiveness that the guilty party
has not sought! The guilty party must recognize his fault. The offended party
must want to receive the entreaties of the offending party. Further, no person
can forgive if forgiveness has not been asked of him by the offender, if the guilty
party has not tried to appease the offended." Here too, I will not follow the subtle
trajectory of this meditation, all the paths and the voices [*les voies et les voix*] that
cross each other in it, all the way to the double limit where, recalling what he
calls the "conditions of forgiveness," Levinas quickly evokes the essential pos-

11. Translator's note: the phrase "healing away" is in English in the original text.
12. Dominique Borel, "Note bibliographique: La *Teshuva* dals la pensée juive du XXe
siècle," in *Retour, repentir et constitution de soi*, ed. Annick Charles-Saget (Paris: Vrin, 1998),
210.

sibility of the offending one's unconscious which should bring one to conclude, I quote: "In essence, forgiveness is impossible." Levinas also evokes in passing, still a bit furtively perhaps, another border, a decisive one, to my mind, a limit touched upon by an opinion that was preserved in the *Gemara*, that of Rabbi Yehuda ha-Nassi, who speaks of a purifying forgiveness, on the day of Kippur, without *teshuva, without* repentance.[13] On the edge of that same limit, in an elliptical text that remained unpublished in his lifetime, on "the signification of time in the moral world" and on the Last Judgment, Walter Benjamin too, spoke of a storm of divine forgiveness which blows to its own limit, but without ever merging with a movement or an economy of reconciliation: a forgiveness (*Vergebung*) without reconciliation (*Versöhnung*). Beyond its legal code and its penal limits, the concept of *imprescriptibility* signals toward a Last Judgment: until the end of times, the criminal (dictator, torturer, nation-state guilty of crimes against humanity) will have to appear before a court and give account. There is no longer an end to responsibility that the guilty one could assume. Ever. It is of this impossible that I would have wanted to speak as the only chance of forgiveness —in all of its ethical and political consequences. It is similar to the avowable and the un-avowable: if I avow only what is avowable, I am not avowing. To avow is to avow the unavowable, much like forgiving is forgiving the unforgivable: doing the impossible.

Well, then, since I will never feel justified in renouncing the necessity of a forgiveness conditioned upon repentance, nor in renouncing the demand without demand [*exigence sans exigence*], and without duty, and without debt, of unconditional forgiveness that gives its sense to any pure thought of forgiveness, the only responsibility I cannot escape is to declare to the other this dilemma; it is to take the initiative, as I do here, of this declaration and to commit myself to drawing its juridical, ethical, political, and historical consequences. By reason of what I have just said, I must do so *alone* and even if I am the only one to take this initiative, without expecting reciprocity, alone and there where I am irreplaceable in this responsibility. It is thus that I understand or accept the concept of election, there where being chosen, well beyond any privilege of birth, nation, people or community, signifies that no one can replace me at the site of this decision and of this responsibility. And this does not erase, on the contrary, the transgenerational or collective responsibilities that torment the sleep of innocents.

3. One would then have to avow a *third aporia* of "living together." I will never

13. Levinas, *Nine Talmudic Readings*, 18.

be able to renounce and to say no to a preference for "my own" [les "miens"], nor, inversely, to justify it, to have it approved as the law of a universal justice. Those whom I call, in this undeniable but unjustifiable hierarchy, *my own*, are not those who belong to me; it is the ensemble of those with whom, precisely, it is *given to me*, prior to any choice, to "live together," in all the dimensions of what one calls so easily a community: my family, my congeners, countrymen, co-religionists, my neighbors [*mes voisins*], my close ones, those who speak my language, and I would go so far as to say, my neighbor [*mon prochain*], there where this word, in the biblical tradition, can designate as well the distant stranger, but on the condition that he be my fellow man [*mon semblable*], man and brother in humanity (I have elsewhere interrogated the ambivalences of this notion of fraternity, I cannot revisit this here).[14] How to renounce it, but also how to justify my preference for all the forms of the proximate, of this proximity that at the limit, in situations of mortal danger, would carry me to the rescue of my children rather than of those of another, rather than to the rescue of all those others who are not only my others, at the rescue of a man rather than an animal, and even of my cat rather than a cat unknown to me and dying in Asia? In the eyes of justice or of universal equality, how to justify a preference for one's own children, a preference for one's own, parents and friends, even a preference among one's own, as far as death and ultimate sacrifice, the privilege of Isaac, for example, rather than Ishmael? My own do not belong to me, nor does my "home [*chez moi*]." So go the declensions of the first person, the belonging of belonging [*l'appartenir de l'appartenance*]. "Living together," I belong to that which does not belong to me, to my own, to a language, a site, to a "my home," that do not belong to me and which I will never possess. Belonging excludes any absolute appropriation, even the radical right of property.

How, then, to deny but also how to justify the interior urgency that will make me first nourish my own, the proximate or the neighbor [*le proche ou le prochain*], before rushing to rescue the billions of famished men in the world? For the eloquent and meticulous militants of the rights of men and of social struggles in their countries should never forget that never, in the entire history of humanity, have so many people on earth been lacking bread and drinkable water; and that indifference or passivity on this subject is the beginning of a crime against humanity, a transgression of "You shall not kill"; and whoever says "you shall not kill," if he restricts himself to my neighbor, my brother, my fellow man, man,

14. Most notably in *Politics of Friendship*, trans. G. Collins (London: Verso, 1997).

also avows, what a paradox, the accepted murder of all living others in general, to wit, what one names stupidly [*bêtement*] and confusedly the animal. Well then, this preference, this hierarchy, can give itself distinct manners, brutal or distinguished, odious or refined — no one will ever be able to deny it, in all good faith, nor renounce it. But no one will ever be able to justify it either, what one calls justifying, judging and proving that it is just before a universal justice. In this regard, I will always be indebted and always be failing to fulfill the first duty. To avow this aporia does not suffice, but it is the first condition of a responsible lucidity and a first gesture to broach the best possible negotiation, to invent and unilaterally to propose its rule to the stranger, to the unknown one, to the other, even to the enemy, beyond even the neighbor, the fellow man and the brother, all the way to the point where "living together" commits life to all living, to the gaze of all the living, to the gaze and even beyond the gaze, and even there where no sacrifice can leave my conscience at rest, as soon as one faults or assails the life of a living other, I mean of an animal, human or not. What remains unjustifiable in all good faith remains, therefore, inasmuch as unjustifiable, unforgivable, therefore, unavowable. And it is therefore that which I must begin by avowing.

4. All these aporias obey a common economy, which is none other than economy itself, *oikonomia*, the law of the house, of the proper (*oikos*) and of property. And one would have had to associate the motif of ecology, this large and new dimension of "living together," with the motif of economy. My last example concerns the relation between the living, in the genetic or bio-zoological sense, and technology. More than ever, and every day faster than ever, the techno-scientific and genetico-industrial intervention upon the fetal cell, the genome, the fertility process, the homo- or hetero-grafts, and so on, much like the deployment of so many prosthetic structures, obligate us to re-elaborate the very norms of our elementary perception as to what is an ensemble or an organic identity, the "living together" of a proper body. For a proper body is first of all a manner of being together, symbiotically, with oneself and in proximity — a symbiosis that, here too, we can *neither deny nor justify*. Well then, the technological resources that affect the globalization of avowal by transforming the public space (informatization, panoptimization of telephonic and tele-visual digital communication, etc.), are the same technological resources that engage the living, all the syntheses of the living, all the dimensions of the living being-together (with oneself or with the other) in the space and the time of a *techno-biological prosthesis* that, here again, we can neither love nor reject, neither desire nor refuse, neither justify nor condemn in principle. If it interrupts the naturality of the ensemble, technology

is nevertheless since always the very condition of this "living together" that it constantly threatens. It is death in life, as condition of life. That chance should also be a threat, here is what one must acknowledge, avow, here is that of which one must begin to respond, precisely there where, like the avowal of the un-avowable, the forgiveness of the unforgivable appears both impossible and the only possibility of forgiveness (forgiving only that which is forgivable is not forgiving). Here too, there could be no "how" that would precede, as would do a knowledge, decision or responsibility whose rule each one, singularly, chosen without election, chosen to an irreplaceable place, must invent.

Hastening to my conclusion, in the ellipsis of an image and the furtive passage of a memory, I will gather one question that never waits, the waiting without waiting of these four aporias from which—that is to say also from Jerusalem—I address myself to you. It is very close to Mount Moriah where Kierkegaard, yet another Protestant, like the Neher of Levinas, said—that is his fiction—that Abraham was tempted to ask God for forgiveness. But he would have asked him for forgiveness not for having failed at his absolute duty toward God, rather for having attempted to obey God absolutely and blindly, and so for having preferred this unconditional duty to the life of his kind, to his preferred son. Abraham would thus have had this movement, according to Kierkegaard: to ask forgiveness of God for having obeyed him.

I do not have the time to deploy, as I would have wished, my interpretation of this interpretative fiction.[15] It associates and dissociates two manners of "living together" with every other (every other is any other, any other is wholly other [tout autre est tout autre]). I return for a moment and to conclude, not far from Mount Moriah, but this time closer to the cemetery of Jerusalem. Return, therefore, to end, in Jerusalem. Maimonides, by the way, said that teshuva also meant the end of exile. Return to Jerusalem, therefore, to end, and close to a cemetery. During my first visit, in 1982, an Israeli friend enabled my discovery of this cemetery, showing me the tomb of her grandfather. Then, I accompany her, for she must resolve a question in the offices of the Hevra Kadisha, the institution responsible for the difficult administration of the famous cemetery: allocation of plots, decisions as to the "concessions," transport of bodies, often costly operations, from distant countries, and most often the United States, and so on. This is before the cell phone, but I find myself there, in these offices, before a group of

15. I attempt to do so elsewhere in Donner la mort (Paris: Galilée, 1999).

"responsible" individuals, busy men, all dressed in black and with a traditional headdress. These men appear to run and to be out of breath; they display a feverish activity around walkie-talkies, telephones and computers that ostensibly link them to everywhere in the world from which one begs them, at any cost, for a place in the cemetery. Everything is becoming substitutable in this world, but the irreplaceable resists there, precisely here, now, not only in this place named Jerusalem, but in this very place, the cemetery, in this corner of Jerusalem, in view of orienting the dead.

I asked myself then: what does "living together" mean when the most urgent is to choose, while living and in the first place, a last place, a place apparently irreplaceable, desire then dictating not only dying and perhaps surviving or coming back to life in order to rise together upon the arrival of someone, but waiting, here and not there, before this door, unique in the world, this sealed door, the coming or the advent, the to-come of a Messiah? And yet, even before the globalization of the cell phone, of email and of the Internet, all these little prosthetic machines, telephones, computers, walkie-talkies were beginning to make, yet another time, all these here-nows infinitely proximate and substitutable. New York could appear closer than Gaza (with or without airport), and I could have the feeling of being closer to some other at the other end of the world than to some neighbor, some friend from West Jerusalem or East Jerusalem. To ask oneself then, on a cell phone, whether Jerusalem is in Jerusalem, is perhaps no longer to trust, like others in older times, the distinction between earthly Jerusalem and heavenly Jerusalem. Yet, this place of promise appeared to resist substitution and telecommunication. What was signified then by the placing of this "taking place" [l'emplacement de cet "avoir lieu"]? And of this messianic taking-place?

But I asked myself first, in anguish—and it was the same question: who can attribute places? Who can authorize himself, while avowing it, to grant here, to refuse there, to grant to one and to refuse to the other the chance to make this place his place, to elect it or to believe himself elected to it, be it in order there to bury his dead or to await some messianic peace, a to-come or a return?

Since this moment and through analogous experiences (a few weeks before this first visit to Jerusalem, I was coming out of a jail cell in Prague), I had to begin thinking that which, in what I have named elsewhere messianic spectrality, or spectral messianicity, exceeds, precedes and conditions all messianisms. And to think a certain faith older than all religions. This must have occurred to me [*m'arriver*] a long time ago in Algiers but also during these last years in Jeru-salem. I do not know, I avow it, how to interpret what then occurred to me—or would occur to me still [*ce qui alors m'arriva—ou m'arriverait encore*]. Nor what was announcing itself above me as a *revenant*, what was announcing itself by return-ing upon me [*ce qui s'annonçait en revenant sur moi*].

# 24

# Stéphane Mosès, Normative Modernity and Critical Modernity

Stéphane Mosès, excerpt from "Modernité normative et modernité critique," *Figures philosophiques de la modernité juive* (Paris: Éditions du Cerf, 2011), 22–31.

Stéphane Mosès (1931–2007), a pioneering interpreter of German-Jewish literature, is perhaps best known for his writings on Franz Rosenzweig and Walter Benjamin. Mosès wrote *Système et Révélation*, one of the first comprehensive analyses of Rosenzweig's *Star of Redemption*, and *L'ange de l'histoire*, a study of Rosenzweig, Benjamin, and Scholem. Together these works helped determine the scholarly itinerary for the subfield of Weimar-period German-Jewish thought. At the same time, Mosès was an important participant in its postwar French sequel: *l'école juive de Paris*, as Emmanuel Levinas dubbed it.

Born in Germany, Mosès was still a child when his family emigrated first to the Netherlands, then to Morocco in 1936. His family was briefly interned in 1942, before the American invasion of North Africa, then naturalized as French citizens in 1949. Mosès was a student at the École normale supérieure (ENS) in 1954 when he became interested in questions of Jewish identity. As a student and then a director at the École d'Orsay, he was an integral part of the school as well as the journal *Targoum*, which was published from 1954 to 1958 and edited by the school's alumni. The year he became director of Orsay, 1961, Mosès was also appointed an assistant professor of German at the Sorbonne. After the Six-Day War, a turning point for many Jews of his generation, he emigrated to Israel, where from 1968 until his retirement he taught comparative literature at Hebrew University, all the while remaining involved in French intellectual life.

The selection that appears here was originally presented as the first in a lecture series at the Catholic Institute of Paris in January 2006, a little over a year before Mosès's death in 2007. In it he outlines an important dichotomy in twentieth-century modern Jewish thought between the two terms of the title: *normative modernity* and *critical modernity*. Not only do these two categories provide a rubric for understanding both Weimar-period German thinkers along with their postwar French counterparts, but the latter category, critical modernity, also provides a formal means for treating such writers as Kafka and Derrida whose thought is often poorly conceptualized when described in theological or recuperative terms. For Mosès it is their very inversion and subversion of biblical and rabbinic forms that define their connection to the tradition.

[ ... ]

At the end of the 19th century and the beginning of the 20th, a reversal was produced in Judaism which inaugurated the second Jewish modernity after Mendelssohn up until today. [ ... ] This rupture with the tradition comes essentially from Nietzsche, but I cannot develop that here. In any case, the critique of rationalist objectivism marks a return to foundational texts. [ ... ]

From here one can move on to the study of the difference between two forms of Jewish modernity: in our terminology *normative modernity* and *critical modernity*.

To illustrate what I call *normative modernity*, it is necessary to treat authors such as Emmanuel Levinas but also Hermann Cohen and Franz Rosenzweig. This same generation of *normative modernity* presents itself as a return to traditional texts, but in a form comprehensible to people today. It is a *translation*. For Levinas this is in the philosophical language of modernity. In this sense, Jean-Luc Marion was right to say: It is Rosenzweig who opened fidelity to the contents of the Jewish tradition, but at the expense of traditional language with its own conceptuality and its own dialectic, for the benefit of their translation into the language of philosophy. Levinas put it this way: "Translating into Greek the wisdom of the Talmud." For him the biblical stories as well as the Talmudic texts with their apparent "disarray," provide witness to more than an archaic and irrational thought. Under these forms of discourse, which have become strange to us today, there hides a truth, according to him, a *universal* meaning out of which it is necessary to decipher the specific rationality. It is not a question of an exotic or obsolete language and formulas that are incomprehensible today. It is a world encased or lost under signs, but these signs are *united* by the thinking that comes to us from the outside. This thought from outside is rightly modern philosophical thought, coming from the other end of the canon, revealing the possibilities that await exegesis: not only the meaning of the transmitted text, but also the meaning of its exegesis. This form of modernity is *normative*, because authors like Levinas and before him Rosenzweig unveiled an orthodox content of the Jewish tradition that they were not calling into question, but reformulating in philosophical language. With Rosenzweig one sees it all the time: those of you who have had a look at *The Star of Redemption* have been able to observe that, in a philosophical discourse very close to that of the great German idealist systems, the contents of the most ancient Jewish tradition are unveiled and developed in the form of explicit citations, for example, referring to this *normative modernity*.

But today even in that which one calls the Jewish school of Paris there is another form of modernity that I will term *critical modernity*.

What is *critical modernity*? In fact it is a category that I myself have elaborated, no one having ever claimed to refer to *critical modernity*, no more so than *normative modernity*; these two categories are thus mine. *Critical modernity* is represented by authors such as Benjamin, Kafka, Celan, Arendt, Jabès and in a certain measure, Scholem, and much later Jacques Derrida.

*Critical modernity* adopts a point of view radically opposed to that of *normative modernity*, to the extent that the contents of the religious tradition no longer possess their original standing as an instance of truth. One could call the representatives of this position *secularized*. In effect, for them the content of the Jewish tradition no longer speaks to us today; to cite from her essay "The Crisis of Culture," Hannah Arendt writes a phrase that by her account represents a formula of Alexis de Tocqueville, "the thread of tradition is broken," and "we cannot reconnect it."[1] We have lost the continuity of the past, such as it seemed to be transmitted from generation to generation and to develop thus a certain autonomy. That which remains for us is the past itself, but a *shattered* past that is no longer capable of inspiring in us judgments of evident value. In this broken time that expresses the discontinuity of the past, the contents of faith—I speak now of the Jewish faith—are no longer audible for us; they no longer correspond to any experience today.

To illustrate this situation I will simply cite a passage of Kafka in *The Letter to His Father*. Kafka who did not send this letter, who himself thought it was too cruel, for all that, in this unsent letter speaks of "the nothing of Judaism," bequeathed by his father and of which he says cruelly that "it was truly nothing, a pleasantry, not even a pleasantry." I have never read anything as cruel. This something that can no longer be transmitted, here is the philosophical horizon of *critical modernity*.

In addition to the great novels, Kafka wrote many much shorter texts and stories that take up a traditional theme, be it borrowed from Greek or from biblical mythology, as though an instantiation of it. By means of commenting on, interrogating and putting in question these texts, these enigmas, Kafka subverts the original sense from top to bottom, but maintains the form. Those who are

---

1. Hannah Arendt, *The Life of the Mind* (New York: Houghton Mifflin Harcourt, 1981), 212.

somewhat acquainted with the world of traditional Jewish parables, which are moreover just like the parables of the Gospels, will find the same forms of rhetorical construction, but without the meaning, without their signification. For example, there is a text of Kafka's titled "Poseidon," consecrated to the god of the sea of Greek mythology. In this text, Poseidon has become an employee of the waterworks company. In another text, "The New Attorney," Kafka transforms this new lawyer named Mr. Bucephalus, the mythical horse of the emperor Alexander, into an obscure lawyer and member of the bar for the administration of horses, in which the perspicacious observers guess his ancient identity as a horse, as it says in the text, "Did I not just lately see even a quite simple court attendant stare at the lawyer with the professional eye of a modest racetrack follower, as the latter, lifting his legs high mounted the outside stairs step-by-step, with a tread that made the marble ring?"

In the same spirit, Kafka consecrated a series of aphorisms to biblical themes whose meaning he ironically reverses. He writes, for example: "If that which was destroyed in paradise was destructible, then it was not something important, but if it was something indestructible, then we live in a false belief."[2]

In the same perspective, one can speak of the French poet Edmond Jabès who in *The Book of Questions* and elsewhere engages in pseudo-Talmudic discussions in which he dramatizes a scene of imaginary rabbis. Rather than debating positive theological questions, these rabbis endlessly debate the emptiness of our world, in which God is absent without hope of returning. One can equally recall Jacques Derrida's work *Glas*, in which the page layout and the juxtaposition of two texts appearing independently recalls the Talmud.

To conclude, I would like to consider with you Paul Celan's "Psalm," a well-known poem from a collection appearing in 1963, in which the author evokes a question one of the audience members just posed to me during the conference break: "You have not spoken of the absence of God during the Shoah." It is not a subject I want to speak about explicitly, but in reading this text of Paul Celan's we will see that this is the central matter. In addition, this text of Celan's is truly, in my opinion, an example of *critical modernity*.

2. Kafka, *Hochzeitsvorbereitungen auf dem Lande* (Hamburg: Fischer Taschenbuch Verlag, 1983), 144.

PSALM

Niemand knetet uns wieder aus Erde und Lehm,
niemand bespricht unsern Staub.
Niemand.

Gelobt seist du, Niemand.
Dir zulieb wollen
wir blühn.
Dir
entgegen.

Ein Nichts
waren wir, sind wir, werden
wir bleiben, blühend:
die Nichts-, die
Niemandsrose.

Mit
dem Griffel seelenhell,
dem Staubfaden himmelswüst,
der Krone rot
vom Purpurwort, das wir sangen
über, o über
*dem Dorn.*


PSALM
Paul Celan

No one kneads us again out of earth and clay,
no one incants our dust.
No one.

Blessed art thou, No One.
In thy sight would
we bloom.
In thy
spite.

A Nothing
we were, are now, and ever
shall be, blooming:
the Nothing-, the
No-One's-Rose.
With
our pistil soul-bright,
our stamen heaven-waste,
our corona red
from the purpleword we sang
over, O over
the thorn.[3]


PSALME
Paul Celan

Personne ne nous pétrira plus de terre et de glaise
Personne n'insufflera plus sa parole à notre poussière.
Personne.

Béni sois-tu, Personne.
Pour l'amour de toi
Nous fleurirons
Contre
Toi.

Un néant
Nous étions, nous sommes, nous
Resterons, fleurissant:
La rose du néant, la
Rose de personne.

Avec
Sa tige claire d'âme,
Son étamine déserte de ciel

3. [John Felstiner's English translation in Paul Celan, *Selected Poems and Prose*, trans. John Felstiner (New York: Norton, 2001).]

Sa couronne rouge
De la parole pourpre que nous avons chantée
Au-dessus, Ô au-dessus
De l'épine.


The Christian theme of the passion at the end will not escape you. In fact this poem represents traditional forms of the Jewish liturgy and the Bible in a complete inversion of the meaning.

The first stanza retells the story of the creation of man in Genesis: "No one kneads us again out of earth and clay." This is the creation of man from clay and divine breath. "No one incants our dust." The verse is a reprise of a very ancient traditional Jewish interpretation; in the first Aramaic translation of the Bible made by Onkelos in the second century after Christ, he *interpreted* the Hebraic verse as affirming that God injected his breath into man to create him and translated it as saying that God had made of man a speaking being, from which Celan gets the formulation: "No one incants our dust, no one." This proceeds in an absolute reversal of the biblical story, like the original form but nonetheless unable ever to be repeated. That which the biblical tradition recounts: the creation of man from the earth, from the breath of the divine, is irreversibly past. Why? There is a response posed by the auditor here: evidently it is necessary to read the poem from the historical experience of Paul Celan, who lived the extermination of the Jews in Romania and whose parents were killed in the course of the Shoah. Where the text says, "And the Lord God formed the human from the dust of the earth and breathed into his nostrils the breath of life and the human being, Adam, became a living being," where the first translation of the Hebraic Bible in Armenian by Onkelos has, "And the human became a speaking being," Celan reprises this as, "no one," "Niemand bespricht uns mehr." No one will speak to us anymore, no one will breath his word into our dust, as the Hebrew Bible established it, evoking the divine character of man. This reality was irrevocably destroyed for Celan by what happened during the war, by the extermination. Man, today, cannot be regarded as a creature, in any case not as a person, as one who could be recreated in the same way as the Bible evokes.

The subject of this phrase, of these three verbs is "no one" repeated three times: "No one, No one, No one." An anaphora that reverses itself in the fourth verse, "Blessed art thou, No One," as in the passage of the *Odyssey* where the Cyclops asks Odysseus his name and he responds, "No one." Odysseus thereby transforms himself into a "no," negatively. Celan does the opposite. The pronoun "no one" is transformed here into a substantive "no one." From the Christian perspective, one knows God is a person [*une personne*]. In Celan he has become "no one [*personne*]," that is to say *there is no more God*, but this "no one [*personne*]" is an interlocutor to whom the poet addresses himself, saying, "Blessed art thou, No one," taking up here the Jewish liturgical expression that introduces all blessings with "Blessed art thou, the Lord our God [etc.]." The inversion performed by Celan is extremely paradoxical because it means both that there is not and that, after what has happened, there is no longer. The same idea of a protector God, of a benevolent God, is no longer thinkable after what has happened. Emmanuel Levinas had offered this terrible formulation in an interview: "The benevolent protector God committed suicide in Auschwitz." It is thus no one. At the same time, there is here a form of address to someone, an incomprehensible form of address, but a form of address, "For your love [*Pour l'amour de toi*] / we bloom / against / You." In German, the "against" is at the same time "up against you" and "in opposition to you." The verse introduces the theme of the flower, of humanity that continues despite everything. Despite this seemingly irrevocable destruction, humanity is comparable to a flower, a rose—the rose of no one (Celan's collection to which "Psalme" belongs is titled *The No One's Rose* [*Die Niemandsrose!*])—and to the rose that blooms, that *will bloom* in the future. "Against / You [*Dir entgegen*]" means simultaneously "in revolt against you" and "right next to you." You see at what point Celan plays here with a form of "negative" theology. Thus, after having evoked the absence of the benevolent God of love in the first stanza, the second and the third stanza turn toward man, toward humanity.

Here again there are forms of traditional Jewish literature that are subverted. "A nothing," this was nothing, "a nothing, we were," no one, this was nothing, we, we are a nothing, a nothing "we were, are now, and ever / shall be"—these formulas reprise the theological definition of God from Maimonides as eternal and invariable substance. "He was; he is; he will be" is an expression repeated each day in the daily prayer from Maimonides' "Thirteen Articles of Faith." Celan has turned again toward man, defined for all eternity as a nothing, a nothing because destroyed once and for all. The Shoah is thus not only an event on the historical, political level, but is also an event on the *metaphysical* level after which nothing, above all, not the idea that we have made for ourselves of humanity, can be as it was.

"We were, are now, and ever / shall be, blooming: / the Nothing-, the / No-One's-Rose. That is, the rose of no one: "no one" is the divine person who is no longer present, no longer thinkable, and "the nothing" is us. After the "we-you" of the second stanza, here we are the "we" of humanity. The last stanza comes back to things and seems truly to manifest a "negative" theology; all these negations are reiterated in order to invert them into something that could resemble a hope—for my part, I will say a *poetic* hope, that is to say, one relevant to poetic language.

"With / our pistil": here we have a series of neologisms. Celan constructs them often: thus "soul-bright," "heaven-waste"; there are all the components of the flower, stem, stamen, corolla/petals.[4] The stem, which is *soul-bright*, is metaphorically comparable to a bright soul, which soars toward the sky under the "stamen heaven-waste," toward a heaven-desert. "Its red corona / from the purpleword": the repetition of the color red is here an allusion to many things: to blood and, naturally, to imperial purple, a symbol of the Roman Empire in the Jewish tradition and, consequently, of power and historical violence.

"Its red corona / from the purpleword we sang"; the "we" here is self-citation. In another poem, Celan evokes this little-known reality: before entering the gas chambers, religious, Orthodox Jews sang hymns to God. The purple word, the bloody word, but also the poetry that we sang. "Over, oh over the thorn": it is a question of the thorn from the crown of thorns of Christ during the Passion. Here again, as often elsewhere in Celan, the extermination of the Jews is comparable to the Passion of Christ. There is a very paradoxical return of traditional Jewish forms that are subverted, emptied of their traditional content. At the same time, with Celan in any case, there seems to surge a new hope out of this reversal, which I, for my part, interpret as a poetic hope: the *song*, the fact that all of this can be said, that all of this can be expressed in a certain sense.

*Translated by Sarah Hammerschlag*

4. [Following the French translation here and in what follows, rather than Felstiner's.]

# Acknowledgments

This anthology could not have come together without a great deal of help. Thanks first to Series Editors Eugene Sheppard and Samuel Moyn for suggesting the volume and for offering help and guidance along the way. Sylvia Fried has been a constant lifeline. P. David Hornik and Susan Abel were masterful in the copyediting and production stages, respectively. Golan Moskowitz lent a necessary helping hand. Thanks to Phyllis Deutsch for her patience and support. Beatrice Bourgogne took on much of the translation work. Thanks go to Jean-Luc Marion for helping me navigate some difficult permissions issues and to Paul Mendes-Flohr and Arnold Davidson for offering feedback on an early draft of the table of contents. Bettina Bergo offered fresh insight into an early translation draft. Maureen Kelly was a veritable hero at the end, reading through the final drafts, finding my mistakes, and making the most elegant editing and translation suggestions. I'm grateful, once again, to Alexandra Garbarini for her friendship and insight into this thorny process. Finally, thanks to Ryan and Lila, for putting up with me, especially in those final days, when it was a race to the finish.

# Suggestions for Further Reading

PRIMARY SOURCES

Atlan, Henri. *The Sparks of Randomness*, vols. 1 and 2. Stanford: Stanford University Press, 2010, 2013.

Blanchot, Maurice. *Writing the Disaster*. Translated by Ann Smock. Lincoln: University of Nebraska Press, 1995.

Derrida, Jacques. *Adieu to Emmanuel Levinas*. Translated by Pascale-Anne Brault and Michael Nass. Stanford: Stanford University Press, 1999.

"Abraham, the Other," in Bettina Bergo, Joseph Cohen, and Raphael Zagury-Orly, eds., *Judeities: Questions for Jacques Derrida*. New York: Fordham University Press, 2007.

Guenon, Denis. *A Semite: A Memoir of Algeria*. Translated by Ann Smock. New York: Columbia University Press, 2013.

Lazare, Bernard. *Anti-Semitism: Its History and Its Causes*. Introduction by Robert Wistrich. Lincoln: University of Nebraska Press, 1995.

Levinas, Emmanuel. *Difficult Freedom*. Translated by Sean Hand. Baltimore: Johns Hopkins University Press, 1990.

Misrahi, Robert. *Un Juif laïque en France*. Paris: Entrelacs, 2003.

Sartre, Jean-Paul. *Anti-Semite and Jew*. Translated by George J. Becker. New York: Schocken, 1965.

Schwartz-Bart, André. *The Last of the Just*. New York: Overlook Press, 2000.

SECONDARY SOURCES

Abitbol, Michel. *Les deux terres promises: Les Juifs de France et le sionisme 1897–1945*. Paris: Perrin, 1989.

Berkovitz, Jay R. *The Shaping of Jewish Identity in Nineteenth-Century France*. Detroit: Wayne State University Press, 1989.

Birnbaum, Pierre. *Jewish Destinies: Citizenship, State and Community in Modern France*. Translated by Arthur Goldhammer. New York: Hill & Wang, 2000.

Brenner, Michael, Vicki Caron, and Uri R. Kaufman, eds. *Jewish Emancipation Reconsidered: The French and German Models*. Tübingen: Mohr Siebeck, 2003.

Friedlander, Judith. *Vilna on the Seine: Jewish Intellectuals in France since 1968*. New Haven: Yale University Press, 1990.

Graetz, Michael. *The Jews in Nineteenth-Century France: From the French Revolution to the Alliance Israélite Universelle*. Translated by Jane Marie Todd. Stanford: Stanford University Press, 1996.

Hammerschlag, Sarah. *The Figural Jew: Politics and Identity in Postwar French Thought*. Chicago: University of Chicago Press, 2010.

Hand, Sean and Steven T. Katz, eds. *Post-Holocaust France and the Jews 1945–1955*. New York: New York University Press, 2015.

Hyman, Paula. *The Jews of Modern France*. Berkeley: University of California Press, 1998.

Judaken, Jonathan. *Jean-Paul Sartre and the Jewish Question*. Lincoln: University of Nebraska Press, 2009.

Kaplan, Zvi Jonathan and Nadia Malinovich. *The Jews of Modern France: Images and Identities*. London: Brill, 2016.

Lazare, Lucien. *Rescue as Resistance: How Jewish Organizations Fought the Holocaust in France*. New York: New York University Press, 1996.

Lee, Daniel. *Pétain's Jewish Children: French Jewish Youth and the Vichy Regime, 1940–1942*. Oxford: Oxford University Press, 2014.

Leff, Lisa Moses. *Sacred Bonds of Solidarity*. Stanford: Stanford University Press, 2006.

Lehr, Johanna. *La Thora dans la cité: L'émergence d'un nouveau judaïsme*. Lormont: Le Bord de L'eau, 2013.

Malino, Francis and Bernard Wasserstein, eds. *The Jews in Modern France*. Hanover, NH: University Press of New England for Brandeis University Press, 1985.

Mandel, Maud. *In the Aftermath of Genocide: Armenians and Jews in Twentieth-Century France*. Durham, NC: Duke University Press, 2003.

Marrus, Michael R. *The Politics of Assimilation: A Study of the French Jewish Community at the Time of the Dreyfus Affair*. Oxford: Clarendon Press, 1971.

Mendes-Flohr, Paul. R and Judah Reinharz, eds. *The Jew in the Modern World: A Documentary History*. New York: Oxford University Press, 1980.

Paxton, Robert O. *Vichy France: Old Guard and New Order*. New York: Columbia University Press, 2007.

Samuels, Maurice. *The Right to Difference: French Universalism and the Jews*. Chicago: University of Chicago Press, 2016.

Schnapper, Dominique. *Jewish Identities in France: An Analysis of Contemporary French Jewry*. Chicago: University of Chicago Press, 1983.

Simon-Nahum, Perrine. *La cité investie*. Paris: Cerf, 1991.

Szwarc, Sandrine. *Les intellectuels juifs: De 1945 à nos jours*. Paris: Le Bord de l'Eau, 2013.

Vidal-Naquet, Pierre. *The Jews: History, Memory, and the Present*. New York: Columbia University Press, 1996.

Weber, Elisabeth. *Questioning Judaism*. Translated by Rachel Bowlby. Stanford: Stanford University Press, 2004.

Wieviorka, Annette. *The Era of the Witness*. Translated by Jared Stark. Ithaca: Cornell University Press, 2006.

Wolf, Joan. *Harnessing the Holocaust: Politics of Memory in France*. Stanford: Stanford University Press, 2003.

# Index

Dostoyevsky, Fyodor, *The Brothers Karamazov*, 107

Dreyfus Affair, xiii–xiv, xx–xxi, 1, 2; André Spire and, 42, 43–44; antisemitism in era of, xiv, xix, xxvn14, xxvn19, 10, 18–19, 30–34, 36, 39, 41; Edmond Fleg and, 54; Herzl and, xiv, xxvn14; Jewish identity and, 31–32, 54–58; Jewish Question and, ix; Zadoc Kahn and, 18, 19; Bernard Lazare and, 30, 31, 33n5, 38n11, 38n13, 40; messianism in era of, 5–9, 48, 52; Zionism and, xiv–xv, 2–3, 5, 31, 42–43, 48, 54

Drumont, Édouard, xiii, xxvn13, 33, 36, 40, 44; *La France juive*, 2, 18, 43

du Gard, Roger Martin, 133

Durkheim, Émile, xx, 157; "Individualism and Intellectualism," xx

earthly city and heavenly city, Atlan's comparison of, 159–70

Eastern European Jews emigrating to France, xiv–xv, xviii, xxvn18, 2–3, 203–4

Éclaireurs israélites de France (EIF), xxvin20, 54, 66, 79, 159, 186

École Gilbert Bloch (École d'Orsay), 67, 79, 159–60, 186, 245

Egypt, modern, antisemitism of, 132

EIF (Éclaireurs israélites de France), xxvin20, 54, 66, 79, 159, 186

Eladan, Jacques, 5n1

Eliezer ben Hurcanus, 168

emancipation and citizenship of Jews in France, ix–xii, xxiv–xxvn5, 50, 53, 139, 157

emigration. *See* immigration/emigration

Esau, 83, 87–88, 89, 95, 96

exile. *See* Diaspora/exile

Fanon, Frantz, 125

feminism. *See* gender issues

Finkielkraut, Alain: "From the Novelesque to Memory," 198–207; *The Imaginary Jew*, 198–99

Flavius Josephus, 33

Fleg, Edmond, xiv, xvi, xxi, 3, 31, 54–55, 66, 105, 106, 151, 181; "Why I Am a Jew," xxi, 54–58

forgiveness, 85, 216–17, 225, 230, 232, 234, 236–39, 242

Franck, Adolphe, xii, 1

Franco-Prussian War and Treaty of Frankfurt, 22n3, 132

French identity, xxii, 64, 66, 123, 138

French Jewish thought, modern. *See* modern French Jewish thought

French Revolution (1789), ix, x, xiii, xxvn10, 2, 6, 18, 39, 43, 48, 49, 52, 138–40, 157, 198

French universalism, 125

Freud, Sigmund, 117, 209, 213, 214; *Moses and Monotheism*, 210

Galileo, 155

galuth. *See* Diaspora/exile

Gamzon, Robert, xvi, xxi, 54, 66–67, 79, 159, 186; *Tivliout: Harmony*, 60, 66–77

Garden of Eden, 173–74

Gematria, 92n9

gender issues: Cixous on, 208–13; history, masculinity of, 130–31; Mesnile-Amar and, 181; patriarchy, 208, 210–13

genocide, 146, 161, 205–6, 233. *See also* Holocaust

geo-theology of Eretz Israel, 152–57

Gide, André, 129

Gideon, 95

Glatzer, Nahum, *Modern Jewish Thought*, ix, xxiii, xxviin36

Gordin, Jacob, xv, xxi, xxiii, 60, 78–80, 186, 187; "The Galuth," 78–98; "Investigation into the Theory of Infinite Judgment," 78

Gordin, Rachel, 78, 79

Gougenot des Mousseaux, 33

Graetz, Michael, 5n1

Grégoire, Henri (Abbé), xi, xii, 50, 53, 138

Gregory VII (Hildebrand; pope), 17

Gross, Benjamin, xxviin35

Isaiah, 69, 72, 85–86, 89, 103, 154, 167, 168, 169n5
Ishmael, 83, 84, 87, 190, 240
Islam, xiv, xvi, xviii, xix, 8, 50, 123, 146, 152, 155, 157n8, 161–62, 172, 186, 190, 236
Israel: birth of State of, xxii, xxiii–xxiv, 113, 123, 139, 142, 184, 230; Diaspora, joint existence with, 137–50; Egypt at war with, 132; emigration of French Jews to, xvii–xviii, xxiii–xxiv, 67, 123, 152, 187, 245; emigration of North African Jews to, 125, 171; French Jewish intellectuals' support for, 126; identity of, 188–90; "new antisemitism" and, 176–77; Palestinians and, 126; Six-Day War (1967), xvii, xxii, 123–24, 145, 152, 245; War of Independence, 137; Zionism and, 139, 141, 152
*Israélites*, as term, xxivn2

Jabès, Edmond, 214, 247; *The Book of Questions*, 248
Jacob, 69, 80–81, 82, 87–89, 91, 96–97, 189–90
Jacob, Max, 184
Jankélévitch, Vladimir, xxi, xxviin35, 60, 105–6; *Forgiveness*, 237; "Judaism, an 'Internal Problem,'" 105–16
Jaurès, Jean, 33, 44
Jerusalem: Derrida on cemetery in, 219, 242–44; heavenly city and earthly city, Atlan's comparison of, 159–70; Mea Shearim, 204; as "navel" of Eretz Israel, 152; "next year in Jerusalem," 170. *See also* Temple
Jew in non-Jewish French writing, the, 118
Jewish Question, the, ix, xiii–xiv, 1, 30, 32, 38n13, 106, 123, 125, 139, 201
Jewish Statutes, xvi, 54, 59, 60, 63–65, 64, 66, 105, 151, 159
Jewish thought, modern French. *See* modern French Jewish thought
Joan of Arc, 128

Joseph II (Holy Roman Emperor), xi
Joshua, 153
Joyce, James, 210
Judah, son of Jacob, 189–90
Judah Halevi, 94, 156, 157, 187
Junger, Ernst, 133

Kabbalah, xii, xv, xxi, 78, 80, 91, 159, 160, 186–87
Kadoorie, Sir Ely, 51
Kafka, Franz, xxiii, 199, 206, 209, 210, 214, 245–46, 247–48; *The Letter to His Father*, 247; "The New Attorney," 248; "Poseidon," 248
Kahn, Zadoc, xx, 2, 18–29, 42, 48
Kant, Immanuel, xv, xx, 78, 79, 118, 222, 231, 234, 235
Kaplan, Chaïm, 201
Keren Kayemeth LeIsrael (Jewish National Fund), 156
Kierkegaard, Søren, 106, 242
Kofman, Berek, 120–21
Kofman, Sarah, 60, 117–18; *Rue Ordener, Rue Labat*, 117; *Smothered Words*, 117–21
Kook, Abraham Isaac (Avraham Y. H.), 167, 187
Kook, Zvi Yehuda, 187
Kornberg, Jacques, xxvn14

*laïcité* (secularism in France), x, xiv, 18, 199
Lamourette, Antoine-Adrien, 138
Lanzmann, Claude, 60, 179
Lassalle, Ferdinand, 157
Lazare, Bernard, xiv, xx–xxi, 2, 30–32, 42, 44; *Antisemitism: Its History and Causes*, 30; "Jewish Capitalism and Democracy," 38–41; "Judaism's Concept of the Social and the Jewish People," 32–37; *Le miroir des légendes*, 30
Leah, 97
Leibowitz, Yeshayahu, 165
Le Roy Ladurie, Emmanuel, 148
Lévi, Sylvain, "L'Alliance israélite

universelle" (radio address; 1932), 48–53, 100n2

Levinas, Emmanuel, 99–100; Ashkénazi and, 186; Atlan on, 164, 165; on Chouchani, xv; Derrida and, 214, 215–16, 220–22, 229, 231, 238–39, 242; on ethics, vii; Finkielkraut influenced by, 198; on forgiveness, 238–39; "From Shylock to Swann," 182; on God committing suicide in Auschwitz, 252; Gordin and, 78; on impact of Hitler on Jewish identity, 179; Jankélévitch and, 106n1, 107n5; "The Jewish Cultural Renaissance in Continental Europe," xvii; "The Jewish Experience of the Prisoner," 60, 99–104; on Jewish suffering, xxi; "Jewish Thought Today," 106n1; Benny Levy as student of, xxviin35; Neher and, 151, 186, 220, 242; "normative modernity" and, 246; Otherwise than Being, 99; as philosopher of "the other," 107n5; postwar French Jewish renaissance and, 245; on receiving light of world through lens of Judaism, xxiv; Rosenzweig studied by, xxiv; on Shoah/Holocaust, 205; Totality and Infinity, 99

Levites, 73, 165, 174, 176, 204

Levitte, Georges, 79

Levi-Valensi, Élaine Amado, xxviin35

Levy, Benny, xxviin35

Levy Itzhak of Berdichev, 84

liberation, 39, 52, 70–75, 82, 84, 90, 112, 139, 147, 157, 163

Libre Parole, La (antisemitic newspaper), 18, 43–44

Linsler, Johanna, xxvn18

Lispector, Clarice, 209

living together, Derrida on, 214–44

Lunel, Armand, 54

Luria, Isaac, 156

Lurianic Kabbalah, xxi, 80

Luzzatto, Moshe Chaim, 156, 157

Lyotard, Jean-François, 118; The Differend, 60

Maharal of Prague, xxviin35, 187

Maimonides, 78, 242, 252; The Guide for the Perplexed, French translation of, xii, 1; "Thirteen Articles of Faith," 252

Mandel, Arnold, xxiii

Manitou, as pseudonym for Léon Ashkénazi, 186

Manuel, Eugène, 49–50

Marienstras, Richard, xxii, 124, 137–38; Être un peuple en diaspora, 137, 138; "The Jews of the Diaspora, or the Vocation of a Minority," xi, 137–50

Marion, Jean-Luc, 246

Marranos, 5, 149, 183, 215, 228

Marx, Karl, and Marxism, 33, 34, 113, 157, 231

masculinity of history, 130–31

Mayanot, 187

May 1968 student revolt, ix, xix, xxii

Memmi, Albert, xvi, 124, 125–26, 144, 146, 179; The Colonizer and the Colonized, 125; "The Jew, the Nation, and History," 125–36; Portrait of a Jew, 126; Le racisme, 125

memory: in Dreyfus era, 25, 26; Jewish identity and, 192, 195, 201–7, 224, 225, 228, 229, 231, 233, 238, 242; Shoah/Holocaust and, 60, 67, 201; in World War II era, 60, 67, 104, 117, 118, 128, 130–31, 137, 140, 143, 148

Mendelssohn, Moses, vii, xi, xxivn5, 246

menorah, 92

Mesnil-Amar, André, 181

Mesnil-Amar, Jacqueline, xviii, 180, 181–82; Ceux qui ne dormaient pas, 181; "The Lost Children of Judaism," 181–85

messianism: in Dreyfus era, 5–9, 48, 52; Jewish identity and, xxiii, 187, 195, 214, 222, 224, 228, 243; universalism and particularism and, 152, 156–58; in World War II era, 69, 86, 95, 97, 105, 111, 115

Meyer, Arthur, 32, 38–41

Midrash, 81, 84, 88, 89, 90, 91, 92, 95, 96, 97, 190–91, 192, 193

migration. See immigration/emigration

minorities and minority culture, xi, xxi, 113, 114, 137–50, 172

Mirabeau, comte de, 53

Misrahi, Robert, 179

modern French Jewish thought, ix–xxiv; continuities and discontinuities in, xxiii–xxiv; correlating texts and historical events, xix–xxiii; defining, ix; historical background, x–xix; significance of, vii. *See also specific persons by name*

modernity: Ashkénazi, "Tradition and Modernity," 186–97; Mosès, "Normative Modernity and Critical Modernity," 245–53

Molière, 52

moneylending and usury, xi, xii, 32–33

monotheism, 121, 152, 160–61, 164, 210

Montesquieu, marquis de, 138

Moroccan Jews, xviii, 135, 171, 245

Mortara case, 49

Moses, xxvn10, 6, 57, 69–71, 81, 83, 89, 91, 139, 153, 161, 162, 183, 187, 212

Mosès, Stéphane, xvii, xxii–xxiii, 180, 245–46; *L'ange de l'histoire*, 245; "Normative Modernity and Critical Modernity," 245–53; *Système et Révélation*, 245

Moyn, Samuel, vii

multiculturalism, 176, 198

Munk, Salomon, xii, 1

Murayama, Tomiichi, 233

Muslims, xiv, xvi, xviii, xix, 8, 50, 123, 146, 152, 155, 157n8, 161–62, 172, 186, 190, 236

Musset, Alfred de, *Rolla*, 11

Nachman of Bratzlav, 81, 92

Nachmanides, 156

Napoleon, xi–xii, 128

Naquet, Alfred Joseph, 138

nations and Israel, relationship between, 93–97

nation-state, Jewish reverence for, 139–40, 144

Nazis. *See* World War II

Neher, André, xvii, xxviin35, 79, 124, 151–52, 186, 215, 220, 242; *Biblical History of the Jewish People*, 151; *Clefs pour le judaïsme*, 152; "The Jewish Dimension of Space: Zionism," 151–58

Neher, Reneé Bernheim-, xvii, 79, 151

Nemirovsky, Irene, 63

Nietzsche, Friedrich, 103, 117, 231, 246

Noah, 173

North African Jews: in battle for Monte Cassino, 130; emigrating to France, xviii, xxii, 123, 171, 209–10; emigrating to Israel, 125, 171. *See also* Moroccan Jews; Tunisian Jews

*Nouveaux Cahiers, Les* (journal), 160, 181

Nuremberg court, 233, 234

Onkelos, 251

other/otherness, xvi, 7, 99, 107, 119, 149, 176, 2229

Pacifici, Alfonso, 158

*pacte civil de solidarité* (PACS; civil unions), 225–26

Palestine: Balfour Declaration, 48; immigration of French Jews to, xvi, xvii; United Nations acceptance of partition of, 141

Palestinians, 126

*Pardès* (journal), 172

Parisian riots of 2005, 199n2

particularism: Jewish, xxii, 60, 123–24, 126, 149, 160, 172, 175–77, 214; of multiculturalism, 198

passivity, Jewish, myth of, 205

Pastoret, Emile Claude de, 138

Patachia of Ratisbon, 36

patriarchy, 208, 210–13

Paul (saint), 93

Péguy, Charles, 31, 44

Périer, Casimir, 44

Pétain, Philippe (general), xvi, 125, 209

Pharisees, 196

Philip IV (king of France), 38
Philippe, Duke of Orleans, 38n13
Pius IX (pope), 33n6
Plotinus, 105
pluralism, xxvin20, 3, 138–39, 149, 178
Pobiedonosef, Georgii, 15
Pola Affair, 40n18
politics, Jewish, 124
postcolonialism, 172
postwar French Jewish renaissance, xvii,
    xxi–xxii, 78, 79, 245
postwar religious revival, 127
Poujol, Louis, xxvn6
prisoners of war, Jews as, 99–104
prophetic tradition, 10–17, 48, 93, 99–100,
    193, 195
Proust, Marcel, 181, 184, 206

Rabinovitch, Wladimir, xxviin35
race and racism, 125–26, 132, 177
race laws in World War II France (Jewish
    Statutes), xvi, 54, 59, 60, 63–65, 64, 66,
    105, 151, 159
Rachel, 97
Racine, Jean, xvii, 52
Rashi, 57, 83, 86
Rawidowicz, Simon, Babel and Jerusalem,
    158
Raynal, David, 44
Rebecca, 88
redistributive justice, 74
régéneration/revitalization, x–xi, xii, 188–91,
    197
Reinach, Salomon and Théodore, 10
Resistance movement (World War II),
    xxvin23, 105, 110, 137, 151, 181
Rigord, 36
Rosenzweig, Franz, vii, xvii, xxiii, 54, 245,
    246; Star of Redemption, xxiii, 245, 246
Rothschild, Baron James de, 25n5
Rousseau, Jean-Jacques, 52, 139, 231
Rudnicki, Adolf, 205n4
Ruth, 95

Sabbath observance, 70–71, 86
sabbatical year, 72–73
Sachs, Nelly, 209
sacrifice, 23, 56, 80, 84, 92, 93, 101, 132, 167,
    183, 214, 234, 240, 241
Sadducees, 196
Salomon, Mathilde, 44
Salvador, James, xix–xx, 1, 5–6; Paris, Rome,
    Jérusalem, 5, 6; "The People," 5–9
salvation coming from the Jews, Gospel of
    St. John on, 95
Samuel, 95
Sanhedrin, xii, xiii, 20
Saint-Simonism, 5–6
Sartre, Jean-Paul, xxviin35, 125; Réflexions sur
    la question juive, 179
Schelling, Friedrich, 105
Schleiermacher, Friedrich, 2n2
Schneerson, Zalman, xv, 160
Scholem, Gershom, 214, 245, 247
Schwab, Moïse, 1
Schwarz-Bart, André, The Last of the Just, 60,
    202n3
scouting movement, Jewish, xvi, xxi,
    xxv–xxviin19–20, 54, 60, 66, 79, 186.
    See also Éclaireurs israélites de France
Second World War. See World War II
secularism: of Finkielkraut, 198–99; in
    France (laïcité), x, xiv, 18, 199; Marienstras
    on non-Zionist, secular Jewish identity
    in Diaspora, xi, 137–50
Sefer Yetsirah, 91
Serge Klarsfeld Memorial, 120
Shechinah (Divine Presence), 82, 90, 94
Shem, 93, 95, 190
Shema, 42, 76
Sheppard, Eugene R., vii
Shoah. See Holocaust
Shoah (film; 1985), 60
Simeon bar Yohai, 84
Simon-Nahum, Perrine, 10
Six-Day War (1967), xvii, xxii, 123–24, 145,
    152, 245

# Publication Credits